T0342449

THE FAMILY OFFICE

OFFICE

*A Comprehensive Guide for Advisers,
Practitioners, and Students*

William I. Woodson and
Edward V. Marshall

Columbia University Press
New York

Columbia University Press
Publishers Since 1893
New York   Chichester, West Sussex
cup.columbia.edu

Library of Congress Cataloging-in-Publication Data
Names: Woodson, William I., author. | Marshall, Edward V., author.
Title: The family office : a comprehensive guide for advisers,
practitioners, and students / William I. Woodson and Edward V. Marshall.
Description: New York : Columbia University Press, [2021] | Includes
bibliographical references and index.
Identifiers: LCCN 2021004239 (print) | LCCN 2021004240 (ebook) |
ISBN 9780231200622 (hardback) | ISBN 9780231553711 (ebook)
Subjects: LCSH: Investment advisors. | Financial planners. | Financial
services industry. | Families—Economic aspects. | Rich people—Finance,
Personal. | Wealth—Management.
Classification: LCC HG4621 .W66 2021 (print) |
LCC HG4621 (ebook) | DDC 332.6—dc23
LC record available at https://lccn.loc.gov/2021004239
LC ebook record available at https://lccn.loc.gov/2021004240

Cover design: Milenda Nan Ok Lee
Cover image: KjellBrynildsen © iStock

Information is not knowledge. The only source of knowledge is experience. You need experience to gain wisdom.

—Albert Einstein

Главное, самому себе не лгите.

—Fyodor Mikhailovich Dostoyevsky

I dedicate this book to my beautiful wife, Cynthia, whose patience and support know no bounds; my wonderful children, Olivia, Chase, Jack, and Henry, who challenge and inspire me; and my many great bosses, colleagues, and clients from whom I've learned all that I have to share.

–Bill Woodson

Once again to Natalia
And to Isabella, Veronika, Emilia, and Evelina
Many Fêtes

–EVM

Contents

Foreword

It is my genuine pleasure to introduce you to a book that I am highly confident will help guide families and their advisers for decades to come. This book's unique pedagogical approach, founded in decades of the authors' experiences, gives family office principals, the professionals who work for them, outside advisers, and students of the industry a front row seat to how the best family offices help families successfully navigate complex issues: managing personal and financial affairs, mitigating numerous risks and threats, raising well-adjusted children, conducting important philanthropy, and providing a legacy.

I have known and worked with Bill and Edward for most of the last two decades. In addition to their formal education and training, they have what is most important: hands-on experience working with many of the world's most successful and iconic families and their family offices. A lot of different things have to add up to produce a superb adviser, but the most valuable thing excellent professionals bring to the table is their *perspective*. That perspective is born out of working for decades, often alongside other professional services experts, to deliver bespoke solutions, while also observing what works and what doesn't. While advisers' expertise can help produce superior financial outcomes, their perspective also helps manage complexity and family dynamics, which in the end often proves to be priceless.

My own perspective comes from past experience at Merrill Lynch, UBS, and Credit Suisse, along with my current role as CEO of Boston Private. One of my final positions at Merrill was serving as Head of the European Private Banking business, which gave me the ability to see up close the services and advisory culture in the birthplace of family offices, Europe. At UBS, I was Head of the Private Wealth team in the U.S. and helped found the group in 2003. As the CEO of Credit Suisse Private Banking–Americas, I had the privilege of working with remarkable clients and advisers. In many cases, the North and South American clients we served were highly complex families with very unique needs. However, no matter how unique the stories and the original nature of their family's path to success, there was always one common denominator—they all wanted to protect the well-being of current and future generations. Bill and Edward often found themselves squarely in the middle of these discussions and provided pivotal guidance to lead families to their desired outcomes.

Anyone who has worked with me over the years has heard me say, "no client ever wakes up in the morning hoping someone will sell them a financial product." They wake up with hopes, dreams, and goals for themselves and their families. They want to work with a trusted adviser who can guide them to the best advice and solutions to produce the most efficient and effective path to their desired outcomes for their families, their businesses, and their legacies. Moreover, they want an adviser who understands their family's dreams and motivations— which is critical to effectively supporting them to achieve their goals. This is the core of what readers can hope to gain from reading Bill and Edward's book. They have synthesized years of hands-on experience to help those who work within and around family offices find solutions for both simple and deeply complex problems.

The importance of the approach outlined in this book and its benefits cannot be overstated. Select few families now control a disproportionate amount of wealth globally, and this wealth—and how it is managed and used—has significant societal implications. Family offices, given the wealth-managerial function they play, have an important responsibility and unique opportunity to assist families in channeling this wealth for good, whether by helping children become responsible stewards of their wealth, investing in game-changing technology, or engaging in meaningful philanthropy and impact investing. The professional maturation of a family office "industry" that includes robust guidance on best practices, expert and peer collaborations, and academic training is therefore of immense importance to families, and to those who serve and advise them. This book will quickly become an important and seminal work in that maturation.

I personally enjoyed reading this book and valued the way it allows readers to engage with realistic case studies. I have always felt that learning from experience—your own or your educators'—is best, and who you learn from is equally important. In reading this book, you will simply be learning from the best. I have often told young executives, along with my own children, to be very deliberate in choosing to whom they apprentice themselves. Try to learn from people who are not only well educated but also have deep experience and a proven track record of success. That's what you have in this book. Enjoy it. I did.

Anthony DeChellis

Acknowledgments

WE WOULD LIKE to express our appreciation for the substantial contributions by so many industry colleagues, without whom this book could not have been written. As will be made clear in the rest of this book, managing a family office properly requires the active involvement of a broad range of professionals, advisers, and service providers, each providing the family and their family office with discrete expertise, experience, and advice.

This is also true with respect to this book, which is intended to be a comprehensive guide for academics, students, principals, and practitioners as they study the industry and/or navigate the challenges of starting and running a family office. As such, the insights and advice shared in this book come, in part, from a number of contributors who developed content for specific chapters, permitted the use of their prior writings on the subject, or provided detailed advice to the authors.

While we have endeavored to list all these contributors in the endnotes and the Appreciations section, we would like to formally recognize and thank those who contributed significant content to the book (in the order presented). Please note that contact information for each of the substantial contributors can be found at www.thefamilyofficebook .com.

Linda Mack of Mack International, for her contributions in human capital and staffing.

Trish Botoff of Botoff Consulting, for her contributions in compensation plans.

William Farren of My Accountant, Inc., for his contributions in accounting and bill paying.

Jason Brown of SEI Archway and Proteus, for his contributions in consolidated reporting.

Stephen Prostano of PKF O'Connor Davies, for his contributions in tax reporting.

Brad Deflin of Total Digital Security, for his contributions in information technology (IT).

Kathy Reilly of Lifestyle Advisors, for her contributions in lifestyle management and concierge.

Anne Lyons and **Judy Boerner-Rule** of Tapestry Associates, for their contributions in estate management.

Keith Swirsky of GKG Law, for his contributions in private aviation.

Daniel Berick of Squire Patton Boggs, for his contributions in regulatory issues.

Joel Palathinkal of Sutton Capital for his contributions in venture capital.

Beth deBeer of iImpact Consulting Network, for her contributions in impact investing.

Mary Elizabeth Klein, for her contributions in art and collectibles.

Chad Sweet of The Chertoff Group, for his contributions in security.

John Prufeta of Medical Excellence International, for his contributions in managing healthcare.

Michael Gray of Neal, Gerber & Eisenberg, for his contributions in legal services.

Suzanne Hammer of Hammer & Associates, and **Vahe Vartanian** of Global Family Office Community, for their contributions in family philanthropy.

Darren Moore of Bourland, Wall & Wenzel, for his contributions in private foundations.

Dennis Jaffe, for his contributions in wealth education.

Al King, **Matt Tobin**, and **Tom Cota** of South Dakota Trust Company, for their contributions in private trust companies.

Robert Casey, for his significant editorial contributions throughout the book.

Jamie McLaughlin of James H. McLaughlin & Co., for his advice, reviews, and guidance.

We would also like to thank **Columbia University Press**, its publisher, **Myles Thompson**, and **Brian Smith** for their guidance throughout and unwavering support for this endeavor.

Disclaimer

THE MATERIAL AND information contained in this book is for general information and academic study purposes only. While best efforts were made to provide accurate and up-to-date information, the authors make no representations or warranties of any kind, express or implied, about the completeness, accuracy, reliability, suitability, or availability of the information contained in this book. The family office world is complex, dynamic, and nuanced. Therefore, the reader should not rely upon the information contained in this book as a basis for making any business, investment, legal, tax, or any other decision. Readers should always seek and rely upon the advice of their business, legal, regulatory, tax, investment, and related advisers prior to and when engaging in any and all of these areas. In no event shall the authors, the publisher, their employees or agents be held liable or responsible to any person or entity with respect to any loss or incidental damages caused, or alleged to have been caused, directly or indirectly, by the information contained in this book. Any acknowledgments, appreciations, or references contained in this book, of or to, a person, company, or organization does not constitute an endorsement or an approval by the authors or the publisher of any of the products, services, or opinions of that individual, corporation, or organization. All names, characters, businesses, and events used in this book are fictional and any resemblance or likeness to actual persons, living or dead, companies, family offices, advisers, and service providers is solely coincidental.

Introduction

FAMILY OFFICES TRADITIONALLY have been repositories of great wealth, and their activities are conducted behind closed doors and shrouded in secrecy. Many families would prefer to keep it that way. Yet as a group, family offices have acquired a dramatically higher public profile over the last decade or so. The Dodd-Frank financial reform legislation of 2010 threatened them with regulation if they served any nonfamily investment clients, and later offered them an exemption if they didn't. It was one of the first times that family offices faced the prospect of being in the regulatory hot seat. Subsequently, several high-profile hedge fund managers jettisoned their nonfamily clients and converted their operations to family offices, thereby escaping regulation through that same safe harbor. The result was a sustained burst of attention to the family office world in the news media that continues to this day.

Equally significant in terms of raising their profile has been the emergence of family offices as major players in the financing of private companies. After the financial crisis of 2008, some notable family offices reduced their exposure to public securities markets and private equity funds, turning increasingly to direct equity investments in private businesses. The participation by family offices in high-profile deals helps them attract more investment opportunities, but it also brings with it a whole new level of attention, allure, and scrutiny from the media. Thus, over time, the public has been getting a bigger and bigger look at the private world of family offices.

And what is to be seen there? Vast wealth, to be sure, but also the vast challenge of managing this wealth and preserving it for future generations of the family. Power struggles among relatives and lack of family cohesion are as perilous to the health of a family office as overzealous spending by family members or investment losses. Keeping things right among family members helps to enable the peaceful transition of control of the family office from one generation to the next, which is essential for continued sustainability. That's the long-term challenge.

The more immediate challenge is the subject of this book: understanding family offices, why families create them, what they do, and how to manage them effectively. It is a formidable undertaking when one considers the complexity and personal dynamics that come into play when advising and supporting wealthy families.[1]

The Family Office is a first-of-its-kind combination academic textbook and comprehensive practitioner's reference manual. It provides an insider's view of family offices to those looking to understand them, whether they be graduate students, family principals, current practitioners, or advisers/vendors. The book presents these insights through a series of **problem-based learning (PBL) cases** across multiple topics designed to provide readers with a foundation of knowledge about family offices, insights into the services they provide, and the practical application of family office management principles. The cases follow a single family's journey from the time of a significant liquidity event; through the creation, staffing, and management of their family office; and on to its succession. Each case study is supported by **detailed reference material** that can be accessed separately. Through this methodology, readers get a practitioner's view of issues that wealthy families face and the solutions they adopt to address them **throughout a family office's life cycle**.

The book is aimed at three primary audiences:

- **Academics and university students**, who can use the learning cases format to better understand why wealthy families create family offices, their various constructs, the services they provide, and how they should be managed and governed
- **Family office principals and professionals**, who can use the detailed reference material provided here across multiple service, advisory, and managerial areas to obtain guidance in one or more discrete areas of interest

- **Service providers and vendors**, who can use the case studies and background information provided here to understand family offices, including their issues and needs, in order to better provide services and advice to their clients and customers

The book is organized into four separate sections arranged by the major components required to start and run a family office. **Section One** focuses on the issues around the formation of a family office, including the different types, the services they provide, their design, and how they are staffed. **Section Two** provides an overview of the key services that family offices provide, including how best to deliver them. **Section Three** discusses governance structures and provides overarching managerial insights. **Section Four** provides important industry data on family offices, as well as a link to access additional educational and industry resources.

Each of the first three sections of the book contains multiple individual chapters that provide insights into and context on the major concepts for family offices. These are introduced through problem-based learning cases and detailed background reference material.

Each chapter is broken into four sections:

- A **case study** that presents topic-specific challenges faced by a family office in a realistic setting, with background information that the reader can use to uncover and solve the specific issues raised
- Extensive **reference material** in each of the topic areas to provide readers with both an understanding of the issues pertinent to the case and technical resources for those looking for advice in a particular area

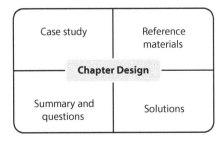

Figure Int.1 Chapter design

- A **case summary and set of questions** designed to analyze the critical components and examine potential future considerations of the case
- **Detailed solutions** to the questions that reveal best practices and informed insights focusing on how to assess, unravel, and address issues raised in each of the cases

For students and academics looking to learn about family offices, the reasons they are created, and the various services they provide, the book is an **educational textbook.** The case studies are an established and effective way to introduce the subject and educate by providing context on real-life challenges that wealthy families face, including when and how they are resolved.

For principals, practitioners, and family members, the book provides **technical reference material** across the myriad of service and advisory needs of a wealthy family. This background information can be accessed directly without having to review the case studies, questions, and answers, including by consulting the glossary and index in the book.

For advisers and vendors to family offices, the book offers deep insights into the numerous service and advisory needs of wealthy families. As such, it gives important **intelligence on customer needs, preferences, and behaviors**.

So long as families have had significant wealth, there have been established approaches and practices that can serve as a guide. These are found by understanding the issues that significant wealth creates, knowing how other families have addressed them, and learning from professionals and organizations that work with similar families.

This book provides a summary of the solutions that apply to the formation, services, and governance of family offices. It also helps readers understand how family offices are similar and different. Understanding these nuances is as important as knowing what to do, when, and with whom.

The Family Office

Formation

BACKGROUND INFORMATION FOR CASE STUDIES 1 THROUGH 3

John always enjoyed hearing the satisfying, quiet squawk as he landed his Cessna 172 at Marshfield Airport (KMFI). Getting up there always meant that he was that much closer to getting away from it all via a weekend in waders.

It had been six months since John sold his company, and even though he was technically not working, he felt like he had no time to himself. John had let go of his baby, Rybat Manufacturing, which he had built over two decades, and now he wanted this time away to think about the next chapter in his life.

John Oskar Thorne was the quintessential Midwestern kid. He grew up in the suburbs and spent summers on Lake Michigan with his large, extended family. He developed an appreciation for manufacturing, helping his father and mother with the small tool and die shop that they had started after retiring from a large manufacturing firm just west of Chicago. John left Chicago and headed for West Lafayette, Indiana, to study industrial engineering and economics at Purdue University. John was a focused student and took on as many internship opportunities to work with manufacturing companies as he could, spending his free time, including summers, learning on the job at companies near campus and out in Michigan, Texas, and far-flung Wyoming.

After college, John landed a job with a manufacturer in Wisconsin and spent five years working his way up the ranks. He realized that while the corporate life was a comfortable environment where he could make a decent living, working for someone else wasn't for him. He decided to strike out on his own. Using his savings and borrowing money from his family, John partnered with two college friends and launched Rybat Manufacturing.

John picked a poor time to launch a manufacturing company, though, as the economy soon headed into a downturn. As a result, his partners went back to their corporate jobs, selling their shares to him. With his wife and a new baby in tow, John continued to struggle for a while, but eventually Rybat Manufacturing took off.

To make it work, John essentially lived at Rybat Manufacturing's offices, and the stresses took a toll on his personal life. He divorced his college sweetheart, and she and his son moved back to her hometown in suburban Detroit. John kept grinding away and expanded Rybat Manufacturing at a fast clip. He augmented the strong organic growth of the company through the acquisition of smaller specialty manufacturers, and he stepped into the international scene with a joint venture with a Chinese conglomerate.

Rybat Manufacturing was starting to pay off for John in terms of his personal financial picture. He bought a nice home in Hawthorn Woods, Illinois, and started having free time to enjoy things outside of work. He joined a prominent national networking club for chief executive officers (CEOs), which became a helpful source of advice as his life became more complicated and he looked to find peers who were in the same boat. Through the networking group, he made friends who were hobbyist pilots and decided to get a private pilot certificate. He bought and leased back to a local flight school a used Cessna 172. John's parents had instilled a love for the outdoors in him, and he eventually started flying prospective clients to his favorite fly-fishing spots, which turned out to be an effective business development method. John pinched some pennies and ended up buying a small ranch in Wyoming, which for him was a fly-fisherman's paradise.

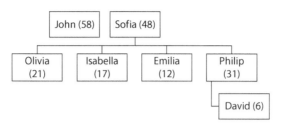

Figure s1.1 The Thorne family tree

John's mother had developed a passion for cars, having grown up in Detroit. This love for cars prompted him to buy his mom a gorgeous 1967 Mustang and to splurge on a 1961 Jaguar XKE for himself during the Concours d'Elegance in Pebble Beach, California, a beautiful part of Northern California's coastline and a place where he loved to play golf while visiting his family on the West Coast.

John eventually remarried and started another family. His new wife, Sofia, was a rising-star attorney whom he helped set up in a practice after the birth of their first child. Sofia was also active on the Chicago charity scene, supporting the arts (including a symphony and a small art museum) and the Children's Hospital. John and Sofia had three children: Olivia (age twenty-one), Isabella (seventeen), and Emilia (twelve), bringing John's total number of children to four with his son, Philip (age thirty-one), from his previous marriage. Sofia's mother was originally from Mexico, and partially in her honor, the couple decided to buy a nice place in Cabo San Lucas, which the entire family could use as a getaway during the cold, harsh, and long winters of Chicago.

Rybat Manufacturing continued to expand successfully, and the industry itself started to attract serious notice. A while ago, John was featured in the *Chicago Tribune* as one of Chicago's Business Leaders. Rybat Manufacturing continued to build its brand through community engagement through active corporate philanthropic efforts supporting financial literacy and science, technology, engineering, and math (STEM) curricula in the local public schools.

At this point in his life, John had accumulated a net worth of roughly $50 million, with $15 million of that being liquid. Over the years, he worked with his high school classmate Tadeusz, a local trust and estate attorney, to set up the traditional tax and estate-planning vehicles for someone with his level of net worth.

He had also acquired a disparate set of advisers to help him with his personal and financial affairs. His personal attorney, Natalia, was a local partner in a national law firm and had supported him with meeting his corporate and personal needs. For example, Natalia worked with John to put all his properties and his plane into separate limited liability companies (LLCs). John also developed a good relationship with a local certified public accountant (CPA), Sam, who had been with him since before he started Rybat Manufacturing. Sam worked closely with Janina, John's indispensable administrative assistant of fifteen years, to help John keep track of his personal financial affairs, which were becoming more complex every year.

Even when John was just starting out, he had developed an interest in investing. John's college roommate, Charles, likely played a part in developing this appetite. Charles had left Wall Street and started his own hedge fund that was doing well, and John had become one of his first limited partners. John also dabbled in some individual stock trades with his local wire house broker, Ted. John wasn't Ted's biggest client, but he enjoyed a regular phone call to catch up on the markets and John would make an occasional trade based on Ted's advice. John had a relationship with a national bank that primarily helped with his commercial banking and limited personal lending needs. In addition, John placed some money over the years with a local asset manager that catered to clients focused on large cap value investing.

Rybat Manufacturing's growth continued to soar. John's college alma mater noticed the growth and hit him up for a donation, and he gladly pledged to support engineering scholarships to encourage talented women to join the field.

Others took notice of Rybat Manufacturing's success as well. John started to receive calls from investment bankers and industry corporate development teams, pitching him potential sale options. John hired one of the top investment bankers in Chicago, Cynthia, who helped him prepare the company for sale, solicit bids, and negotiate contracts. At fifty-eight years old, John wasn't ready to give up the reins of his baby, but a large manufacturing conglomerate made him an offer he just couldn't refuse: $900 million in a mix of cash and stock in the acquiring company (80 percent cash, 20 percent stock).

After long deliberation with his wife, set of advisers, and friends at his CEO networking group, John decided to sell Rybat Manufacturing. As part of the deal, John signed a two-year noncompete agreement.

For the first time in a long time, John was out of the workforce.

SUMMARY OF CASE STUDY CHARACTERS

For ease of recollection, the following is a list of characters introduced throughout the various case studies in this book.

Companies

- Rybat Manufacturing—name of the operating company sold
- Left Seat Management—name of the family office

Family Members

- John Thorne—principal (fifty-eight);[1] former business owner, active pilot, and hobbyist direct investor
- Sofia Thorne—John's wife (forty-eight); born in Mexico City; active in philanthropy
- Gabriella—Sofia's mother (seventy-two); lives in Los Angeles; has medical issues
- Philip—son from John's first marriage (thirty-one); teacher in Chicago, divorced, with one child from the first marriage (David); remarried (Song), with a second child (Maggie)
- Olivia—oldest daughter from John's second marriage (twenty-one); married to Brecken, who is the daughter of a very large and well-known family that owns a large closely held family business; adopts two girls (Devin from Ethiopia and Katie from Russia); equestrian; attends Columbia University and has an investment banking career on Wall Street
- Isabella—second daughter from John's second marriage (seventeen); attends the Massachusetts Institute of Technology (MIT); and joins a start-up in Silicon Valley
- Emilia—third daughter from John's second marriage (twelve); avid tennis player and skier; attends the University of Colorado Boulder; degree in environmental studies

In-laws

- Brecken (wife of Olivia)
- Song (second wife of Philip)

Family Office Staff

- Michael—First CEO
- Tracey—Second CEO
- Jack—Chief investment officer (CIO)
- Jason—Chief financial officer (CFO)
- Chase—In-house legal counsel
- Henry—Chief pilot
- Evelina—IT specialist
- Janina—John's executive assistant
- Ed—Tax professional
- Veronika—Estate manager and, later, operations manager
- Cara—Master of business administration (MBA)
- Katya—An accounts payable clerk who gets fired

Advisers

- Natalia—lawyer
- Sam—CPA
- Charles—Hedge fund professional; John's former roommate
- Ted—Stockbroker
- Tadeusz—Trust and estate attorney
- Cynthia—Investment banker

CHAPTER ONE

Types

CASE STUDY

Summary

- Six months after the sale of Rybat Manufacturing
- The challenges that come with substantial wealth
- The background and history of family offices
- Different types and attributes of family offices

Key Words/Concepts

- History of family offices
- Types of family offices
- Attributes of family offices

Challenge

His life after exiting his business turned out to be much more complex than John could have imagined. The magnitude of this sale hit the news wires nationally, and he was getting interview requests left and right. The calls and uninvited suggestions of what he should do next started to come in. Having parked some of the cash proceeds into his bank account and some with his stockbroker, Ted, John wanted to hit the pause button to contemplate this new chapter in his life.

John did do one thing up front. He made a quiet, multiyear pledge to Purdue to support a chair in the engineering department and expansion of the internship and co-op programs that he felt had been instrumental to his success early on. His big splurges came in the form of real estate. He bought a large lot in Glencoe, Illinois, and started building his dream house, which would eventually become his primary personal residence. He also started to buy up the properties adjacent to his ranch in Wyoming, which seemed to become more expensive once sellers began using the Internet to find out that John was nearly a billionaire. Furthermore, he decided to keep his Cessna 172, but he spent some money on upgrading its interior and technology, including high-end external cameras so he and the kids could make flying videos to post on social media sites.

Six months after the sale of Rybat Manufacturing, John felt like he was juggling too many balls. He realized that he was spending too much time on things he didn't enjoy, and far too little time on the things he did like doing. John felt guilty that he had not yet done anything with all the money sitting in his bank account. He was well aware that he needed to start putting some of the sales proceeds to work in the market, although he had never managed a portfolio of this size before and wanted to be cautious.

He also needed to visit his ranch in Wyoming and more closely oversee the acquisition of adjoining significant land parcels and leasing some of the land out for cattle grazing. The house in Glencoe was now well underway, and there was a never-ending need for him to meet with contractors to iron out details, select building materials, and approve change orders. And while Sofia was helpful, she was also spending a great deal of time in Mexico overseeing the purchase and remodeling of their new vacation home in Cabo San Lucas. She desperately wanted him to go down there with the children so they could enjoy the warm weather, do some activities together, and spend more time with her side of the family.

Sofia was also increasingly drawn to other activities, including her work with the Children's Hospital, the art museum, and the local symphony, including hosting a number of events to help these charities raise money. Not surprisingly, each of these institutions also seemed to be taking a greater interest in both her and her husband, inviting them to fundraisers, introducing them to other prominent supporters, and sharing ambitious plans for expansion and new programs.

And then there was the jet he wanted to buy. Over the last couple of years, John had become accustomed to flying privately, whether for himself in the Cessna 172, or via charter for the occasional business trip or family vacation. He was beginning to think that he should just buy a private jet and hire his own pilots to avoid the hassles of dealing with charter operators, flying in the older planes they typically provided him, and interfacing with the mixed bag of pilots they employed. After all, he was a pilot, knew planes, and had the money and need to justify such an expense.

Finally, the administration, bill paying, and reporting for all these activates was starting to outstrip what Janina was able and comfortable to provide in her capacity as John's executive assistant and bookkeeper. The same could be said for all the various travel, scheduling, event planning, and related needs with which she helped both John and Sofia.

With whatever new free time John had, he started attending his chief executive officer (CEO) networking group more often and connecting with his friends, asking them what they did after their individual liquidity events. Some of them had started single-family offices (SFOs) or worked with multifamily offices (MFOs) to manage their personal assets and affairs.

After getting advice from his network and weighing his options and requirements, John decided that he wanted to start his own SFO. However, there really wasn't a good instruction manual to help with that effort.

"Where do I start?" John thought.

BACKGROUND INFORMATION

For Emperors and Kings

Family offices are attracting growing attention as the vehicle of choice by the megawealthy to manage their assets, both in the United States

(U.S.) and elsewhere. Yet they are by no means a new phenomenon. Family offices have been around in some form or other since civilization began in order to provide a vehicle for wealthy families to manage and safeguard their assets.

Before the Renaissance, only emperors, kings, and nobles had the political power and resulting economic might to amass great fortunes. The family office emerged to serve them, from the Roman majordomos to the chief stewards employed by noble families throughout the Middle Ages.

The Renaissance brought a flowering of commerce and international trade, which in turn generated great wealth for the leading merchant families. Their complex and far-flung business activities—as well as dynastic ambitions for their offspring—encouraged them to seek help managing their family affairs. They adopted sophisticated family office functions, such as systematically collecting, accounting for, safeguarding, and reinvesting their assets. Those tasks remain essential services of family offices today. These families came to understand the key qualities needed of those who would serve them by running their family offices. Those qualities were—and remain today—loyalty, discretion, attention to detail, timely execution, business acumen, and faithful stewardship.

The ninenteenth century brought a surge in economic growth, industrialization, and wealth creation that far surpassed anything in history. Business empires sprang up and grew to enormous size. Family fortunes, as well as the need for family offices, expanded accordingly. Also encouraging the formation of family offices were the increased use of tax and estate-planning vehicles and the role of separate management companies.

One of the first modern family offices was established by John Jacob Astor in 1835. Astor, a German immigrant, made three successive fortunes, as a fur trader, an international merchant, and a Manhattan landlord, becoming one of the first multimillionaires in the United States. Astor's family office headquarters was built like a bank and served as collection point, counting house, and vault for rents generated by his real estate empire. Known by its address, 85 Prince Street, it was designed to be impregnable—burglarproof, fireproof, and earthquake resistant. The building sported thick masonry walls reenforced with iron bars, an iron roof, iron doors, and iron-grated windows. It is sometimes said that family offices are established because of the founder's desire for privacy, control, and continuity. That certainly seems the case with Astor, who oversaw his empire from within a fortress.

Another high-profile family office was set up by John D. Rockefeller in 1882. The cofounder of Standard Oil was estimated to have been worth over $1 billion in 1937. The Rockefeller family office continues to operate today, and indeed it established a number of businesses and nonprofit consulting firms that serve other wealthy families in the areas of wealth management and philanthropy.

Classifications and Attributes

There are generally nine distinct classifications of family offices (figure 1.1): traditional family offices, virtual family offices (VFOs), commercial

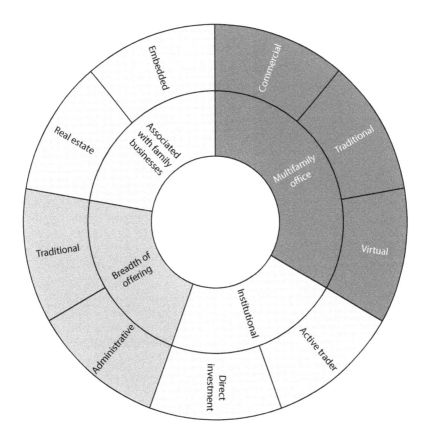

Figure 1.1 Family office archetype wheel graphic

MFOs, traditional MFOs, direct investment family offices, active trader family offices, administrative family offices, embedded family offices, and real estate family offices. These nine archetypes are subsets of four distinct classes of family offices based on common characteristics: breadth of offering, multifamily offices, associated with family businesses, and institutional.

Tables 1.1 through 1.4 summarize these classifications and illuminate how best to understand and distinguish them.

Understanding the various categories of family offices and their distinctive attributes is the first step when learning about this industry, whether as an academic, practitioner, or vendor.

TABLE I.I
Breadth of offering

Classification	Description	Attributes
Traditional family office	These family offices provide solutions over a broad range of service and advisory needs, historically through their own staff (although this is shifting somewhat as families increasingly look to outsource noncore service needs).	Newer family offices in this category exhibit many common characteristics. Maybe the most notable is the extensive involvement by their founding principals and its impact on strategy and decision-making.
Administrative family office	This type of family office typically limits itself to noninvestment-related activities. These families choose to outsource investment management to third parties and focus their efforts on managing personal assets, administration, wealth education, philanthropy, and other areas.	More established family offices in this category often have long-established policies and procedures, carried out by employees who are longtime family retainers who are culturally tied to the founding principal.

TABLE 1.2

Family offices associated with a family business

Classification	Description	Attributes
Embedded family offices	Embedded family offices are not separate business entities, but rather integrated into closely held family businesses.	These have a similar range of behavioral proclivities as SFOs. They are categorized together largely because of their association with a closely held family business (whether real estate or not).
Real estate family offices	Real estate families deserve their own category of family office because of the similarities in their investing behavior and family office needs. It is only a slight exaggeration to say that families that made their money in real estate tend to reinvest most of it in real estate. While these families do accumulate and invest liquid assets, they generally do so in a modest and less active way than other families relative to their real estate activities.	

TABLE 1.3

Institutional family offices

Classification	Description	Attributes
Active trader family office	These family offices take an institutional approach to managing money. They usually are larger family offices that focus on active investment strategies in liquid capital markets, an approach seen among former hedge fund managers who convert their operations to family offices.	These family offices are often quite large, staffed by finance or private equity professionals, and take an institutional approach to their jobs. It is not uncommon to see these types of families formally separate the investment management business from the personal family office.
Direct investments family office	These are institutional family offices that focus their investment activities almost exclusively on private investing. The professionals who run these family offices often come out of investment banking and private equity. They focus their considerable (and expensive) resources on finding, evaluating, and managing direct investments, often in partnership with other family offices and private equity funds.	

TABLE I.4
Multifamily offices

Classification	Description	Attributes
Traditional MFO	MFOs provide a broad range of family office services and advice to multiple wealthy families, whether or not they are related to each other.	These are, for the most part, professional organizations despite the delineation as to whether they are owned by a financial services firm. And while they operate under senior leadership and are affected by their personalities, views, and preferences, the diversity in staffing and clients generally moderates the impact of this relative to SFO principals. Further, as service providers to wealthy families that can more easily choose to go elsewhere for advice and services, these businesses are held accountable in a way that is not necessarily the case with SFOs.
Commercial MFO	MFOs that are created (or acquired) by financial services firms and/or professionals as a way to attract and serve wealthier, more complex families.	
Virtual family office	Executives at a professional or financial services firm coordinate the delivery of services through a combination of in-house staff, typically in their area of expertise, and third-party providers drawn from their network.	

ASSESSMENT AND ISSUES SURFACED

What Did We Learn?

After his large liquidity event, John is determined to start a family office. He has decided on this course after facing the growing complexity of his life. He is also spending time on too many things, many of which he has no interest in and for which he knows he can hire others to oversee. John wants to leverage his good fortune so he can focus his time on the things that are the most important to him in this new chapter of his life.

Case Questions

- What is a family office?
- What are the appropriate considerations for John to keep in mind while establishing his family office?
- What types of family offices could John consider?
- What are some of the risks that John has expressed or is not anticipating?
- What should be the most time-consuming part of establishing the family office for John?

RECOMMENDED SOLUTIONS

Responses to Case Questions

What is a family office?

Family offices are entities set up by a single family, or by or for a group of families, to manage their assets and affairs. They are used to address the issues that come with substantial wealth, including dealing with complexity and helping family members achieve their goals (e.g., simplicity, purpose, legacy, family harmony, passing down wealth, investment management, philanthropy, and so on). In this context, family members are called "principals," and the senior staff of a family office are referred to as "family office executives." Principals are the primary members of the family that the family office supports, although there are situations where multiple generations and/or extended family members can use the services of a family office. Family offices vary in design, operations, and services delivered, depending on the needs of the principals.

What are the appropriate considerations for
John to keep in mind while establishing his family office?

In John's case, there are three major groupings of considerations that he should think about as he is contemplating creating his own family office: the magnitude of his wealth, the depth and breadth of his activities, and his stated (and often unstated) desires and aspirations.

At his new level of wealth (nearly $1 billion), he has sufficient means to support a family office. Family offices tend to be pricey ventures to start and maintain. Principals also tend to want to resource the family office lightly, which can lead to issues with budgeting, cash flows, and the ability to attract top talent for key positions. In John's case, he is liquid enough that a family office makes sense.

As evidenced in the case study, John's life was relatively complex anyway, but it has gotten even more so after the sale of Rybat Manufacturing. He needs a better structure to support the depth and breadth of activities he is already coordinating among himself, Janina, and his set of professional advisers. For example, John's time is being spent on managing his new property additions in Wyoming and the new dream home he is building locally. While he enjoys the idea of these new additions to his estate, it is hard to imagine John being thrilled about taking calls from contractors about construction that is past due.

The world of investments has also become more of a headache to John than it previously had been. He used to satisfy his penchant for investing by talking about the markets with his broker or dabbling in private markets with friends and family. Now it feels like an avalanche of sales calls, with no clear strategy or method to pick the right horse—or maybe he shouldn't even be betting on horses at all. He's done what many newly ultrawealthy people have done: sit in cash for the most part. However, this is only a short-term solution, and he will need to focus on developing a more responsible approach to managing his money. There is also the likely expansion into private aviation. As a pilot, with the financial wherewithal to responsibly own and charter private planes, John is likely to increase the amount of time he devotes to this area.

Principals in John's position often struggle after the sale of their business with what to do next, and how to achieve new desires and goals. He initially thinks about going back to running an operating company because for him, those were the "good old days," when he was sure of what needed to get done. However, as he becomes accustomed to this new chapter in his life, he knows that things will need to change and that a family office could be part of that. Moreover, John's passions and hobbies are evident, and they have grown in scope and depth from his humble beginnings of building a struggling company and ending with a very successful sale. It is likely that flying, fishing, and direct investing "hobbies" will take more of a precedent going forward, and any family office structure should take these into consideration.

There is also Sofia's and his interest in philanthropy to consider. They now have the financial ability to be significant contributors, but they have not spent the time to think about what they want to do, nor have they got the experience to determine how best to do it.

What types of family offices could John consider?

While all of them generally support the same types of services and activities, there are several major types of family offices. For John, the types that are most relevant for his situation are the SFO, MFO, and VFO.

An SFO (also sometimes referred to as a "traditional family office") is a full-service entity set up to address a wide range of requirements and services for an individual family. This type of family office tends to keep some functions in house and outsource others, depending on the proclivities of the principals. Think of this type of entity as a family office that allows a principal to be more hands-on in areas of personal interest and importance to them. Based on John's situation, an SFO is the best choice for him to set up.

Of the other family office archetypes, John could possibly have his personal and financial affairs managed by an MFO or a VFO. MFOs are designed to support the needs of more than one family. Sometimes they are established by a group of wealthy families that band together to spread costs and enhance services. Other times, they are established by professionals to serve several families. In either case, MFOs help families who want to outsource the majority of their family office needs, do not have the means to set up their own SFO, or both. The outsourced nature of MFOs is in contrast to SFOs. Because of John's stated desire to be more hands-on with his personal affairs and investments, the MFO would not be an effective solution for him.

VFOs have some similarities to MFOs, in that they often are employed to take care of more than one family. However, they are set up by a professional adviser (usually an attorney, accountant, or wealth manager), who acts as a coordinator for the services typically provided by an SFO. Similar to MFOs, VFOs would potentially make sense for John if he wanted to delegate more of his affairs to someone else, if his life were less complex, or his requirements were not as diverse. However, for someone who is as likely as John is to want to be involved in his family office, a VFO would likely not be a good solution for him to consider.

What are some of the risks that John has expressed or is not anticipating?

John intimated that he is having trouble evaluating and benchmarking solutions for this new chapter in his life. While he was a skilled operator and had built an incredible business, he is unprepared for this part of his life—he doesn't know what he doesn't know. Some of the risks that he could anticipate would be executing without a plan or context of what a family office can and should do for him. This could lead to overspending or underspending on critical staff, challenges around managing the increased flow of information and requirements that he has levied on himself, or potentially getting into a position of illiquidity because of a series of haphazard direct investments.

With John's new wealth and increased public profile comes an increased risk of liability. His new homes, ranch expansion, and other dealings will expose him to new liabilities. Given his higher profile, he should start to consider a number of other privacy and security issues, such as the lack of resources dedicated to risk and threat management in comparison to what he likely invested with his prior company. There is also an outsized access to his personal financial information in the hands of a small number of people who work for him but are not properly trained or equipped to handle the additional scope, focus, and risks.

Another issue that he faces is his inability to plan and act in a strategic manner when his personal affairs drag him into the most tactical and minute planning details. He is mired in the day-to-day, and until he builds a proper team around him, he will struggle with thinking about the long game.

What should be the most time-consuming part of establishing the family office for John?

Even though John is an incredibly talented business operator, he lacks the experience, context, and strong network to make effective decisions around his family office at this point. He should focus his time on becoming educated about family offices, the services they provide and their various constructs, and on prioritizing solutions around his immediate service and advisory needs. This will prompt him to make an important first hire of someone who can help him build out the office. This person then will help him determine the services that it should provide, ensure that his immediate needs around reporting and managing his personal assets are being addressed, and identify and mitigate new risks.

CHAPTER TWO

Services

CASE STUDY

Summary

- More than nine months after the sale of Rybat Manufacturing
- Setting up the family office
- Determining which services to provide, when, and by whom

Key Words/Concepts

- Advice and services
- In-house versus outsourced
- Priorities

Challenge

It had been over nine months since the sale of the business, and John was feeling more comfortable with his decision to start his own family office. However, he had lingering questions on how to start the office, what it should look like, and what it should do. He received a great deal of advice on this topic from both professional advisers and his peer groups. While this advice was helpful, John often felt that the recommendations posed more questions than they answered.

As John began to put his family office plans into action, his lawyer, Natalia, was very helpful in describing the type of formal corporate entity that he should create to serve as the separate management company for the family office. This new entity would initially employ the various family office professionals, contract for office space, and pay all the bills. However, this still left open questions as to *what* the family office should be doing, *how*, and *by whom*. These were all questions that John needed to get answered.

His lawyer also suggested that John speak with Sam, his certified public accountant (CPA), to determine how best to fund the family office to ensure the greatest available tax benefits. John did reach out to Sam, but his impression was that Sam's experience with clients in his situation was limited. Sam's bread-and-butter business did not include working with family offices. Moreover, Sam indicated that he planned to retire in the next five years, which prompted John to start looking for a more suitable, long-term tax adviser.

John's various existing financial advisers were obviously ecstatic about helping him after the liquidity event. John couldn't recall ever receiving so many calls, e-mails, and invitations to play golf, including from numerous financial advisers whom he had never met. It was becoming challenging to keep up with all this outreach, and he knew that he needed to find a way to sort through and evaluate all these new contacts.

John wondered how investment decisions would be made once he created his family office. He had always managed his own investments, relying on advice and recommendations from his stockbroker, Ted, and hedge fund buddy, Charles. However, he never gave anyone the complete discretion to make investment decisions for him. While John certainly was comfortable making investment decisions and wanted to stay involved, he now faced handling a personal investment portfolio that was orders of magnitude greater than he had overseen in the past. Based on his research of similar-sized families, he was certain that investors for this level of assets did things quite differently, and likely with a different set and type of advisers.

Finally, John was starting to connect more frequently with his chief executive officer (CEO) networking group, and with renewed purpose. He was eager to understand how they structured, staffed, and managed their offices. However, the feedback he received about structures, governance, and approaches varied greatly.

All this advice was helpful, but John believed that he was struggling to place the specific recommendations into context. It felt as if that every time he learned about a new element of how to start and run a family office, he was opening doors to even more parts of such an office that he needed to understand.

John decided to get started by hiring someone to help him manage this increasing level of complexity. After all, he had run a successful and sophisticated business in the past, with lots of people and moving parts. John thought that overseeing a family office should be similar. Of all the people he knew and trusted who could help him, there was no one better than Jason. Jason was the chief financial officer (CFO) at his operating company and stayed in that role after the sale. John had stayed in touch with Jason and sensed that he was not happy with the new owners of the company and the demands of being part of a public company. John asked Jason to join him as the second employee for the family office (Janina, John's trusted administrative assistant, was the first hire). Jason agreed, and he was tasked with establishing a formal family office, overseeing the accounting, and helping manage all the various and increasingly complex personal activities and requirements.

BACKGROUND INFORMATION

What to Do, When, and By Whom

Family offices are responsible for a wide range of advice and services. While there are numerous ways to classify them, for the purposes of this discussion, we have organized them into seven primary areas (see figure 2.1). Details regarding the delivery of many of these services are provided later in the book.

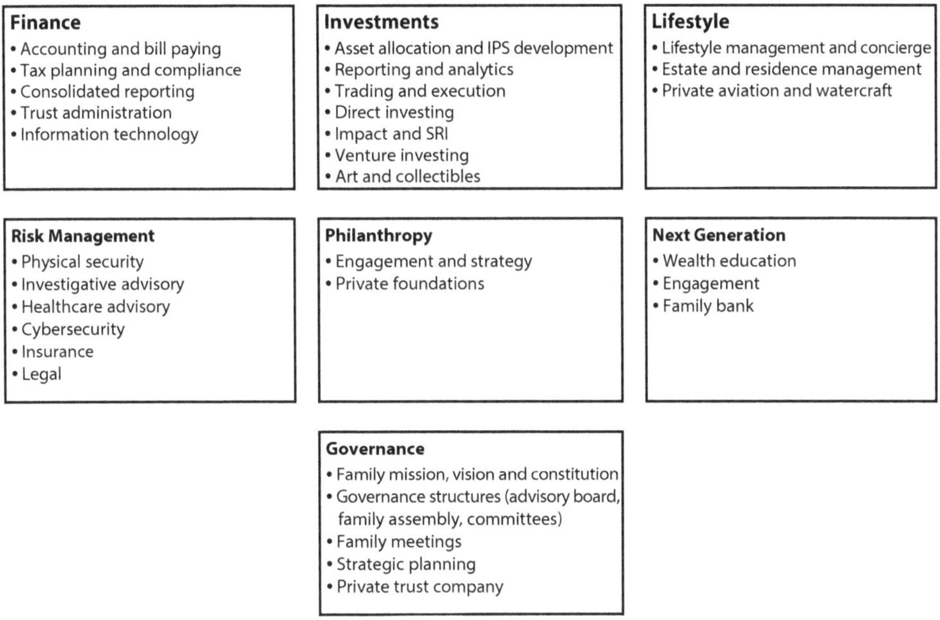

Finance
- Accounting and bill paying
- Tax planning and compliance
- Consolidated reporting
- Trust administration
- Information technology

Investments
- Asset allocation and IPS development
- Reporting and analytics
- Trading and execution
- Direct investing
- Impact and SRI
- Venture investing
- Art and collectibles

Lifestyle
- Lifestyle management and concierge
- Estate and residence management
- Private aviation and watercraft

Risk Management
- Physical security
- Investigative advisory
- Healthcare advisory
- Cybersecurity
- Insurance
- Legal

Philanthropy
- Engagement and strategy
- Private foundations

Next Generation
- Wealth education
- Engagement
- Family bank

Governance
- Family mission, vision and constitution
- Governance structures (advisory board, family assembly, committees)
- Family meetings
- Strategic planning
- Private trust company

Figure 2.1 The seven service verticals of family offices

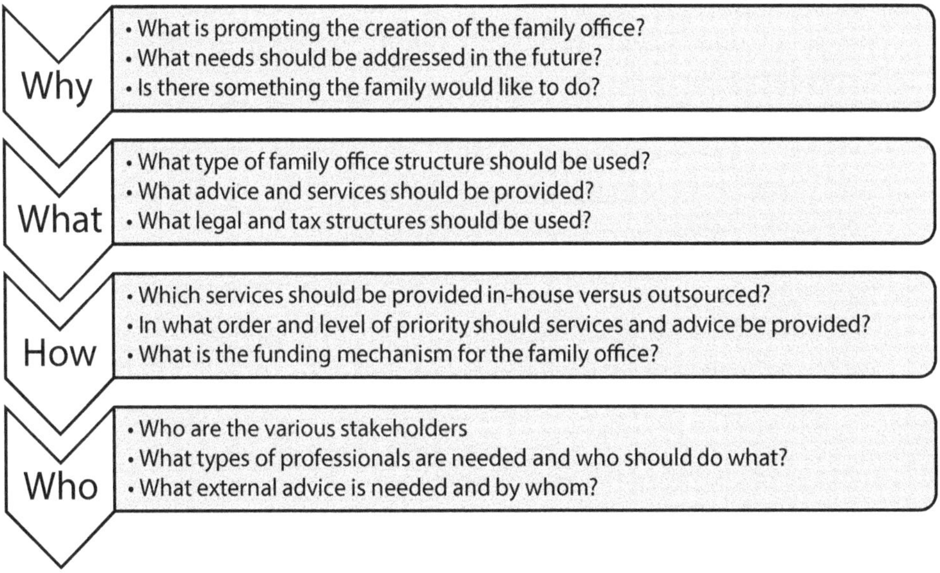

Why
- What is prompting the creation of the family office?
- What needs should be addressed in the future?
- Is there something the family would like to do?

What
- What type of family office structure should be used?
- What advice and services should be provided?
- What legal and tax structures should be used?

How
- Which services should be provided in-house versus outsourced?
- In what order and level of priority should services and advice be provided?
- What is the funding mechanism for the family office?

Who
- Who are the various stakeholders
- What types of professionals are needed and who should do what?
- What external advice is needed and by whom?

Figure 2.2 Determining the right advice and services to deliver to a wealthy family

While every family office will provide different types of services, and potentially additional specializations, figure 2.2 shows a good checklist to review broad areas of need for wealthy families. There are traditional needs, approaches, and prioritizations that apply broadly to family offices. However, what services to provide, how, and by whom will vary by family because of the differences in the types and evolution of challenges that families of substantial wealth face.

Determining the right advice and services to deliver to a wealthy family should be based on an assessment in four critical areas—namely, why, what, how, and who. The answers to these questions will form the foundation for important determinations regarding details of the delivery.

Family offices often grow initially by hiring professionals to conduct most services in house. At this stage, many do not take the time to strategically think about what they need, want, or should do themselves versus outsourcing to a third party. The reasons for this behavior stem from the way in which family offices are typically created and evolve.

Most family offices are created to address a growing level of complexity in living, managing assets, paying bills, and providing financial reporting. This growth in complexity usually is incremental, and families often meet these initial needs simply by hiring professionals to work in the family office. It should be noted, however, that decision-making around the formation and initial staffing is heavily influenced by the experience and interests of both the principals and the senior professionals in the family office.

Regardless of how the service requirements arise and solutions are provided, it is a best practice for families to evaluate what they should, and should not, be doing internally before making significant investments in people, processes, technology, and other resources.

Table 2.1 summarizes each of the key service areas and lists important considerations as to whether the family should outsource them. The table also provides some important insights into the priority with which particular services should be provided.

ASSESSMENT AND ISSUES SURFACED

What Did We Learn?

Having decided to start his own family office, John was confronted with numerous questions about execution. He was inundated with advice from multiple professional and personal relationships, but he did not have the experience or context to evaluate this advice properly. He questioned whether his needs and requirements might be different given his new level of wealth, and therefore warrant new approaches and solutions. John is starting to appreciate all the things he has on his plate that are reducing his ability to do other things he wants.

TABLE 2.1
Key service areas

Key Areas	Services	Delivery Considerations
Finance	• Accounting and bill paying • Tax planning and compliance • Consolidated reporting • Trust administration • Information system management	**In-house versus outsourcing:** Consideration should be given to the relative level of complexity, need for direct control, and privacy concerns. For example, bill payment and reporting require close involvement of the family and timely oversight and decision-making. Taxes and information technology (IT) are more easily outsourced and often require technical expertise not available within the family office. **Priorities:** Finance is one of the primary functions for a family office and should be one of the first solutions adopted. It is also a task that should be focused on throughout the life of the family office, even when it expands to provide other, more strategic services. Failure to deliver timely and accurate reporting will hamper the family office's ability to provide valuable advice in other areas.
Lifestyle	• Lifestyle management and concierge • Estate and residence management • Private aviation and watercraft	**In-house versus outsourcing:** Typically, these services require a combination of internal staff and external vendors. The actual oversight and management of the activity or asset is done by third-party specialty service providers on site and/or with technical expertise, scale, and the like. However, these services, which are often near and dear to the family, require coordination and oversight by internal family office staff. **Priorities:** Lifestyle needs may also be one of the first areas of focus, depending on the lifestyle, assets, and activities of the principals and the family. These activities affect the quality of life for the principals and the family and, therefore, should be (and remain) a priority.

(Continued)

TABLE 2.1 (*continued*)

Investments	<ul><li>Asset allocation and IPS development</li><li>Trading and execution</li><li>Direct investing</li><li>Reporting and analytics</li><li>Venture investing</li><li>Art and collectibles investing</li><li>Impact investing</li></ul>	**In-house versus outsourcing:** As with lifestyle needs and assets, albeit for different reasons, these types of investment usually require a combination of both internal and external resources. For direct and socially responsible investments, the family office is often involved in developing strategy, while the execution is carried out by third parties such as asset managers. Investments in art and collectibles are very personal to the family, although acquisition, appraisals, and storage require the use of expert third parties. **Priorities:** Investments, while of great importance to a wealthy family and a considerable focus by many family offices, is usually an area where the ultimate solutions evolve over time. First, the assets are often illiquid and therefore do not require significant oversight, aside from knowing about and managing around public or private single-stock exposures, where possible. Second, principals generally evolve in their thinking and practices around investments as they become more liquid, engage with investment professionals, and learn about the capital markets. As a result, while important, the family office should address investments in a measured way, often following the lead of the principals, who may dictate the approach, which advisers to use, and other decisions.
Risk management	<ul><li>Physical security</li><li>Investigative advisory</li><li>Cybersecurity</li><li>Insurance</li><li>Legal</li><li>Heathcare advisory</li></ul>	**In-house versus outsourcing:** With very few exceptions, these services are almost exclusively provided by third parties that specialize in each area. While a family office may have internal legal counsel, that person is usually coordinating services across multiple external law firms. **Priorities:** A family office should focus intently on risk management from the beginning, whether or not the principals express an interest in that or direct them to do so. Wealth comes with considerable risks, not just from publicity but from the personal assets that wealthy families acquire, the investments they make, and the lifestyle they lead.

Philanthropy	• Engagement and strategy • Private foundations and other philanthropic vehicles	**In-house versus outsourcing:** Philanthropy usually begins within the family office and expands to involve third parties over time as the family develops its philanthropic mission and increases the amount of money dedicated to charitable causes. A private foundation, while a separate legal entity, is often overseen and administered by the family office itself (until it is quite large). **Priorities:** Philanthropy, as well as the level of involvement by a family office, vary greatly from family to family. Senior executives in the office should be attuned to existing or evolving interests in philanthropy and assist the family when and where they can. Over time, this may become an area of great interest to a family, and therefore of considerable focus to the family office.
Next Generation	• Wealth education • Family meetings • Family bank	**In-house versus outsourcing:** Educating children about the challenges that come with wealth must begin with the family, while assistance is often provided by the family office. Selectively, the family or family office will use vehicles such as a "family bank," governance and educational forms such as "family meetings," and outside experts for things such as meeting facilitation, education and training, and the drafting of governance documents. **Priorities:** Wealth education delivered in its various forms is another area where assistance by the family office is very dependent on, and often set by, the principals. So much of the need is based on whether the principals are personally interested in and committed to providing such education, the age of the children, and the investment and/or philanthropic activities of the next generation. Regardless, it is an important area for wealthy families for reasons that are discussed later in this book. Senior executives within a family office should be aware of ways to provide the children with wealth education, periodically raise the issue with principals, and be mindful of behavioral issues among children that would warrant making this a priority.

He recognizes that in large part, the family office will need to be responsible for overseeing and managing these areas.

Case Questions

- Is John talking to the right people?
- Who else should John be talking to?
- What services should the family office focus on first?
- What services might the family office be required to provide in the near future?
- What should the family office do in house versus relying on others?
- How can John better manage his time so that he can pursue his passions?

RECOMMENDED SOLUTIONS

Responses to Case Questions

Is John talking to the right people?

Yes and no. John is talking to many of the right people, inasmuch as they are part of his current contingent of professional advisers. However, he is starting to appreciate that his advisers may not have the relevant experience with larger investors or family offices. This is not to suggest that their advice is not sound or that they should not be considered as advisers for him going forward. Rather, it means that John needs to be mindful of possible gaps in both his *and* their knowledge as it relates to the questions currently being asked and the answers that he is being provided.

Who else should John be talking to?

Because John understandably does not have experience managing a family office, he should seek to learn what he can about family offices and their various constructs, understand how they are organized, and identify the services that they typically provide, when, and by whom. This research will help put into context the advice that he is receiving. He should also seek advice from individuals who currently have family offices (as he has with the CEO networking group), as well as consultants who advise principals on setting up a family office.

What services should the family office focus on first?

Family offices are generally established to manage an existing, and often growing, level of complexity in the personal and financial affairs of a family. As such, the services that initially should be provided largely center around mitigating these complexities. In John's case, they would be his various personal construction projects, including general management and oversight. Related to these are the accounting, bill payment paying, and reporting for the sizeable expenditures that these projects require.

In addition, family offices should focus on ways that they can help the principals engage in their passions. While many of these activities may not be creating complexity right at the moment, addressing them early can be of great value to the family. In some cases, this support is provided by simply freeing up the principals' time so they can engage in other activities. In other cases, the family office can provide direct assistance to the principals. For John, this assistance could help him with the possible acquisition of a new plane or with his direct investing activities. For Sofia, the focus might be her philanthropic ambitions. The combination of the two factors—managing complexity and assisting the principals in pursuing their passions—provides the greatest immediate impact on improving the quality of life for them and therefore should be a main focus for the family office.

Related to both of these points would be the legal structures, tax planning, and managerial agreements related to establishing the family office, owning assets, and ensuring that appropriate tax planning is done.

What services might the family office be required to provide in the near future?

Investment management is obviously an area of great importance for the family office, given the long-term significance of properly managing John's significant investment portfolio. However, investment management should be considered after his immediate needs in finance, lifestyle, and risk management are addressed. This does not mean waiting to begin a discussion regarding investment management or considering strategies. Developing an appropriate investment solution requires a great deal of time, and sometimes the hiring of additional professionals. Focusing on investment management in a manner that compromises effective execution on the other, more immediate needs, therefore, is a risk to the family office. Keeping that in mind, helping John with the development of an investment management solution should be one of the family office's next major priorities.

What should the family office do in house versus relying on others?

John has the requisite wealth to support all the family office functions in house if he wants. He has not expressed an overt desire for extraordinary privacy, nor has he demonstrated that he must be in absolute control of all services. Given this, his immediate needs regarding managing his personal assets, improving accounting and reporting, and allowing him to pursue a diverse range of personal passions suggest that a mix of internal versus external service solutions will be best for him.

The ranch in Wyoming and the house in Cabo San Lucas cannot be managed daily by the family office, given their locations and the experience required to do this well. John's family office should expect to outsource much of the ongoing management of these properties to third-party residence managers. Furthermore, while they are complicated and expensive assets, they do not rise to a level where the family office needs to hire a dedicated estate manager to oversee these; instead, it should rely on interfacing with local property managers. The house in Glencoe, in contrast, is both a local project and the family's primary residence. Families typically want to oversee the construction and management of these projects personally, albeit with the help of contractors, and can manage the ongoing needs of the property personally.

However, the record keeping, bill paying, and reporting for all these properties can and should be provided by the family office. The vast majority of family offices of this size conduct their own bill paying, record keeping, and reporting, largely because the family offices are doing so for other activities, and because most principals prefer to have greater oversight and control of their expenses.

It is too soon to determine whether the investment management functions should be outsourced by the family office. John certainly has the appropriate level of wealth to hire a chief investment officer (CIO) for the family office, although his interests and needs regarding the investment portfolio have not yet been discussed in enough detail to explore the idea of having a dedicated person in this position. John's interests in private aviation will likely be handled by him, at least initially, given his familiarity with planes. Their interest in philanthropy is still in its early stages, so it should be a focus in the future.

How can John better manage his time so he can pursue his passions?

One of the reasons for setting up a family office is so that John has more time to pursue his passions. However, he has both an interest and a need to stay involved with the oversight and management of his various personal assets, investment activities, and philanthropic pursuits. To do so, John will need to staff his family office properly and establish the appropriate reporting, communication, and governance mechanisms. This is where his experience running an operating company will be relevant, although there are important nuances that come up with family offices with which both he and the family office should be aware.

CHAPTER THREE

Leadership and Staffing

CASE STUDY

Summary

- One year after the sale of Rybat Manufacturing
- Senior leadership positions
- Hiring considerations

Key Words/Concepts

- Leadership
- Staffing

Challenge

The first thing that Jason had to do in his new role as the chief financial officer (CFO) for John's family office was to learn exactly what a family office is. He had certainly heard the term before and knew some former public accounting colleagues who worked at family offices. However, his background of managing the finances for a private operating company, and most recently a public company, did not overlap much with professionals managing the affairs of very wealthy individuals. Nor did he personally have the high level of wealth or complexity of affairs that would give him great insight into the issues that John and Sofia were now facing.

Despite this, Jason was confident that he could quickly develop an understanding of family offices and help John manage his. This was certainly true with respect to the accounting, bill paying, and reporting responsibilities. Jason was also confident that he could effectively oversee the various projects around personal assets because he had run large, complex, and expensive projects at Rybat Manufacturing. However, Jason was concerned about being relied upon to help John better manage his investments and buy a plane. And then there were Sofia's needs connected to her philanthropic ambitions. She was starting to write much larger checks to various charities and was spending more time volunteering at the Children's Hospital.

Jason also knew that he had to set the family office up properly from a legal standpoint and ensure that all the appropriate tax-saving strategies were being considered. As a certified public accountant (CPA) who had spent ten years in public accounting before joining Rybat Manufacturing, Jason was broadly familiar with management companies, asset ownership vehicles, charitable vehicles, and tax-planning strategies used by small businesses and their owners. However, he had no direct experience with family offices.

Jason began his new role in learning mode. He met with John's various legal, tax, and financial advisers to introduce himself, understand their current roles, and assess what they could do for the family office. To get to know about and better understand the managerial needs across the personal properties, Jason spent time speaking with the various contractors and local property managers and made plans to visit each of them.

Jason began to develop an organizational chart for the family office and created an initial budget. He relied on Natalia and Tadeusz to help integrate the organizational design with the various legal entities that would need to be set up. However, the design for the family office was going to be more challenging. He would have to develop one that listed the personnel he needed, their roles, and the various reporting lines. He would also need to develop an initial budget that reflected staff costs, related overhead, external service provider fees, and any other costs and fees that the family office would incur.

BACKGROUND INFORMATION

Roles and Responsibilities

When creating a family office, it is critical to understand the professional profiles and expectations for the key family office positions. The profiles presented in table 3.1 provide insights into the scope of responsibilities for key roles and the qualities and experiences required to fill those roles. Larger family offices will need people in the C-suite

TABLE 3.1
Roles and Responsibilities

Role	Definition
Chief executive officer (CEO)	The most senior executive at the family office, who manages the organization and establishes the strategy for the single-family office (SFO) to ensure that its mission and goals are fulfilled. This person is often the primary liaison between the SFO and the principals of the family.
Chief investment officer (CIO)	Designs and executes investment strategy for the SFO and manages overall assets. This person manages the internal investment team and external asset managers, and may report to the CEO, family principals, and, occasionally, board of directors.
Portfolio manager	Experienced investment professional who works under the direction of the CIO or senior managers. Assists in selecting, monitoring, and managing investments and investment managers. Completes special investment performance research studies.

Investment analyst	Analyzes and values potential acquisition opportunities and monitors the performance of the existing portfolio; reports to the CIO.
Chief financial officer (CFO)	The key executive responsible for financial policy and planning. Oversees budget, tax, insurance, and treasury functions, and ensures that financial policies and procedures meet the SFO's objectives and regulatory requirements. This person typically reports to the CEO and, occasionally, board of directors.
Controller	Oversees accounting, budgeting, and facilitation of relationships with lawyers, prime brokers, and tax advisors; typically reports to the CFO.
Tax manager	Prepares and reviews complex annual returns and provides ongoing strategic tax planning services; typically reports to the CFO.
Accountant	Maintains the ledger, manages payroll, and performs financial statement preparation and analysis; typically reports to the controller or CFO.
Bookkeeper	Executes daily accounting and administrative tasks; typically reports to the accountant, controller, or CFO.
General counsel	Advises on routine legal matters, reviews investment and management structures, and oversees outside counsel regarding tax, estate planning, insurance, and other issues.
Chief operating officer (COO)	Ensures the efficient and effective operation and business administration of the SFO; oversees administrative and staff functions such as technology and human resources; typically reports to the CEO.
Executive assistant	Supports a senior executive in a staff capacity by handling a wide variety of situations involving the administrative functions of the office that need not be brought to the attention of the senior executive.
House/property manager	Controls residential properties within the organization. Oversees and coordinates property and landscape maintenance, security plans, and issues. Attends public meetings on behalf of the employer and secures needed permits and approvals.

Source: Trish Botoff, "Compensation Trends, Best Practces, and Market Data," 2020.

providing oversight over all these functions. Smaller ones may not require them, they may not have the resources to fill them, or executives may be able to wear multiple hats.

The C-Suite in Family Offices

Leadership matters in all organizations, including in family offices. This is true across all senior roles, although the CEO role at a family office is particularly hard to fill, and for many family offices, the responsibilities cannot be successfully outsourced to a service provider or vendor. That is why it is not uncommon to see smaller or newly formed family offices headed by family members. They may not want the job particularly, but no acceptable candidate can readily be found to take it. Similarly, the looming retirement of a longtime CEO can pose an existential threat to the sustainability of a family office, particularly if it coincides (as it often does) with a change in generational control of the family itself.

The position of CIO likewise poses a challenge to fill. Top candidates all sport large salary requirements and may insist on bringing with them well-paid staffs of analysts, strategists, and other support people. Competition to hire CIOs comes not just from other family offices, but from all corners of the asset management industry, pushing up compensation levels. Faced with this kind of expense, small and midsize family offices often decide to outsource their investment function to one of the growing number of firms providing external CIO services.

The remaining two positions listed here, CFO and operations manager, tend to be easier to fill because candidates can be drawn from a broad range of industries, not just the upper tiers of the wealth management business.

Tables 3.2 and 3.3 list the key areas of responsibility for each of the senior leadership positions within a family office.

Hiring for Both Fit and Function

A common refrain among professionals in this industry is, "Working in a family office is different." Family offices require employees to be both good at their job responsibilities and able to manage the unique dynamics that come with working for wealthy families. As with other diverse and complex businesses, success in hiring for a family office depends greatly on the development of, and attention to, a human capital plan

TABLE 3.2
Senior Leadership Positions within a Family Office—CEO, CFO

CEO	• Oversight of all family office operations
	• Strategic planning for the family office enterprise
	• Management and review of investment policy
	• Strategic financial planning and forecasting
	• Management of personnel hiring, training, and mentoring
	• Responsible for family office board meetings
	• Management of planned and ad hoc projects for principals
	• Wealth education of the next generation of the family
	• Engagement with legal counsel for family office and related matters
	• Supervision of risk management and continuity of operations planning
CFO	• Management of finance, accounting and tax personnel
	• Overseeing of financial management operations
	• Development of financial management strategy across the family office enterprise
	• Consolidated financial reporting of the family's personal and business affairs
	• Generation of the monthly/quarterly financial package for principals, which includes profits and losses and a consolidated report of investment assets
	• Supervision of annual and ad hoc audits of the system of controls, assets, and finances
	• Regular reviews of insurance policies and insurable assets
	• Coordination with the CEO and operations manager of personal asset forecasts and budgeting
	• Preparation and filing of tax reports
	• Support for bill payment capabilities for family members
	• Partnering with internal and external advisors

that specifically defines each position in the organizational structure. The definition of each position includes the following two essential components: position specifications (i.e., function) and cultural "fit."[1]

Position Specifications

- Scope
- Reporting relationships
- Responsibilities and accountabilities
- Performance expectations
- Metrics for measuring success

TABLE 3.3
Senior Leadership Positions within a Family Office—CIO, Operations Manager

CIO	• Management of investment personnel, including hiring, training, retention, and mentoring • Oversight of family office portfolios managed in house and/or by third-party managers, including liquid and illiquid investments • Support for principals to achieve and express their investment strategies and goals • Developing, maintaining, and measuring the family office investment policy statements (IPSs) • Sourcing of investment opportunities in public and/or private markets • Coordinating with the CFO on performance reporting across all assets and portfolios • Coordination with in-house and external wealth management teams on investment decision-making processes • Supporting the next generation's wealth education and incorporating external advisors as necessary
Operations manager	• Responsible for nonfinancial family assets, such as artworks, personal residences, aircraft, and yachts • Hiring, training, and mentoring of administrative and operational staff • Project management and reporting • Managing select third-party relationships, including residence managers, lifestyle and concierge service providers, pilots and captains, and other professionals • Overseeing personal staff, including chauffeurs, maids, chefs, housekeepers, and others

Once the position specifications have been clearly defined, the family can determine the skill, knowledge, experience, and competency requirements, as well as the education, certifications, and designations required for each role.

Ideal Candidate Profiles/Culture Fit

Defining the personal characteristics and attributes, values, behavioral characteristics, decision-making and interpersonal styles, and other motivators needed to ensure a good culture fit with the family are also an essential part of this process. Getting the fit right is critical for success and effectiveness.

Compensation philosophy is an important dimension of culture fit and may differ significantly from family to family. On one end of the spectrum, a family believes that they are hiring an employee to help them achieve their objectives and will compensate that person only in the form of a salary and annual bonus. On the other end of the spectrum, a family believes that they are hiring a partner to help them achieve their objectives and will compensate the person accordingly. In addition to salary and bonus, they will offer coinvestment opportunities and/or carried interest and other forms of long-term incentive (LTI) compensation.

While it is tempting to shortcut or skip this part of the process, investing the time to define the position *and* the culture fit requirements carefully is the only way to ensure success. Making the wrong hire costs much more than money; it also can cause wasted time and potential derailment of the family mission and legacy. The two primary causes for the failure of family office searches are

- Hiring an individual who is known and trusted but lacks the requisite skills and experience to perform the job (because the position, performance expectations, and metrics for success were not clearly defined up front and assessed before the hiring decision was made)
- Hiring someone who has the requisite skills and experience but is not a good culture fit (because the culture fit requirements were not clearly defined up front and assessed before the hiring decision was made)

Two other reasons for failed searches are

- Lack of an effective search process
- Ineffective onboarding, compensation, performance management, and/or retention strategies and processes

Assessment Process

Once the family has completed human capital planning, including the definition of leadership roles, position descriptions, and ideal candidate profiles, they have the information they need to develop a comprehensive assessment process that will be used to identify and select candidates. Each family is unique, so the criteria for culture fit will be unique to each family. There is no industry standard for assessment criteria.

ASSESSMENT CRITERIA The first step is to define selection criteria consistent with the position description, ideal candidate profile, and culture fit requirements. These criteria will also enable candidates to be consistently assessed both in an absolute sense against the requirements and in a relative sense, benchmarked to one another.

For consistency, and to identify the best candidate, it is important to use the same criteria and process to evaluate all candidates—this includes internal and external candidates as well as family and nonfamily candidates.

ASSESSMENT TOOLS The next step is to determine which tools will be used in the assessment process. Numerous tools are available, and they are often used in combination. The following represents a list of the tools we consider to be most effective:

- **Structured interview:** Structured interviews involve asking each candidate the same questions in order to compare the responses afterward and assess them consistently.
- **Behavioral interview:** A behavioral interview is a technique that requires candidates to be introspective and asks them about past behaviors in order to predict future behaviors; candidates are also asked to discuss specific experiences and stories to clarify and explain their behaviors and motivations.
- **Open-ended questions:** Determining in advance what you want to learn from a candidate and then preparing and asking open-ended questions are important in all assessment interviews; the interviewer can then ask follow-up questions to clarify the meaning or intent of each candidate's responses. Open-ended questions are important; the interviewer is not effective if they put words in a candidate's mouth.
- **Behavioral assessments:** There are numerous behavioral assessment tools in the market, and a number of these can be very helpful. However, a behavioral tool is no substitute for comprehensive interviews in which you truly get to know candidates, their values, and their experiences in depth to assess fit. These tools are not intended to be a shortcut or "silver bullet."
- **Evaluation forms:** Evaluation grids or matrices that indicate the specific criteria to be assessed using a rating scale are an effective way to assess and rank candidates consistently.

- **Case studies/presentations:** In instances where the family wants to gain a deeper understanding of how a candidate approaches an analysis or problem-solving situation and/or a client advisory interface, or they are torn between finalist candidates, case studies or presentations can be helpful.

Proper assessment is critical to making the right long-term hire decisions. Families who do not have an effective assessment process have a high risk of failure. In other words, if you do not know what you are looking for or how to assess whether you have found it, you cannot succeed—or if you do, it is only a fluke and unrepeatable. A family cannot rely on a miracle to occur. They need a process that can produce a reliable, consistent, and successful outcome.

Recruiting Process

INTERNAL SELECTION PROCESS It is important to identify and assess internal candidates, including family members, for potential succession to leadership roles. The assessment process outlined here should be applied to all internal candidates. If these criteria are deemed important for success and effectiveness, they should apply to everyone equally, including any family members being considered for positions.

EXTERNAL EXECUTIVE SEARCH PROCESS The family conducts an external search in cases where a leadership role cannot be filled via internal succession, for whatever reason. Whether the family decides to manage the search process themselves or engage an outside professional search consultant (i.e., an executive recruiter) to conduct the search, it is extremely important to have a well-defined, structured process to ensure a successful outcome. The search process's time line, milestones, and deliverables must be established. The individuals involved in the process and their accountabilities and responsibilities should also be clearly laid out.

An effective search process will include the following elements:

- **Market research:** Conduct market research to identify the universe of potential candidates.
- **Search and candidate target strategy:** Based on the market research, create a target pool of potential candidates to approach.

- **Contact and screen the target pool:** Access and engage potential candidates in discussion about the position; through screening conversations, determine the best-qualified candidates to interview.

INTERVIEW, ASSESSMENT, AND SELECTION PROCESS Once potential candidates have been sufficiently screened, it is time to implement the formal interview and selection process. As noted earlier in this chapter, candidates should be assessed using the appropriate tools and criteria on an absolute and relative basis. This will enable the family to effectively select the best candidate.

NEGOTIATE AN EMPLOYMENT OFFER Once the final candidate has been selected and compensation and other employment terms agreed upon, an employment offer is typically made contingent upon satisfactory professional reference and background checks. Some families may do preliminary referencing prior to making the offer, but it is crucial that the candidate's current employment situation never be compromised. If preliminary referencing is desired, it is best to ask the candidate for the names of references with whom they would be comfortable having the family or search consultant speak. When conducting background checks (e.g., criminal), it is very important to use an outside firm that specializes in doing this work.

Development Plan

In defining the ideal candidate, people often come up with a wish list—a list of ten requirements, with the hope that the individual will score 10 on each criterion. However, this person may not exist. The reality is that an individual will likely score 12 in one or more areas and 8 in one or more. The family will select the individual who represents the best composite fit for the position. If there are any gaps in the candidate's technical knowledge or skills, a development plan should be implemented to ensure the success of the new hire. The individuals responsible for carrying out the plan and evaluating progress toward completion should be clearly designated. Commitment from all constituencies concerned is necessary to the success of the new hire and the development plan.

Onboarding Plan

The onboarding plan is designed to help the new employee become acclimated to their new role, to the family and family office culture, and to the family's advisers. The goal is also to help the new employee build relationships and achieve results quickly and effectively. Creating early wins for the new hire promotes credibility with the family and among the other employees. It also gives the new employee confidence that they can be successful. Commitment to the success of the new employee and to creating an environment that fosters success is critical.

KEY QUESTIONS AND CONSIDERATIONS

- Who will design the onboarding plan for the new employee?
- How will you prepare the new employee in advance to build relationships with key family members, staff, and advisers?
- If issues occur with the family dynamic, how will you help resolve them?
- In the case of succession, how will you help transition relationships from the departing executive to the new executive?

Performance Management Plan

An effective performance management plan defines the expectations and metrics to use to evaluate success; they must be objective, results-driven, quantitative, and qualitative. Performance expectations and metrics must be aligned with family philosophies, values, and objectives. They must also be mutually agreed upon and clearly communicated. Ongoing, open communication and feedback regarding performance and achievement of goals and objectives are also critical. Solving an issue and getting back on track quickly constitute the best way to avoid creating a chronic issue that could result in failure.

Compensation and reward systems also need to be designed and structured in alignment with family values, philosophies, goals, and objectives. Incentives absolutely drive behavior. The family needs to be sure that compensation and incentive plans will drive behavior that leads to desired results.

Compensation Plans

While compensation plans vary across family offices, the most common is a traditional salary and bonuses (or annual incentives), with recent survey data suggesting that the practice is followed by more than 80 percent of families. Decisions regarding bonus amounts are typically made on a discretionary basis, as opposed to a formal incentive compensation plan that may or may not include delineated metrics. This is not surprising, given that family offices are just now starting to emerge as a separate industry, with benchmarks around both compensation level and performance measurement.

However, family offices should consider using more structured incentive plans as opposed to simply providing discretionary bonuses. These plans provide the family with an opportunity to use compensation to drive targeted performance and improve alignment with strategy.[2]

Methods for Determining Annual Incentives

Whereas discretionary bonuses are usually determined at the end of a performance period, more formalized or structured incentive plans define certain criteria at the beginning of the performance period. These can include the following:

- **Participation:** Establishes which positions or employees will take part in an incentive plan.
- **Incentive opportunity:** Often defined as a percentage of base salary.
- **Performance criteria:** Outlines which performance categories will be considered for earning an incentive.
- **Performance targets:** Establishes performance expectations, potentially at threshold, target, or maximum defined performance and payout levels. Typically incorporates key financial metrics, such as investment returns versus key benchmarks, but may also include more qualitative measures. A mix of quantitative versus qualitative metrics, as well as which financial metrics are used, are established to align with the family's strategic direction, varying substantially among family offices.
- **Performance period:** Defines the work period that will be used to assess performance (typically aligned with calendar year, but

not in all cases), as well as the expected timing of payouts, which often depends upon the timing of investment or other year-end financial results.

Long-Term Incentive Plans

As previously mentioned, compensation arrangements and practices for executives and other key team members at family offices are becoming more formalized and sophisticated. The use of LTIs, particularly based on assets under management (AUM), is one such trend. Reasons for implementing LTI plans include the following:

- Increasing competitiveness of compensation levels with industries from which key family office employees and executives are recruited
- Motivating employees to achieve performance levels above what would normally be accomplished
- Increasing the office's value to the family, encouraging an ownership mentality
- Providing a retention mechanism through the use of "golden handcuffs"
- Creating an opportunity for long-term financial security and retirement planning for key executives
- Allowing participants to defer LTI payouts (and taxes) when implemented concurrent with a nonqualified deferred compensation (NQDC) plan

LTI DESIGN CONSIDERATIONS Designing formalized incentive plans for senior employees at a family office, whether they are annual or over a longer term, is challenging due to the unique needs, issues, and dynamics of family offices. This helps explain the higher percentage of LTI plans used by investment-centric family offices.

However, this should not be a reason to disqualify the use of LTI plans. Rather, it is an opportunity for family office executives to initiate discussions with the family about requirements and expectations, which would serve them greatly. There is an increasing number of compensation consultants that specialize in family offices, which can, and should, be used as a professional resource.

The following are a number of reasons why family offices are implementing LTI plans:

- The long-term goals of the family and the family office.
- Award structures that drive performance.
- Aligning the value of annual LTI awards to current performance.
- Sequencing cash payouts to encourage retention, which results in a program that works less like a bonus plan and more like an equity plan.

LTI PLAN PREVALENCE AND VESTING Coinvestment opportunities are the most prevalent type of LTI plan used by family offices, followed by deferred bonuses and incentives and carried interests.

The use of vesting provisions is a common practice and is especially recommended to be used with LTI plans as a retention mechanism. In family offices offering LTI compensation, most incorporate three- to five-year vesting provisions. However, some firms report that no vesting provisions exist. Vesting provisions are an important tool for retaining talent and can also be seen as an opportunity to align compensation programs with the long-term goals of the family office.

Table 3.4 presents a list of typical LTI programs and their best uses.

TABLE 3.4
LTI Programs

Plan Type	Best Uses
Coinvestment opportunity	• Allows participants to have minority participation, alongside the family, in investments to which they would not have access normally • Family offices with a private equity function or similar investment opportunities • Participation limited to a select group of key employees
Carried interest	• Provides participants with a share of investment profits in excess of a specified return, typically in alternative investments such as private equity or hedge funds • Family office with a private equity function • Participation usually limited to CEO/CIO/private equity roles
Deferred bonus/ incentive compensation	• An incentive compensation opportunity based on longer-term performance; typically vests over time and pays out in the future • Implemented by SFOs that focus on managing the family's affairs and investments • Can be offered to an array of employees depending on their seniority and roles

Source: Trish Botoff, "Compensation Trends, Best Practces, and Market Data," 2020.

ASSESSMENT AND ISSUES SURFACED

What Did We Learn?

Jason is obviously an important first hire for the family office, and John will rely heavily upon him to help manage the delivery of services and advice across each of the areas of need. However, Jason is not an expert in all these areas, so he will need significant help from others. His initial focus is on organizational structures, staffing, and financial management.

Case Questions

- Why was Jason the first person John hired to help him with setting up and managing the family office?
- What resources should Jason use to learn about family offices?
- Is Jason focusing on the right things?
- How should Jason find and evaluate potential employees?
- What staffing solutions should Jason consider to obtain help with the residential projects in Glencoe, Wyoming, and Cabo San Lucas?
- What should Jason start to do about helping John better manage his investments?
- How can Jason help John with finding and buying a new plane?
- Is there anything Jason can do to help Sofia with her charitable activities?

RECOMMENDED SOLUTIONS

Responses to Case Questions

Why was Jason the first person John hired to help him with setting up and managing the family office?

Principals new to setting up a family office often choose initial employees around their priority needs, familiarity, and trust. As the CFO for John's former company, Jason had the required background to help manage the immediate and pressing issues that John faced—namely, better accounting, bill paying, and reporting on the numerous activities. Given Jason's background at Rybat Manufacturing, John also had confidence that he could help initially staff the family office for its needs in other areas where project management was a high priority, including residence management and lifestyle/concierge.

John also knew and worked well with Jason, and he trusted him. It is difficult for principals who are only recently coming into significant wealth and setting up a family office to hand off important and sensitive personal matters to outsiders, even if they are, in theory, more qualified to help given their greater background and experience.

What resources should Jason use to learn about family offices?

Very few technical resources are available to tell family office professionals how to do their jobs. As a result, most family office executives rely on advice from the professionals who serve them and peers who play similar roles for other families. There are also a number of family office industry trade organizations, networks, clubs, conferences, and executive educational programs. In addition to speaking with John's advisers, Jason should seek out and develop a network of peers with whom he can connect periodically, as well as join relevant trade organizations and clubs, attend family office conferences, and consider attending a family office–focused executive education program.

Is Jason focusing on the right things?

Yes, because helping John gain control over the financial, operational, and reporting issues is a critical task, and thus it should take immediate priority. Jason is also right to start with the organizational imperatives, including setting up the necessary legal structures, determining required staffing, and budgeting costs.

How should Jason find and evaluate potential employees?

The answer depends on the function for which Jason is hiring. The finance and accounting needs of a family office are very similar to those of small businesses, so finding professionals who can assist in these areas is relatively easy for Jason, and likely similar to what he did when he worked for Rybat Manufacturing. The same can be said for information technology (IT), albeit less directly; however, hiring for other service responsibilities such as estate management, lifestyle and concierge, and investment management will be more difficult for Jason. He does not yet know which of these services John and he may decide to bring in house versus relying on external service providers to deliver. Neither does he have connections within the industries that employ these types of employees. As a result, John should consider using a recruiting firm that specializes in working with family offices, in addition to consulting his network of peers, trade organizations, and clubs.

What staffing solutions should Jason consider to obtain help with the residential projects in Glencoe, Wyoming, and Cabo San Lucas?

Because Jason has neither the expertise nor the time to personally manage, on a day-to-day basis, the numerous needs related to the various residential projects, he must rely initially on third-party property managers. The challenge for him, as well as for many family offices, is that large estates, particularly those under construction or remodeling, require a unique expertise and level of ongoing oversight that exceeds the capabilities of traditional and local property managers. For this reason, many family offices with substantial residential management needs often contract with external estate managers or hire a dedicated in-house professional. At this stage, it is likely best for Jason to engage the services of an external estate management firm until the construction and remodeling projects are completed. He can then assess whether he should bring this service in house, depending on the ongoing supervisory and managerial needs across all the properties.

What should Jason start to do about helping John better manage his investments?

At this point, it is too early for Jason to make this a major priority, given everything else he has on his plate. Furthermore, Jason has little sense of how John will ultimately want to manage his investments, whether via an in-house CIO or by leveraging some or more of his current or future financial advisers. This subject, however, should be a point of discussion with John only once Jason has addressed the more immediate needs.

How can Jason help John with finding and buying a new plane?

Because John is a pilot and aircraft enthusiast, it is unlikely that he will delegate to Jason the primary job of finding and selecting a jet and determining the best way to employ pilots (e.g., whether by relying on a local aircraft management company or creating a small flight department). However, Jason should get up to speed about private aviation because without a doubt, John will ask him for help in such areas as comparing the financial implications of different types of planes, ownership options, and pilot staffing. He may also be responsible for interfacing with various aviation professionals and attorneys regarding contracts, insurance, employment agreements, and other issues.

Is there anything Jason can do to help Sofia
with her charitable activities?

While Sofia has not yet expressed an interest in doing something more substantial with her philanthropy, nor has she asked for his help, Jason should consider that this will be an important area where the family office can eventually provide a great deal of support. It is not uncommon for principals who are already engaged in philanthropy to want to expand these efforts, sometimes significantly, once they have both the resources and the time to focus on them. In addition, because the financial magnitude of charitable gifts is increasing, Jason should make sure to consult and involve John's attorney and CPA to ensure that the proper philanthropic vehicles are being considered and that available tax planning is being conducted.

Services

BACKGROUND INFORMATION
FOR CASE STUDIES 4 THROUGH 9

It had been eighteen months since John sold Rybat Manufacturing, and a year after he decided to create his own family office, Left Seat Management,[1] and hired Jason, his former CFO, to help him get started (figure s2.1). A lot has changed since then, as John's and his family's needs expanded and both he and Jason became more familiar with the needs, structures, and management of a family office.

At this point, the family office had eleven full-time staff members and 5,000 square feet of office space in Evanston, Illinois, and it had made a few important hires. This included the formal family office chief executive officer (CEO), Michael, whom John met through one of his CEO networking peer groups.

Michael had the relevant experience that John needed to set up his family office. He started his career as an investment banker before migrating to private banking, where he advised private clients on wealth management, banking, investments, and numerous related issues.

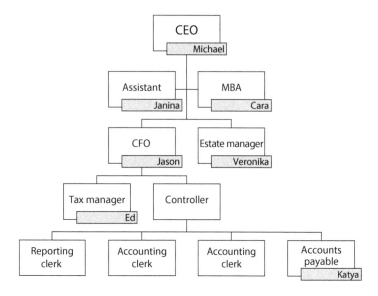

Figure s2.1 Updated staffing diagram for the Left Seat Management family office

He ultimately rose to a position running the wealth management business for a boutique private bank. Michael was eager to bring his broad experience working with wealthy families to help John and Sofia, as the capstone to his career.

Because of his diverse background, Michael was also intimately involved in helping John with his substantial investment portfolio and served as the informal chief investment officer (CIO) for the family office. Since the sale of his company, John had taken his time to learn what he could about investment management options and best practices, particularly from families that invested similar-sized portfolios. John came to appreciate that there was a great deal of variation in how families managed their wealth. Some family offices hired their own CIOs to oversee and control virtually all aspects of investment management, including elements such as strategy development, research, and execution. Others were much more delegatory, handing off the investment management (including strategy and execution) to third-party investment management firms, including private banks, brokerage firms, and investment consultants.

In addition, direct investing in small to medium-sized private companies was something on which John was spending a great deal of time these days. He had a penchant for these investments because of his background as a founder and operator. John was starting to see an increased level of private deal flow and had already invested in a number of companies, both individually and in partnership with other wealthy families. The number of deals grew significantly after his increased profile due to the well-publicized sale of his business.

John decided to split the difference between conducting his investment activities all in house and outsourcing them to third parties. That's why he decided to hire Michael. Michael was the senior executive who could run the family office but also was familiar with managing a diverse set of investments. Michael was well suited for this position, given his background in investment banking and his experience in wealth management as both adviser and manager. Moreover, because he was a former investment banker, he could help John with the growing number of private investments that John was exploring. To that end, Michael hired a new master's of business administration (MBA) graduate, Cara, the daughter of one of his former colleagues, to help both him and John manage the liquid investment portfolio and private investments.

The family office also built out its accounting, bill paying, and reporting functions under Jason's leadership. Jason ran the finance group in a professional manner, with defined roles and responsibilities distributed across a five-person staff. Jason also decided to bring in house the tax-planning and tax-compliance services because they had become a large and expensive responsibility of the family office. The tax needs for the family office had become quite substantial, with numerous tax/estate planning and asset ownership vehicles that were created. Jason hired Ed, a senior tax manager at one of the national public accounting firms. Ed valued this opportunity because it enabled him to better balance his personal and professional time and avoid tracking billable hours, and because he could help a large client beyond his usual day job, which centered around tax compliance.

The ranch and various other residential properties continued to be an area of major time commitment and challenge for Jason and the family office. While each home had a local property manager assigned to it, care and maintenance issues continued to arise. There were also the employees at the Wyoming ranch, who needed to be supervised. Jason was increasingly frustrated with various property management issues and knew that he needed someone in house to help with these assets. He hired Veronika as an estate manager, leveraging his relationship with a family office trade organization through which he was able to post an informal job search.

Jason set up most of the technology and systems himself. He decided that the family office wasn't big enough to warrant an internal information technology (IT) resource or an outsourced IT provider or managed security service provider. Jason was familiar with the basics of what the family office needed in terms of computers, networks, and office technology. He did not believe that the family office needed a sophisticated security system because the family office was so far off the radar. Each family member and staff member in the family office had a personal laptop issued by the office and used their own mobile phones to access family office–related e-mails and messages.

The family office used external hard drives to back up data on a sporadic basis and augmented this with a free cloud storage provider for storage and large document sharing. Both the family office professionals and family members commonly used free, personal e-mail providers instead of the e-mail addresses set up by the family office. While at the family office itself, people accessed the Internet via a public Wi-Fi service provided by the commercial real estate manager for the building. There was no firewall or filtering of website traffic. Jason permitted all the family members to use social media on corporate laptops and their personal cell phones.

John continued his research into buying a private jet, but he had yet to pull the trigger on it. Instead, he was using the local FBO (fixed-base operator) at the airport where he kept his Cessna 172 to charter planes for his and the family's various travel needs. He was eyeing a couple of planes, including a King Air 350 that he used extensively for the shorter trips such as to Wyoming. He had also grown fond of using a Challenger 350 to fly down to Cabo San Lucas.

Car collecting also continued to be an important hobby of John's, although he seldom found time to enjoy this particular passion. He would occasionally take his 1963 Jaguar XKE out for a spin when the weather in Chicago was nice, but the car spent most of its time in the garage. The 1969 Ford Mustang, however, was constantly being driven by his son Philip, who had permission to drive this car only.

Sofia started to become much more active with a number of charities, particularly those that help children and the arts. She was starting to think about ways that she can make a difference in these areas in addition to the substantial contributions that she made to the Children's Hospital and a local arts museum. Sofia raised this question with Michael to find out how other families have gone about starting a charity and building out programs in very specific areas. She was also starting to ask how they could have a greater impact with their wealth and support broader causes that exceeded what they had allocated to their philanthropic pursuits. This seemed to be a recurring topic at the dinner table, often brought up by his daughters Olivia and Isabella.

John also continued to be active in his philanthropic pursuits, but not with the same enthusiasm as Sofia. He enjoyed helping his alma mater when he could, as well as the local public school science, technology, engineering, and mathematics (STEM) programs. He felt that he didn't have the same amount of time to devote to it as Sofia. However, he was happy to see Sofia become so engaged in her charities and welcomed involving the family office to help both of them with their philanthropy.

CHAPTER FOUR

Finance

CASE STUDY

Summary

- Six months after the creation of the Left Seat Management family office
- Professionalizing the finance functions
- Improving processes and upgrading technology

Key Words/Concepts

- Accounting and bill paying
- Consolidated reporting
- Tax planning and preparation
- Information technology (IT) infrastructure

Challenge

Jason had done a great job of gaining control over the finances for Left Seat Management. As would be expected given his background, he had established a well-equipped finance department. John was pleased with this development and was finding that he had both more time and better information. Jason hired the people and put in place the systems that he needed to make sure that bills were paid on time and reporting on the personal assets and investments were more clear, accurate, and timely.

Bill paying still took up a significant amount of time for the family office and was migrated away from Janina's daily responsibilities. She was more than happy to give these responsibilities up because that allowed her to spend more time helping with calendars, travel, and numerous other personal needs for John, Sofia, and (selectively) for the kids.

Under the new bill-paying system, the family office followed processes and procedures that were much more in line with what small businesses used. However, the family office did not use a formal budgeting and procurement system to authorize, create, and post purchase orders (POs). In practice, anyone in the family office was authorized to make purchases as needed. However, John and Michael were the only two people in the office with signing authority. Payroll was handled by an established third-party vendor that provides similar services to small businesses.

For reporting technology, the family office used a combination of (1) a ubiquitous small business/ultra-high-net-worth (UHNW) general ledger system, (2) a well-known asset management data aggregation system that links directly to their various custodians, and (3) a spreadsheet software program to combine reports from these systems. These systems were used to create a single monthly financial report for John and Michael.

The general ledger reporting system was effective for the family office's needs with respect to accounting for office costs, payroll, bank reconciliations, and expense management and budgeting. The consolidated reporting system was helpful for monitoring marketable securities. However, the system did not account for nonliquid investments or have certain functionalities that the family needed, such as partnership accounting. In addition, because there are two separate systems, information had to be combined and summarized each month. This process entails (1) posting the activities from nonmarketable securities that data aggregation software cannot capture electronically; (2) calculating and separately reporting the various family members' interests in the various asset ownership vehicles (so-called partnership accounting); and (3) preparing the combined monthly financial report via the spreadsheet software.

Taxes were being prepared by Ed, with the occasional help of the finance department staff, particularly during the busy season. Ed used one of the larger online tax software and research services to prepare and file the tax returns. He created tax files for each of the individuals and entities and used them to maintain important supporting documentation and work papers. Having a tax expert in house was valued greatly by John, Michael, and Jason. They could now easily seek advice in real time with someone who intimately knew them, and the entire family and other entities, without having to pay external advisers an hourly fee each and every time they had a question.

BACKGROUND INFORMATION

Accounting and Bill Paying

Accounting and bill paying are some of the more traditional and important responsibilities for a family office.[1] These needs naturally grow out of a wealthy family's need to account for, report, and manage what can be a very high volume of financial information related to their various personal and investment activities.

As opposed to other services, accounting and bill-paying services are provided by family offices in a manner quite similar to those for small businesses. As a result, many of the processes, personnel, and technologies needed are the same. For these reasons, it is relatively straightforward for family offices to initially staff and deliver these services. However, for reasons that are discussed at length elsewhere in this book, not all family offices deliver these services well. In fact, the timely and accurate delivery of financial information for wealthy families is one of the more challenging and time-consuming tasks for a family office.

One of the reasons for this is that, despite the similarities with small businesses, family offices often do not initially provide accounting and bill paying with a level of staffing or professionalism commensurate with their needs. As a result, the finance department within a family office often struggles to catch up with the increasing level of activity and complexity commensurate with wealthy families.

The following practices should be considered and, where appropriate, incorporated into the family office's finance function.

Payment Approval

Family offices often make purchases based on immediate need, with review and approval being applied at the time that the bill is paid and the check is written. The family office should institute traditional accounts payable policies such that there is a level of oversight and control with respect to whether a product or service is needed and ordered, the terms under which it will be delivered, and, as needed, whether it stays within budget.

Relatively straightforward and common payment controls provide tremendous improvements in the areas of expense management, fraud risk, and financial privacy. They also give the principals comfort that there is proper financial stewardship over their money being applied by the family office. Family office professionals are often surprised by how closely principals monitor expenditures, even relatively small ones. This is understandable inasmuch as principals are used to spending their own money, have their own sense of the value of goods and services, and do not want to be financially irresponsible (or feel irresponsible) despite the magnitude of the wealth they control.

The following are a number of controls in the area of payment approval and execution:

- Determine who is authorized to sign checks and institute additional signer requirements based on threshold payment amounts.
- Use numbered checks in a sequential order so that out-of-range checks can be easily identified.
- Maintain all checks, signature stamps, and ledgers in a secure location.
- Separate the responsibilities for printing checks and signing them.
- If a signature plate or stamp is used to sign checks, make sure that there is a particularly strong and independent check approval and review process.

Purchase Approval

In practice, most family offices have limited preauthorization purchase approval processes in place, certainly compared to their payment approval policies. Purchase orders (POs) require that proposed expenditures be submitted, approved, and documented before a commitment to purchase a product or service is authorized. While it might be a best practice to establish a PO system, most family offices do not do so until they are quite large. Making sure that appropriate purchase approval policies and procedures are in place is critically important to all family offices.

If POs are to be used, the finance department generates a PO that has to be approved before the payment obligation is entered into the system. Once the products are delivered or services provided, the finance department matches the invoice with the PO. The existence of both an approved PO and a vendor invoice eases and speeds up the authorization to remit a check by appropriate personnel.

Common Accounts Payable Group

It is a best practice to ensure that all accounts payable functions are centralized and carried out by the same personnel on behalf of the entire organization. While this is often done naturally by newer family offices and small family offices (SFOs), large family offices often have numerous departments, each of which is responsible for ordering products and services, engaging with various vendors, and authorizing payments. A centralized accounts payable department is used so that common policies regarding approvals, financial controls, and documentation are followed by all departments initiating requests.

Using Others for Accounting and Bill Paying

Family offices are able to outsource accounting, bill-paying, and reporting functions. However, this tends to be a solution for smaller family offices, which do not have a level of activity or a need for oversight and control that would warrant keeping this function in house. For those family offices that are open to outsourcing bill paying and the related accounting and reporting functions, there are a number of important things that they should keep in mind:

- The family must be comfortable with sharing considerable financial information about the family and its spending behaviors with those outside the family office.
- The family office must establish information-sharing protocols through the use of a secure technology platform.
- Controls should be placed on any bank accounts used for bill paying (including maximum and minimum funding amounts) to reduce their financial exposure.

If outsourcing is chosen, the family office should be cognizant of the following issues.

BANK ACCOUNT ISSUES Over the years, many third-party bill-paying providers have learned that sharing bank accounts with clients is a bad idea. It is essential that the firm providing bill-paying and book-keeping services have an accurate picture of the account balance in the account that they are using for payments. If the family office shares the account, it is very likely that they are writing checks and making other payments as well, which makes it impossible to have an accurate balance at any given time. While most family offices will have relationships with banks that monitor accounts and ensure that overdrafts are corrected so that checks will not bounce, sharing bank accounts creates constant problems.

One solution that has been adopted with much success is to create disbursement accounts, which are new checking accounts based at the family office's preferred bank for which the bill-paying provider has limited power of attorney. In these cases, the third-party bill-paying provider is the only one using such an account, which is funded periodically by the family office, their banker, or another trusted adviser.

RECURRING PAYMENTS—NO BILL Very often, recurring payments have to be made, for which there is no bill. A good example would be sending a monthly check or wire to a son or daughter in college for rent, living expenses, and other monetary needs. These payments have to be sent regularly, and they must be scheduled accurately.

Because there is no bill (usually there is only a one-time e-mail or phone request from the family office or family member), there will be nothing in the vendor's in-box to trigger payment.

Calendars and schedules drive this business, and bill-paying providers must fine-tune the process to deal with issues like this. Often, the provider employs software that sends reminders and task lists to the bookkeepers to assist them with scheduling payments for which there is no current bill or invoice.

E-MAIL INVOICES Another issue related to receiving bills and invoices has to do with the fact that more and more vendors are sending their invoices via e-mail rather than regular mail. Typically, they would go to the family office's or a family member's e-mail address in the hope that the family office will forward them for payment. One solution to this problem is to establish a client e-mail address at the office of the bill-paying provider and give it to vendors so they can send a copy to the bill-paying company or individual, with a copy to the family office.

ONE BILL—MULTIPLE PAYMENTS Quite often, bills arrive that require multiple payments—quarterly, semiannual, or at other intervals. These are often real estate and personal property tax bills, which are time sensitive. Keeping track of payment due dates is important, and future payments (and cash requirements) must be scheduled accurately, with payment reminders available to bookkeepers and supervisors.

MULTIPLE NAMES Bills and invoices will come in many different names. If manual data entry is being used, this is not much of a problem, as the bookkeepers will (or should) know that they all belong to the same family. But if optical character recognition (OCR) or other automated data entry is in place, this becomes a bigger issue. Somehow, that system has to know that items addressed to "Mr. John Smith," "Mary and John Smith," "Mr. and Mrs. John Smith," and "Lindsay Smith" (the daughter) are all for the same family and must be paid from the same account. Getting vendors to change names is very difficult (e.g., a mortgage is a legal document and nearly impossible to change). Cross-reference sheets are needed in such cases to ensure that the mailroom personnel sort the mail properly. In the case of OCR, there must be a cross-reference database to make the connections.

CREDIT CARDS Credit cards can create a number of problems because of the wiggle room on credit card payment preferences (e.g., approved purchases, whether the family office wants to make the minimum payment versus paying the full balance, and other options). These statements usually have to be approved by an individual who is a family member or someone in the family office who is familiar with and in frequent contact with the family. (Many other bills are fixed or with very little change month to month, so they are simply paid as they arrive.) There are several ways to deal with the approval process to pay a credit card. The one used most often is to have each paper billing statement go directly to the family office, which in turn authorizes the bill-paying company to access the card online. The bill-paying vendor then makes the payment, and at the same time downloads and categorizes all the transactions on each statement.

In cases where the statement comes directly to the third-party bill-payer, they can e-mail it to the family office for approval. Care should be taken to ensure the use of a secure messaging system so the document is sent in encrypted form, despite the fact that this is a more cumbersome process.

Another issue related to credit cards is that family members often have recurring charges automatically paid by their credit cards to earn points or miles. While this seems convenient, it creates a problem in cases where a card is lost, stolen, or damaged and must be replaced. Some card issuers are good about transferring those recurring charges to the new card, but others are not. This means that at some point, vendors will be left unpaid until the family office or bill-paying provider connects them to the new card.

WIRE TRANSFERS Many wealthy individuals are invested in private equity funds, and other investments. These normally require wire transfers for capital calls. Other large purchases and commitments also require wire transfers. Issuing these wire transfers for family offices creates a whole new set of issues, mostly relating to security and fraud prevention. It is imperative that steps be taken to ensure that the originator of a wire request is actually the family office or a family member and that the request is legitimate.

It is important for the family office and bill-paying provider to lay out the steps under which wire transfers can be processed, and that these include a rigorous callback process similar to what banks use. Whatever the solution, it is important that adequate approval processes be in place for the protection of the family office and the bill-paying firm. International wires add an increased level of complexity and risk, given the high rate of e-mail hacking and regulatory issues.

OTHER ISSUES Wealthy families have complicated financial lives. Quite often, they own assets through entities such as limited liability companies (LLCs). These create problems insofar as they may require separate bank accounts, have stricter reporting requirements, separate tax IDs, and other features. At the end of the day, however, these related entities are part of the wealthy family's personal financial picture, and they should be incorporated into reports.

Posting and tracking debit card transactions can be problematic. This comes into play if a family office is using a full bookkeeping service rather than simply a bill-paying entity. Debit card transactions show up on the bank statements, and quite often, they have very limited descriptions, making accurate categorization difficult. In many cases, there are large numbers of debit transactions, so posting (or downloading) them becomes an issue.

It is preferable for family offices to allow the bill-paying provider to change the mailing address on as many bills as possible to avoid the "round trip," wherein bills go to the family office or a family member's home first and then get forwarded to the bill-paying company.

Investment Reporting

One of the principal responsibilities for any finance department is periodic and robust reporting. In this case, reporting includes not only financial reporting via a general ledger system, but also investment reporting for both liquid and nonliquid investment activities. It might also include various ancillary needs of the family, including budgets, cash flow analysis, portfolio analytics, and project management reports.

Delivering accurate consolidated investment reporting on a timely basis is surprisingly difficult for most family offices. The reasons have to do with how the needs of wealthy families differ materially from those of small businesses and asset management firms, for which most investment reporting solutions are developed. These differences include the following:

- Family offices invest in a wide variety of asset classes, both personal and business, liquid and illiquid.

- Assets owned by a wealthy family are often held through numerous planning entities and trusts, in which each family member has a different pro rata ownership interest.
- The way in which principals would like to see their financial information reported is subject to idiosyncratic preferences, and therefore varies greatly.
- The process by which information is obtained, organized, and reported varies greatly between traditional general ledger and portfolio management systems.
- Ancillary information from a customer relationship management (CRM) system, documents storage and retention, and project management is valuable to integrate but very difficult to do.

As a result, there is no ubiquitously used consolidated reporting system for family offices. The following discusses some of the considerations when evaluating consolidated reporting systems.

Consolidated Reporting Challenges for Family Offices

While advances in technology continue to contribute to operational success in most industries, the private wealth community has fallen significantly behind in effectively deploying advanced technologies and corresponding best practices in the management and support of core family office business functions.[2] The same enterprisewide accounting and finance platforms that other industries employ have not historically satisfied the unique information and reporting requirements of complex families.

In addition to the limitations of these large platforms, which have inhibited their adoption, there are several other factors that have contributed to the lack of technological growth, including the following:

- The complex, lengthy, and resource-intensive solution assessment and decision-making process
- The high degree of variability in operations, information needs, and reporting conventions, which makes technology standardization difficult for potential vendors
- The hesitation of technology firms to invest in research and development for smaller, niche markets

As a result of the need for highly customized, specialized products and the limited technological solutions available to meet these
needs, it is common to see family offices that have adopted the practice
of using a unique combination of nonindustry-focused tools. These
solutions—invariably a mix of spreadsheets, small business accounting
platforms, and portfolio management tools—while disparate, are readily available and have provided a critical flexibility that family offices
need and want in order to solve very specific information challenges.
They are as follows:

- Spreadsheets are the tool of choice because they are cost effective,
  have a wide base of users, require little direct overhead to support, and include embedded functionality to facilitate complex
  equations and requisite customizations.
- In addition to spreadsheets, other systems such as general ledger
  and portfolio management applications are utilized heavily by the
  industry, often as data sources in the compilation and preparation
  of the spreadsheets.

The challenge of using these various tools is that their inherent structural limitations and lack of integration not only create significant
operational inefficiencies, but result in poor data quality.

The end product of endeavoring to operate a business using a combination of systems designed and intended to do something different than how they are ultimately used is invariably an ever-growing
maze of spreadsheets that grows exponentially with each passing year
and each changing of the guard. Auditors, accountants, and advisers
will often find significant gaps in the resulting reports and statements,
which frequently do not reconcile with other spreadsheets and/or
across the disparate systems.

Three Phases of Technology Evolution

Family offices tend to solve their IT needs via an evolutionary process
(table 4.1) moving from *getting the job done*, to using *best-in-class discrete technologies*, to adopting truly *world-class, enterprisewide solutions*.
However, for legitimate reasons discussed next that have to do with
needs, costs, required sophistication, and other factors, many family
offices remain at different phases by design.

TABLE 4.1
Tech evolutionary process

	Gets the job done	Best in class	World class
Overview	• Highly disparate systems • Pervasive use of spreadsheets • Many manual system interactions • Core general ledger, but always the recipient from a multitude of data sources • Labor-intensive, requires manual reconciliation and data QA	• Moderately disparate systems—individual "best of breed" solutions • Specialized technologies for specific business functions • Automated (or semiautomated) system interactions, but still typically overnight and batch in nature • Core general ledger maintained for reporting purposes, but usually only accurate, at best, to the "end of yesterday" • Multiple reconciliation points, but supported through automated exception reporting	• Tightly coupled/integrated enterprise applications • System modules for specific business functions • Real-time integration with the general ledger, driven by business rules and configuration • Core general ledger and chart of accounts driving module behavior and being updated in real time • System-managed, rules-based reconciliation
Advantages	• Effective—inefficient, but gets the job done • Simple reporting and presentation	• Purpose-built solutions • Some controls • Some efficiency	• Enterprisewide system • Full accounting, financial, and CRM • Fully integrated and cross-functional reporting • Easily reconciles • Natural data aggregation • Robust controls and efficiency
Risks	• Data accuracy • Minimal control and security • Tribal knowledge reliance	• Disparate/segmented systems • Reconciliation burden; lack of aggregation • Integration failures • Difficult reporting • Fragile technology footprint	• Change management • Stakeholder buy-in • Additional infrastructure considerations

Source: Jason Brown, "Innovations in Private Wealth Technology and Reporting," strategic advisor, SEI Family Office Services, and chair, Proteus Capital, 2018.

Note: QA, quality assurance.

Family Office and Information Reporting Challenges

The family office vertical within the private wealth management market has had a heightened interest in technology solutions for a protracted period of time. When considering technology solutions, however, family offices tend to independently consider the needs of the various business units found in the office itself until they arrive at the topic of reporting, where there is not only an expectation, but also a real need for information that spans multiple reporting concepts, functions, and business units. Examples include, but are certainly not limited to, the following:

- Performance attribution on an "exposure" basis, which requires both investment and partnership data
- Performance evaluation across multiple custodians leveraging a custom grouping schema
- Risk evaluation of a family branch and/or an individual
- Liquidity analysis across the office to understand the ability to raise cash for a call without having to liquidate positions
- A generally accepted accounting principles (GAAP) system of accounting, with the ability to understand the tax basis of investments

However, because business unit needs are generally evaluated independently, the solutions that family offices implement often can report only within the domain limitations of their respective functionalities. The private wealth management industry, and family offices specifically, appear to be largely stuck in the best-in-class phase of its technology life cycle.

Because of the paradox created by simultaneously looking for function-specific solutions that are capable of meeting cross-functional reporting requirements, solving the family wealth information-reporting problem requires reexamination of the family office structure itself. Families should continually assess how they do things, similar to how all complex operating businesses innovate and grow, and ensure that the technology follows.

CHALLENGES IN VENDOR SELECTION Despite the availability of consolidated financial reporting technology platforms for family offices ranging from best-in-class, function-specific solutions to cross-functional, world-class enterprisewide applications, finding and evaluating the right software vendor can be a challenge. As the industry that supports family offices has grown, so has the number of companies who purport to provide consolidated reporting systems to address the unique challenges faced by family offices. While many of these vendors are indeed well suited to provide function-specific solutions, such as in general ledger accounting, portfolio reporting, and CRM, very few are capable of addressing the needs of family offices on a cross-functional basis.

The reasons for this are understandable, inasmuch as the family office industry remains relatively new, and many companies that now market to family offices build solutions for discrete functional reporting needs, such as small business accounting, portfolio management, and sales management. As a result, many of these technologies are well suited for those functional aspects of a family office and indeed make up the best-in-class solutions mentioned here. But while these companies have endeavored to serve family offices on an enterprise basis by providing solutions in new and different areas, many have struggled to do so with the level of cross-divisional functionality that is required.

There are, however, a number of new and existing technology companies that have successfully developed or integrated capabilities that allow them to offer enterprisewide financial reporting solutions. Many of these companies grew up providing financial reporting software to industries that have needs similar to those of family offices, such as portfolio management or fund accounting. Others are newer businesses established by wealthy families themselves, or multifamily offices (MFOs), built from inception with an eye toward meeting the diverse, cross-functional financial reporting needs of family offices. These companies have the benefit of not being burdened by legacy businesses, or they have successfully evolved their technologies around serving the complex needs of wealthy families.

FAMILY OFFICE CONSULTANTS The challenge for principals and family office executives is to determine which solution is best suited for their office given their needs, sophistication, level of complexity, and budget. A number of dedicated family office consultancies have emerged that specialize in financial reporting needs assessment and technology vendor selection. Regardless of whether a family office is looking for assistance in finding a best-in-class, functional-specific technology or a cross-functional enterprise solution, they should consider hiring one of these consultants to assist them. The value of finding the right solution for the family, given the challenges and complexities faced, cannot be overstated. As mentioned previously, providing timely and accurate financial information is mission critical for family offices, their professionals, and their principals. Getting these important responsibilities right can help the office evolve to provide other higher-level services and advice, improve decision-making around investments and expenditures, and greatly assist with risk management.

Tax Reporting

Income tax planning and preparation constitute an area of significant focus for wealthy families, and therefore the family offices that serve them. What follows is a discussion of the best approaches to delivering and receiving tax advice.[3] Tax planning and tax strategies are beyond the scope of this book.

Wealthy families spend a significant amount of time with their advisers developing, implementing, and administering complex income and estate tax-planning strategies. There are obvious reasons for this, inasmuch as taxes (income, sales, estate, and others) can be significant expenditures, and ones that can be mitigated through prudent planning. It should be noted, however, that much of this planning is not designed specifically to reduce or avoid income taxation. Rather, some of the most widely used tax mitigation strategies are legitimate components of broader philanthropic, multigenerational, and asset ownership/governance plans.

The administrative complexity that robust tax planning imposes upon a family office can be overwhelming. Wealthy families can have dozens of entities set up to oversee every facet of their personal and financial affairs. The majority of these entities require a combination of federal and possibly state income tax returns, estimated tax payments, and periodic annual disclosures. They also require ongoing professional attention and planning with respect to each and every transaction so as to respect the formalities of the structures and to avoid unanticipated tax consequences.

Family offices are heavily involved in the tax function for wealthy families, and it is not uncommon for the first few hires in the family office to have deep finance and/or tax experience. Indeed, the ongoing oversight and compliance complexity created through tax planning is one of the reasons why family offices are set up.

Outsourcing Tax Services

Initially, wealthy families outsource the tax planning and compliance function, largely because this is how they addressed this need in the past, long before their complexity grew to a level where they had the means and motivations to oversee them themselves through a family office. Family offices, even large and complex ones, continue to outsource their tax planning and preparation needs to tax firms, despite the fact that they could bring those services in house. This approach is not inconsistent with addressing these challenges, although it does raise a number of considerations, which are discussed next.

PROACTIVE INVOLVEMENT OF ADVISERS When the tax preparation and compliance functions for a complex family are outsourced, it is critical that the various tax and legal advisers be kept abreast of transactions and activities within the family in as close to a real-time basis as possible. This responsibility should be shared by both the family office and their outside advisers. However, ensuring that it gets done should be a priority of the family office. Top tax and legal advisers are very busy and, despite a legitimate interest in staying involved with families, are often unable to do this.

Some family offices address these needs by hiring senior executives who have a tax background. These professionals can help spot issues that warrant the involvement of outside specialists, respond to questions more easily from these advisers, and translate technical information for the principals and family members.

ADVISERS MUST EVOLVE WITH THE FAMILY It is not uncommon for wealthy families to use the same tax advisers that they employed for the past twenty years. One challenge that this presents, however, is that the issues, complexity, and planning opportunities for the family today are very different from those with which that adviser had been familiar. As a result, many wealthy families will need to upgrade their tax advisers at some point. This is understandable, and normally not too much of a surprise, for legacy advisers, who may often stay involved given their ability to cost-effectively address more traditional and less complicated compliance needs.

RELATIVE COSTS Outsourcing the tax compliance and planning function can seem expensive to family offices relative to what it would cost them to deliver the services in house. While this is not an unreasonable view, the decision of whether to bring tax services in house should be informed by a number of other important considerations, as discussed next.

MAINTAINING PROFESSIONAL STANDARDS One of the issues that family offices need to address if they decide to staff their own tax departments is how many professionals they need. Proper tax preparation involves more than just putting the correct numbers on a tax form and filing it. Tax departments must have sufficient personnel to provide a level of quality control, including ensuring that multiple professionals are involved in preparing and reviewing the returns and that appropriate work paper documentation is maintained.

Related to this issue is the ongoing training that is required of all tax professionals. Large firms devote a significant amount of time and money to ensuring that their professionals are kept abreast of the latest tax legislation and planning concepts. These firms also have the benefit of multiple wealthy clients, with whom they both learn and share experiences. Family offices will struggle to provide these elements for their professionals and thus should go out of their way to ensure ongoing professional education and access to peer networks.

ADDRESSING MANAGERIAL ISSUES Family offices will also have to handle the traditional managerial issues that come with overseeing multiple staff members. This would include ensuring that the staff is properly supervised and supported. Related to this issue is "key man" risk, especially in tax departments where only a few highly technical professionals are employed. These professionals have a tremendous impact on the family office if they were to leave because of the detailed legacy information they possess.

Information System Management

Trends Shaping the IT Landscape for Family Offices

Making IT-related decisions for a family office is markedly different than it was in the early 2010s.[4] Without understanding the dramatic changes that have taken place in technology, it is easy for family office executives to make decisions that are costly and ineffective and can needlessly burden the family office enterprise for years to come. Family offices struggle with finding IT talent and solutions that can help satisfy their desire to have someone with both large-enterprise experience and strategic thinking, as well as the ability to roll up their sleeves and solve acute problems.

Historically, the IT industry was built around hardware and software sales, proprietary protocols, and long-term service and support commitments. Over the last handful of years, this paradigm has shifted dramatically as a result of significant advances in software, hardware, and cloud computing that moves the server rooms off site and enables remote operations and shared resources.

A robust industry of IT companies has sprung up to provide support services for small and medium-sized enterprises (SMEs) and large, multinational corporations. These firms, known as "managed service providers (MSPs)," have benefited from the trend toward outsourced IT functions. The value proposition includes lower and more predictable costs from shared economics and a preemptive as opposed to reactive position for managing issues as they arise.

Family offices, however, are not SMEs, nor are they large, multinational companies. Family offices are rarely started as de novo entities built with a robust strategic planning process. They are often put together in an ad hoc fashion or are simply the outgrowth of management companies formed informally over time to manage the personal and financial affairs of the principals and their families. Therefore, the following challenges and questions tend to arise as family offices look at building and maintaining their IT capabilities:

- Do we use the IT assets of the operating company (if one exists related to the family office principals)?
- Do we hire an IT professional in house to develop and maintain our systems?
- How do we hire the right IT consultants and firms to design, build, maintain, and/or review our IT services?
- How do we determine what IT services and devices we actually need, and how much should we realistically spend to obtain them?
- How can we build a flexible model that can adapt to future needs?
- How can we build security into these systems?
- How will we handle mobile devices?

- How can we communicate electronically in a secure and efficient manner?
- How do we store and protect our digital "crown jewels"?

Unfortunately, many third-party IT service and support providers are not familiar with the vicissitudes and characteristics of a family office. They view family offices as an emerging client type and often confuse significant wealth with significant resources to spend on IT. The reality is that family offices rarely have significant IT budgets, but they do have to cater to the specific needs of principals who value efficiency and convenience.

Furthermore, most IT service providers have not adapted as quickly as digital technology has advanced. In many cases, the providers' business model is "break-fix," a term used to describe a typical business transaction in which the customer breaks something and calls the IT services company for support, a technician is dispatched to the job, more hardware and software are sold, and the enterprise receives a bill for labor and other expenses.

The prevailing break-fix model supports the antiquated structure of the IT services provider. In many cases under this scenario, family offices are left not just with unexpected expenses, but also over-engineered solutions that leave executives and principals confused, frustrated, and struggling to realize value from the expenditure. As a result, the interests of all family office constituents are compromised.

Technological progress is disrupting the traditional IT service and support industry for the benefit of consumers. Software is increasingly replacing the need for local hardware. Cloud computing is providing the ability to monitor and manage IT operations remotely, with resources and expenses shared across multiple customers for increased service levels and cost benefits. This "as-a-service" approach provides preemptive service to reduce unforeseen operational interruptions and unpredictable IT expenses.

Another important consideration for the family office when making IT-related decisions concerns technological protocols. Protocols are set rules for technology operations and the coordination and communication across various components. Many entrepreneurs and technology companies have made a fortune by developing and enforcing proprietary protocols for their products and services. Once again, advancements in technology are challenging the legacy model by shortening product cycles and opening standards. As a consumer, the family office gains by having access to increased options, lower prices, and greater compatibility across components. However, this access is not always easily understood, given the amount of jargon and orientation of current IT service companies. When making IT-related decisions, family office management should consider and weigh alternatives carefully with a view toward these changes in technology, and remain open to benefiting from advances in innovation and increasing value from products and services.

Developing an IT Infrastructure Strategy

While some aspects of IT infrastructure will vary by the family office and its particular circumstances and needs, the most important elements to consider are held in common by all. The best place to start to look at IT infrastructure is at a macro level, where family offices can view the overall topology. Once this is well understood, executives will be better positioned to consider the various components and their relationships within their domain of operation. For the family office, when including the logistics of member-families and remote offices in the purview, it is clear when complexities are compounded and risks are increased.

See figure 4.1 for a framework that family offices can use to design, establish, and support their IT infrastructure strategy. This framework

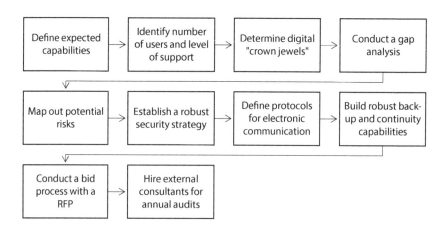

Figure 4.1 IT flowchart

can be used with external consultants, internal IT experts in an operating company, dedicated family office IT staff professionals, or a mixture of all of these.

The Topology

Grasping the physical and virtual nature of IT infrastructure requires an element of visualization that sorts and arranges the various components. An end-to-end module approach is increasingly effective for planning and plug-and-play provisioning of components. The strategy is consistent with technological trends and extracting maximum value from IT-related expenditures, including service and support.

Office management should solicit input from family members when defining the scope of IT-related responsibilities. The possible scenarios range from full centralization and integration into the core functions of the family office, including service and support, to a hard line between office professionals and family members, where each population is served separately. Anywhere on the scale, it is increasingly effective and affordable to provide digital autonomy without compromise while reducing risk.

While illustrating a modular view of a family office's IT infrastructure is helpful, it is important to remember that the landscape is constantly shifting and the future will continue to present tremendous change and new challenges. Exponential increases in Internet-connected devices, such as the Internet of Things (IoT), is propelling the expansion of the surface of IT-related concerns and requirements. The role of family offices in providing a technology infrastructure that serves their constituents is increasing, as is their role in managing the associated rising risks. As a result, all IT should be considered infrastructure for cybersecurity and risk mitigation.

Software-Defined Wide Area Networks

A technology trend that family offices should be aware of and consider is the software-defined wide area network (SD-WAN). This technology uses the public Internet to provide a private Internet experience. The results are bandwidth improvements and better network performance with significantly increased security over traditional networks.

SD-WAN solutions provide comprehensive protection across the network and devices, including:

- Next-generation firewalls
- Secure and intelligent direction of traffic
- Real-time antivirus protection
- Intrusion prevention system (IPS)
- Application control
- Secure Sockets Layer (SSL) deep-packet encryption inspection
- Web filtering to block browser risks and threats
- Data loss protection (DLP)
- Bot and distributed denial of service (DDoS) attack protection
- Phishing prevention
- A virtual private network (VPN) with end-to-end security
- Automatic Internet service provider (ISP) failover

SD-WAN technology can potentially assist family offices to manage the proliferation of personal information on the Internet and the increased number of Internet-connected devices, and to protect dynamically against threats across the IT network.

Leverage Specialization for Planning and Implementing

Resources to manage the challenges of IT infrastructure for a family office today should include some kind of a specialist, whether in house, outsourced, or a hybrid model. The value of good advice will skyrocket, while uninformed decisions can be damaging on multiple levels.

The specialist should be instrumental in the mapping of the macro view; consider IT infrastructure, physical security, and cybersecurity as one; and have advanced knowledge and experience in both aspects. The specialist should be intellectually and conversationally proficient and current with all subcomponents and be able to identify best-in-class providers for each. Depending on the family office size and budget and the level of expertise in house, the specialist can be an internal or external individual or team. Typically, for most family offices except for the largest, an outside specialist is recommended. Finally, IT specialists who focus on cybersecurity are rarely completely conversant on developing and maintaining an IT infrastructure. The skill sets for these two roles are very different, and family offices should be cognizant of these while leveraging internal resources or seeking outside consulting.

ASSESSMENT AND ISSUES SURFACED

What Did We Learn?

John initially sought out Jason to help him because he was familiar with the issues around bill paying, reporting, and taxes. Jason is well suited to help him given his background as the chief financial officer (CFO) for an operating company. The challenges are that the needs, technologies, and personnel resources available to a family office are both similar to and different from businesses. Finance professionals new to the family office often struggle to find the right solutions and invariably go through a learning process as they try to adapt technologies and use vendors that were not designed for the unique needs of wealthy families. Jason must also learn how best to conduct services in house as opposed to outsourcing, while balancing cost efficiency and quality control.

Case Questions

- What are some items that Jason should consider to improve the family office's bill-paying policies and procedures?
- Should the family office consider a different general ledger accounting system?
- Should the family office consider a different consolidated reporting solution?
- Should the family office use a technology system that automatically integrates the general ledger system with the consolidated reporting system?
- How can the family office improve their tax preparation and planning?
- How should a family office establish and maintain their IT infrastructure?

RECOMMENDED SOLUTIONS

Responses to Case Questions

*What are some items that Jason should consider to improve
the family office's bill-paying policies and procedures?*

As would be expected given Jason's background, the bill-paying procedures for the family office are professional. He has adequately staffed
the office for what is a necessary, important, and very time-consuming
responsibility for all family offices. This size of a team allows him to
assign specific roles and responsibilities and to segregate duties, which
provides an important level of fraud control. One area for improvement
to consider would be a more formal expense procurement, documentation, and approval process. This would help ensure a greater level of
budgetary controls because new purchases could not be authorized
before orders are placed. Further, while it is convenient for Michael
to be able to sign checks, the family office should consider setting a
limit to the expenditures that he can approve before requiring John's
authorization.

Should the family office consider a different general ledger accounting system?

There is an important balancing act with family offices between ease
of operations and breadth of general ledger capabilities. Many family
offices should err on the side of ensuring the former in light of their
primary needs because there are legitimate costs (staffing, complexity,
and other issues) of using general ledger systems that are more complex than what a family really needs. In this case, the general ledger
system is meeting the needs of the family office for reporting on office
costs, bank reconciliations, expense management and budgeting, and
other items. Issues tend to arise when the general ledger system isn't
integrated with the consolidating reporting system. Many times, the
integration takes place by manually using a spreadsheet to combine
key elements from each reporting system. For now, the system that
the family office has in place seems to be working for them. However,
the inclusion of a manual process for combining the two reports is less
optimal and introduces both inefficiency and the risk of human error.

Should the family office consider a different consolidated reporting solution?

The current consolidated reporting technology used by the family office is more limited than the general ledger system in meeting their needs. This situation exists because the consolidated reporting solution was designed to report on a liquid portfolio. In this case, the family has significant nonmarketable investments and an additional need for partnership accounting. For these reasons, the family office should consider using a different consolidated reporting system that is built more specifically to meet their unique needs. This system would allow them to better report on nonmarketable securities, across all entities, where the pro rata interest of each of the constituent owners is accurately represented without requiring manual intervention via the spreadsheet summary report.

Should the family office use a technology system that automatically integrates the general ledger system with the consolidated reporting system?

A significant issue with the family office's current reporting technology and procedures is that the general ledger system is not integrated with the consolidated performance reporting system. As discussed previously, this requires a manual interface each month that not only is time consuming, but also introduces the risk of human error. There are integrated general ledger–consolidated reporting technology solutions built specifically for these types of family offices. The trade-offs when using integrated versus stand-alone technology are depth of functionality and complexity of use.

One consideration for the family office would be to change its consolidated reporting technology to one that addresses broader, more family office–specific needs but does not integrate with the general ledger. If they did so, they would have satisfactory solutions for both reporting needs. They might also review whether they really need to summarize the general ledger and investment reporting for the monthly financial reports because this is a time-consuming process that is prone to human error. Many family offices are fine with reporting the two separately and welcome the efficiencies and data safeguards that doing this provides.

How can the family office improve its tax preparation and planning?

Professional tax planning and compliance can become quite expensive for family offices, given the number of entities they use, the level of activities, and the need to integrate tax planning into most of their significant financial decisions. For these reasons, many family offices bring tax preparation and planning in house to reduce costs and more easily integrate tax expertise into their decision-making. However, there are downsides to preparing tax returns internally including key person risks, ensuring quality control, providing ongoing training, and having access to a diverse set of experiences and expertise. This is particularly true if the tax department is small, as is the case with Left Seat Management.

Jason should consider augmenting his tax team at Left Seat Management by hiring a junior tax preparer and/or having an independent tax firm review their tax returns and be available for consulting and planning. Under this approach, it will be important for Ed to keep the external advisers abreast of transactions and planning within the family office so that they can stay current and add to his expertise.

How should a family office establish and maintain their IT infrastructure?

Few professionals who work for family offices have a deep background in IT. As discussed previously, traditional professional backgrounds for family office employees are finance and accounting, investments, legal, and tax. Furthermore, because family offices are established to meet the needs of principals and their family, they are generally structured to make interactions as efficient as possible. IT strategies are no different. These characteristics influence the development of IT infrastructure greatly and introduce potential risks as a result. Security is often sacrificed over convenience, IT budgets are light despite the fact that the data that needs protecting is extremely sensitive, and the family office rarely grows to a size where they can hire an internal IT expert. However, just because an internal resource is rare, family offices have plenty of excellent outsourced and managed IT solutions available to them to support their activities. The key is to find an IT vendor or consultant who has experience working with family office clients.

Jason should focus on IT infrastructure, policies, and training to a much greater extent than he would in a traditional corporate environment since he no longer has the luxury of having an operating company's IT department to rely on. As with numerous other areas where he has needed specialized guidance, he should use his network of other family offices and professional advisers to find technology solutions and a risk management consultant who specializes in working with family offices and SMEs.

CHAPTER FIVE

Lifestyle

CASE STUDY

Summary

- One year after the creation of the Left Seat Management family office
- Complexity of overseeing properties and lifestyle needs
- Considerations when flying privately

Key Words/Concepts

- Lifestyle management and concierge
- Estate and residence management
- Private aviation

Challenge

With the creation of the family office a year ago, daily life for both John and Sofia became quite enjoyable. They were still just as busy as they had always been, but now they were spending more time on things they wanted to do and enjoying the finer things in life. The family was living in their dream house in Glencoe and had a beautiful ranch in Wyoming to visit in the summer and a luxury estate in Cabo San Lucas in the winter. Getting to each property was also much easier, as the family started to fly privately for almost all their trips, albeit in chartered aircraft as opposed to in their own personal plane. John and Sofia were also becoming much more engaged in the Northshore social scene, attending and hosting numerous dinners and parties, holding charity fundraisers, and taking weekend getaways with friends.

What came as a surprise to them, however, was the amount of time they still needed to devote to the planning for each event or trip, including managing invitations and guest lists, making reservations, securing venues, and preparing their homes before the visits. There always seemed to be something that needed to get done, was overlooked, or could have been done better.

Despite the great help that Janina provided, she was still mostly John's executive assistant; she did not have the time, experience, or resources needed to take over these responsibilities for the entire family. The family office's finance staff also tried to help, but their availability varied based on whether they were in the midst of preparing monthly financial reports or helping Ed with the family office's taxes. It was becoming clear to both John and Sofia that they needed dedicated help in these particular areas.

John was also getting ready to buy two private planes at last. He had done all his research and knew what he wanted—a King Air 350 and a Challenger 350. The King Air was perfect for the relatively short trip to Wyoming, while the Challenger could take the whole family to Cabo San Lucas. While John was a pilot and owned a small plane, these were significant investments that required management and staffing beyond his means. He knew, though, that the Challenger was more plane than he needed for the trip to Mexico and that there were certainly less expensive options given the number of hours he flew each year.

Michael and Jason were asked to look into hiring someone who could help with the scheduling and perhaps the residences. John was comfortable taking the lead on acquiring the new planes, although he mentioned to both Michael and Jason that they would have to help him get up to speed on all the various ownership, tax, insurance, and related issues.

BACKGROUND INFORMATION

Managing Lifestyle

Wealthy families typically travel a great deal; own multiple homes; enjoy going to premier sporting, social, and artistic events; and often collect wine, artwork, and automobiles. When the responsibility for ensuring that these activities are executed effectively falls on the shoulders of the family office, it is incumbent on the office to hire staff properly to meet these needs. The family office must also become expert in these areas, or at least know where to go to obtain this expertise and these services. With few exceptions, it is typically best to outsource these responsibilities to qualified service providers in each of the areas. However, outsourcing the duties does not absolve the family office of their responsibility to oversee, coordinate, and periodically reassess how services are being used and delivered.[1]

As with consolidated financial reporting, an industry has developed around helping wealthy families with these needs, and a number of specialty service providers have emerged. Despite this, providing concierge services to wealthy families is still very challenging, so it warrants a great deal of attention by both staff and senior management. Problems will always surface in the delivery of these services, and because they affect the principals and their families directly and are very important to them, they become important to the family office. Family offices often will dedicate a number of staff members to managing these functions and the chief executive officer (CEO) will oversee the service delivery personally.

For the purposes of this discussion, services include the following:

- Event planning
- Travel advising
- Special events and extraordinary experiences
- Dining reservations
- Errands

- Household services
- Personal assistants
- Personal chefs
- Personal shoppers
- Professional organizers

The challenges that family offices face when providing these services generally fall into one of the following categories: how to find and hire the right staff, knowing about and working with the right third-party service providers, and managing expectations and the delivery of services. They are discussed in the next sections.

Finding and Hiring Qualified Staff

When making hiring decisions, the most important things to look for in a concierge and lifestyle management professional is a genuinely warm personality and a desire to be of service. This is a challenging job for the reasons described herein, and it requires a particular type of person in addition to job experience. Key qualities include the following:

- In-depth knowledge
- Attention to detail
- Responsiveness
- Sense of ownership
- Flexible and able to multitask
- Resourceful
- Ability to stay on top of lifestyle trends via reading blogs, magazines, and other lifestyle resources
- Ability to juggle multiple family priorities and interests when planning
- Discretion
- Ability to negotiate contracts and manage outsourced vendors when required
- Ability to budget and account for expenses accurately
- Sense of taste and style that aligns with the hiring family's sensibilities

Typically, the world of hospitality management (e.g., hotels, corporate or residential buildings, and sports arenas), event planning, and public relations are great places to start to find this individual.

Needs Assessment

To ensure the right solution, it is helpful for the family office to first understand the family's needs—the frequency, the complexity, the type of access and dedicated attention required, and modes of communication. After the needs assessment has been completed, the family office will be in a better position to search for, reach out to, and begin evaluating providers.

Finding and Evaluating Third-Party Service Providers

The same qualities stated previously that apply to in-house staff are true for evaluating and engaging a third-party provider. While many providers say that they do many things and/or provide services across all industries, most providers have an expertise that may or may not dovetail with what the family office requires. Some companies handle real estate, some professional athletes, some celebrities, some hedge fund principals, and others deal with wealthy families. Each has different approaches and areas of expertise. It's a good idea to inquire about their core base of customers because the needs of the audiences vary greatly.

The industry is comprised of everything from small boutique purveyors with niche specialties to vast multinational call centers with global reach and capabilities. There has been a great deal of consolidation in this space over the last ten years to achieve better access and economies of scale. One of the challenges as the industry evolves and the players grow in size is maintaining an appropriate level of client engagement and intimacy, particularly with multicity call center companies.

Types of Service Providers

One of the first considerations is to understand the kinds of services and transactions that are required. Some firms are geared more toward everyday, transactional types of work, while others have deep reach in creating extraordinary experiences (although rarely do the two coincide at a fundamental level). It is also important to try to match the personalities of the service providers to the family. Some lifestyle concierges have a flashy style of interaction and delivery, while others are more behind the scenes and private. The service delivery will be more seamless if the company and its representatives match the desired style and approach of the family.

Another critical element of needs assessment is to determine how the majority of services are delivered and how they stack up against the family's wants and expectations. Answer the following questions:

- Does the family want to be able to call a professional and have a lengthy discussion and weigh alternatives when they have a request?
- Would they prefer to e-mail their requests and get an answer back?
- Do they prefer a mobile app that would allow them to select from a range of services and perhaps even see real-time availability for selected options?
- Once the company is engaged, will tasks be managed by a team or by one individual?

In all cases, it is important to ensure that there is good chemistry and communication between the provider and the family office manager.

Fees

One important area to consider is fees. Should the family office engage service providers on a project-by-project basis or on a monthly or annual retainer? If a retainer, how is that bounded by the scope of work so there is a fair expectation of service delivery on both sides? Concierge service providers typically make money both from fees from their clients (which could be annual memberships, monthly retainers, or a guaranteed number of requests, with a cost associated with each type) and from referral fees or commissions from the vendors that they refer. It is important to understand the economic model of the proposed provider. The family office will want to have some insight and transparency into the economics that the concierge provider relies upon so they can accurately assess their recommendations and identify where there might be biases or conflicts of interest.

Extended Service Providers

Another challenge in managing experiences is when service delivery is done by extended third parties, often in other states or countries. For this reason, using and relying on trusted partners that have experience with the unique needs and demands of wealthy families are very important. It is also critical to have a written scope of work detailing expectations, communication frequency, and type and budget/accounting requirements. Having a clear delineation of the engagement up front will give both parties a road map for how best to manage service delivery.

Credit Card Concierge Services

If the family is just beginning to evaluate their lifestyle needs and wants to minimize costs and try the service benefits, one area that may be effective is using their credit card provider's concierge solution. There are many benefits—it is typically staffed around the clock, has access to a vast database of content, is knowledgeable about past requests, and has access to top managers at the property or venue to help expedite requests. In addition, these companies will have negotiated relationships with all sorts of desirable partners that may provide great access, value, and a first look at many types of lifestyle activities, including restaurant reservations, travel upgrades, and premier experiences.

The downside to using this type of service is that depending on the level of card, the family may not have a dedicated provider and may have to engage with different employees each time they have a request. The service can also vary widely, and while the service representatives are helpful and service oriented, they typically sit in a call center, occasionally in other countries, far from the areas where the family lives, works, and plays. They also understandably will not have intimate knowledge about the family and their proclivities.

Credit card concierge services are a great solution if the family knows exactly what they want (and when) and simply needs someone to help them get it. But it is not a great resource for meeting highly curated desires based on personal experience and expectations.

Managing Expectations around the Delivery of Services

For lifestyle and concierge staff, managing service providers, delivery of services, and expectations of the principals and/or family members is a critical part of the job. It is also the reason that these services should often be overseen in house and delivered by the most qualified and experienced third parties. Senior management of the family office, including the CEO, must stay involved and be aware of what is being requested by the family, how it is to be accomplished, and what issues may come up in the delivery of the services.

A recurring challenge when delivering concierge services is that expectations regarding services are often set based on prior experiences. This can be challenging for family office professionals because both poor service and exceptional service can cause challenges. Poor experiences obviously reflect negatively on the family office regardless of whether the office could have anticipated or better managed the delivery. No matter how well a family office is prepared, one small thing will come up and could derail the experience and lead to dissatisfaction of a principal or family member. Family office executives and staff must be prepared for these inevitable occurrences and be able to handle the issue graciously. It is a good idea when evaluating a company to ask about instances where things have gone awry and how they have handled and rectified the situation.

Somewhat counterintuitively, great experiences by the family can also have a negative effect, in that prior experiences often set an expectation, or high-water mark, for what can and should be achievable each and every time. Sometimes lifestyle management and concierge professionals are able to accomplish the impossible (e.g., get backstage passes to a sold-out concert, obtain impossible-to-get dinner reservations on short notice). However, these achievements are not always possible for every request. Therefore, setting expectations about what can be accomplished should be part of ongoing discussions with the principals and their family. It is important to note that at times, the issue is not lack of access or expertise by the concierge, but rather circumstances outside their control (e.g., not being able to secure a reservation at the French Laundry because the restaurant is full for the evening).

One key point is to let the service provider know when the family has flexibility and can accept alternatives so that they can be provided with choices—room type, dates, theater seating, choice of cuisine, time of reservation, and so on. It is always helpful for the concierge to be provided with guidelines so that, in the moment, they can make decisions on the family's behalf. This is critical when rooms, tickets, or reservations are in high demand and are selling out fast.

Managing Estates

Wealthy families rely on a circle of trusted advisers, both inside and outside the family office, to oversee their financial assets. However, much of their wealth is often invested in multiple residences, art, aircraft and watercraft, and other luxuries whose value often exceeds their other investments taken in the aggregate. Given the unique nature of these assets and the ecosystem of services they require, a family's personal service organization—the other side of the family office—is frequently run separately or in parallel to the family office.

The sheer scope of the responsibilities involved in running a significant estate, if misunderstood or underestimated, can present a serious risk to the family and their property. Understanding the ecosystem and the pressures and risks that it accrues is key to building an organizationally coherent and skilled estate management and private services team.[2] An equally important benefit of this understanding is being able to quickly assess risks and identify when to bring in additional or outside resources.

Understanding the Ecosystem of Physical Assets and Personal Service

Estate management and personal service organizations that support wealthy individuals and families can be understood to form an interactive, interconnected network of parts that together create the framework for their lifestyle. The strength of this network can be evaluated based on the health of nine core components and their related areas of focus, as illustrated in figure 5.1.

Performing a situational assessment of each of these areas regularly can identify strengths, opportunities for improvement, and most important, risks to the family, their property, or both. An unaddressed weakness in one area will ultimately affect others. For example:

- A poorly integrated technology system can undermine communications, compromise security, and put the physical safety of the family and property at risk.
- Deferred maintenance can lead to erosion in asset value, insurance claims arising from safety issues, and inconvenience to the family.
- Careless or inadequate staffing can result in costly turnover, personal theft, and endangerment of family privacy and security.

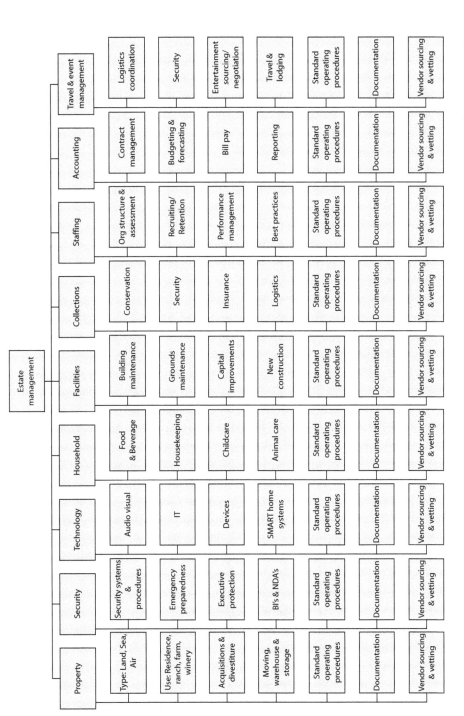

Figure 5.1 Nine core components of estate management *Source:* Anne Lyons and Judy Boerner-Rule, Tapestry Associates, LLC, 2019.

The family, their personal staff, or the family office can use the assessment findings to develop and implement solution strategies, either internally or with the assistance of outside experts. Next, we discuss three of the more challenging aspects of the estate management ecosystem: (1) property and facilities management; (2) operations: staffing and personal services; and (3) special projects: capital projects and new construction. Tools are provided in each section to help illustrate and assess some of the risks associated with each one and to help families and staff know when to engage outside resources.

Property and Facilities Management

Property acquisition happens organically. Over time, a property portfolio will often become geographically dispersed or, by virtue of their asset class, will literally span land, sea, and air. By the time a third home or a yacht or private jet is added, personal enjoyment can be overwhelmed by the unforeseen time, investment, and staffing infrastructure that managing these assets demands.

Estate properties at this level are "commercidential"; that is, a hybrid of highly finished, personalized architecture combined with an infrastructure of commercial size and complexity. These residences and estates are frequently custom built, occupying significant square footage, associated acreage, or both. In addition, it is not uncommon for at least one property in a family portfolio to have a commercial aspect, such as a ranch, farm, or vineyard. Privacy and recreation interests frequently equate to homes in remote locations subject to extreme climates—the tropics, for example. If a property is not a primary residence, a family's use pattern can vary considerably, affecting the property's security profile and vulnerability.

Without a mechanism for strategically analyzing and organizing the management of these properties when they come into the portfolio, families risk staffing and operating redundancies and an exponential increase in the risk to the physical asset itself. The following questions will help a family understand the impact of a property acquisition to the portfolio and themselves personally:

- Has there been sufficient due diligence prior to acquisition to determine whether local resources can support and service the property?
- What will it require to meet the family's needs?

- What are the anticipated operating costs at one, two, and five years after purchase relative to the expected time that the asset will be used annually, its projected long-term hold, and its expected return on investment? Inevitably, the answers to these questions will affect how much a family is willing to invest in staffing, maintenance, and capital improvements.
- Will the property be staffed full time or part time?
- Will staff be shared or relocated from another property? If new, will they be hired in house or outsourced?
- Will the property be available for guests as well as family members?

Operations: Staffing and Personal Services

The delivery of personal services is the product of staff and operations. No two families are the same. There is no boilerplate model for how a family may choose to live in and operate their residential assets. When evaluating the operations of a property and its associated staffing requirements, a balance needs to be struck between the physical requirements of a property and a family's specific expectations regarding their privacy, cost tolerance, and personal services.

Many families have strong, well-functioning staffing models in place to support their property and personal living requirements. However, when families add to their portfolios and move into substantially larger and/or more complex residences, the models that worked previously can quickly become strained. This tension may be evidenced in a variety of ways:

- Reduction in personal privacy and security due to increased staff or vendor presence, access, and opportunity
- Failure to consistently maintain physical assets at levels required to protect their value
- Increase in costs related to the repair and triage of insufficiently maintained assets
- Strain on previously well performing staff members or vendors due to expanded responsibilities
- Service quality reductions or inconsistencies due to inherited service assumptions incompatible with new requirements
- Steep learning curve and communication requirements for both family and staff

- Lack of resource expertise and surge support in specific operational areas, including security, collection management, event management, specialty housekeeping, and storage management

Staffing Considerations

Private family staffing is a delicate and expensive process. Families of significant wealth, along with the advisers who serve them, face unique challenges and high stakes when recruiting a crucial member of private family staff. With confidentiality concerns, personal and financial risks, and highly specific or broad skills requirements, the process and final candidate selection can be precarious if handled improperly. When hiring senior or executive-level staff, an objective placement adviser, in addition to a recruiter, can help ensure a placement's success. The layer of cost that this adds should be viewed as an investment in ensuring successful, long-term placement.

When embarking on a staffing search, families should always inquire how their safety, security, and confidentiality will be handled throughout the process and how they will factor into recruiting candidates. A solid placement process should be initiated with a presearch interview and needs assessment with the family to craft a job description to target desirable candidates most effectively. Ideally, the process should also include a postsearch position integration and performance measurement plan that lays the foundation for a new hire's success and a family's long-term satisfaction. All candidates should undergo and pass a thorough background investigation prior to the final interview with the family or family office.

As a standard practice, or with the addition or sale of a property, a family and their personal service organization should consider engaging an estate management consultant to undertake periodic organizational and operational assessments to identify new staff subject matter or skills requirements, or to realign current staff responsibilities with service expectations and property needs.

For example, such an assessment can highlight the skill-leveraging that evolves when staff members assume responsibilities beyond their core expertise for fear of dismissal if they decline such duties. Over time, if the performance of an otherwise functionally effective employee is compromised, families can end up receiving mediocre results or services. This circumstance increases the likelihood that the employee will leave or be terminated. The resulting staffing gap increases the risks to both the family and their property and generates costs in both the time and expense required to find and train a replacement.

These assessments also support the design or update of staff retention and development strategies and compensation and benefits packages, and serve to identify and underscore best practices to improve operating efficiencies without sacrificing personal asset values.

Special Projects: Capital Projects and New Construction

Estate managers are often required to have project management experience, which is put to the test when they are tasked with overseeing capital improvement projects, renovations, or new construction. Subject to serious financial risk and combining the complexity of a commercial building with the personal nature of a home, estate construction projects present a significant commitment of time, money, and emotion. As such, they can strain even the most accomplished staff and personal service organizations.

Depending on the size, a typical estate construction project can involve multiple contractors and consultants. Monthly billings can quickly escalate to six or more figures. Those metrics alone are equivalent to establishing a stand-alone company for the duration of a project, but without the benefit of a dedicated CEO or chief financial officer (CFO).

Communicating the workload required to oversee and manage such projects is crucial to executing the family's overall vision. Given these realities, the family, their family office, or their personal service organization should consider engaging an owner's representative or construction manager to oversee their project. These professionals generally have many years of experience working in design and construction and can provide the family with the necessary guidance for them to define and balance their scope, cost, time, and quality expectations.

The following questions and principles can help in determining whether outside professional assistance for a project is necessary:

- **Is there a strategic project plan?** Families should take the time to assess their scope, cost, schedule, and quality goals before starting a project. Developing a strategic project plan will help the family understand their project priorities and save time and money.

- **How has the project been budgeted?** Knowing the difference between a construction budget and a project budget, an owner's representative or construction manager can accurately budget the project's hard (building) and soft (consultants, legal, insurance) costs so that the family is sparred unforeseen budget surprises.
- **Does the staff have the time and skills necessary to devote to the project?** Identify knowledge or experience gaps that can pose a risk to the family and a well-executed project.
- **Understand that every project is unique.** Project support should be scaled to the individual needs of a family and their project. A family may have the internal resources to support some projects but not others.
- **Understand the purpose of a project schedule.** A sound project schedule allows a project to evolve, while reducing impact to the family's budget, minimizing compromises to quality, and providing adequate time for operational turnover.
- **Keep a lid on surprises, but know that they happen.** Surprises and bad news happen with projects of this level of complexity. Bad news delivered early allows a family to exercise their full capacity in decision-making and saves them the added aggravation of surprise if the news is delivered too late.

Special Projects: Event Planning and Management

Families of substantial wealth and their personal service organizations often have the opportunity and challenge of executing significant and complex events at their personal properties and/or unique destinations, both domestic and foreign. These events can range from social milestone celebrations to corporate, philanthropic, or political gatherings, where the personal and financial stakes are quite high.

Understand That It's Never "Just a Big Party"

The project management requirements of significant events are frequently underestimated by both the family and their personal services organization. Given the nature of milestone events and celebrations, whose costs can run into the millions, the assumption that an event is anything other than a complex project can create avoidable pitfalls. Household staff, regardless of their relevant experience, can be tasked to lead this planning. Having the staff do more in house may appear to make economic sense, as they are already intimately familiar with personal family entertaining preferences and their household management protocols. However, such assignments can tax their skills, compromising their ability to perform their normal daily responsibilities. The risks here are threefold: (1) failing to meet the family's expectations for the event, (2) causing strains on the staff's day-to-day service to the family, and (3) incurring budget overruns.

As with the delivery of all personal services, working with the family to define and balance event scope, cost, time, and quality expectations is crucial to successful delivery of a complex event. An experienced estate manager would not hesitate to bring in an outside caterer or valet-parking service to support a large, complex event. The same consideration should be given to outsourcing event project management and coordination, especially in the case of high-profile political fundraisers, business gatherings, or multiday social milestone celebrations.

Event Management Components

Strategic partnerships with an event manager or event management firm can be highly beneficial to a family, their family office, and personal staff. The following is an overview of the key event project components required to successfully manage a significant event. A careful review of these components will help guide the determination if outside professional assistance is needed:

- Event branding and creative concept design, including invitation design
- Guest RSVP and personal service support
- Complex event production services, including thematic set design, stage build-out, lighting, sound, creative media content production, livestreaming, and photo and video services
- Lodging and transportation management (over air, land, and sea)
- Premier entertainer sourcing and contract negotiations
- International protocol considerations
- Physical and personal security logistics: guest and venue, event staff background screening, and press and social media monitoring and control

- Complex reporting and communication matrices between inter-related entities (i.e., key corporations or philanthropic organizations, governmental agencies, etc.)
- Rigorous financial budgeting, forecasting, and reporting
- Culinary menu design and catering services
- Family communication mechanisms
- Current personal staff workload, projects, and priorities and what will be affected if attentions are turned toward them

Engaging a Third-Party Specialty Business Provider

Wealthy families and their family offices surround themselves with a variety of trusted advisers for counsel on their legal, financial, investment, and other related matters. While risks to their property and personal experience are arguably as serious as risks to their nontangible assets, families and staff can discount these challenges. The family may view third-party advisers as an unnecessary expense, or the staff may see them as a threat to their employment or comfortable status quo. Instead, families and staff should be encouraged to regard these providers as invaluable resources that can ensure that properties are overseen with the same rigor as their business assets and who can allow personal staff to remain focused and successful in their core areas of responsibility.

When advocating for a third-party provider, it's advisable to assess the need and perform a cost-benefit analysis—essentially develop a business case that supports the request. Proper due diligence in sourcing a third-party adviser mandates speaking to multiple providers to compare their skills and experience, confirming that nondisclosure agreements (NDAs) are in place before such discussions, and verifying each provider's references and insurance coverage before requesting proposals and presenting them for consideration.

Situations That Warrant Third-Party Service Providers

In addition to the areas of risk already noted, engaging a third-party provider in the event of any of the following circumstances will return meaningful benefits to the family and their staff:

- The scale or complexity of a personal property portfolio has become overwhelming in both size and service requirements.

- A family feels that their lifestyle needs are being subjected to wealth stereotyping or no longer feel that their priorities are understood.
- The property portfolio contains five or more homes in unique destinations, changing the relationship between a family and their real property from enjoyment to work. A third-party adviser can help a family rediscover the enjoyment of owning these special assets.
- Service requests and property maintenance are falling behind, rendering properties unavailable for use or disappointing the family when they are in residence. A third party can help triage property issues, develop a plan for getting caught up, identify ongoing staff needs, or surge support to avoid recurrence of problems.
- Greater accountability is desired in contracting, budgeting, and managing estate expenses. A seasoned estate management expert can create a valuable bridge between the family office and the family's personal organization.
- The family office is charged with requests outside their fiduciary charter due to the limitations of a family's personal service organization, whether staff size or experience. Third-party advisers can be a strategic partner in this instance, enhancing the family office understanding of the family and enabling them to provide insightful, effective service.
- The family needs diagnostic assistance to address and solve operational issues related to staffing, maintenance, or special projects, or to partner on alternative uses and divestment strategies for underutilized properties.
- There are desired acquisitions and planned or unforeseen divestments that change the property portfolio and family lifestyle needs. Third-party advisers such as real estate consultants, due-diligence experts, and estate sale managers can help families and their staff uncover potential operational challenges, avoid unnecessary costs, and offer valuable objectivity, especially if the change is precipitated by a personal loss.

Managing Planes

One of the perks of having substantial wealth is the ability to fly privately. Of all the luxuries that come with wealth, this is one of the greatest. Private aviation not only allows greater scheduling flexibility, it also provides families with privacy and security.[3]

Options for Accessing "Lift"

Families who wish to fly privately face a fairly steep learning curve in terms of options to access aircraft, costs, appropriate plane types, managing pilots and staff, tax considerations, and other issues. Generally, families enter this market over time, choosing first to charter aircraft and then to consider purchase options, whether through a fractional ownership program or outright.

While there are many considerations as to the best approach, families generally find that outsourcing to charter or fractional ownership companies makes the most sense unless they fly a considerable number of hours each year (e.g., more than 100), have unique service needs in terms of the types of aircraft they need or airports they fly into, or have developed a hobbyist interest in the industry.

The same approach is often taken with respect to hiring and managing flight departments. Numerous service providers can provide pilots to owners of private planes without the family having to include them as part of the family office. Considerations for whether to formally employ or simply access the pilots and support staff with the plane include the number of aircraft owned, aircraft operations oversight capabilities, budgetary analysis, and the personal preferences of the principals.

Alternatives Available to Access Private Aviation

The following are the most common arrangements for accessing private air transportation:

- **Full ownership:** A family purchases an aircraft and either directly or indirectly (through a third-party service provider) employs a crew to manage all aspects of aircraft operation. Unlimited use of the aircraft is available within the constraints of the aircraft, operating budget, and availability of flight department personnel.
- **Shared ownership:** Two or more families jointly purchase an aircraft to lower the effective costs; in all other ways, this option resembles full ownership.

- **Fractional ownership:** A family purchases a fraction of a plane that is managed as part of a fleet overseen by an aircraft management company offering what is known as a "fractional program," typically starting with a minimum purchase of fifty hours of equivalent annual flight time, and thereafter in twenty-five-hour increments. The aircraft is fully managed by the fractional program, with the family having flexible privileges to use other (larger and smaller) makes and models offered by the fractional program. It is worth noting that fractional programs offer the unique perk of one-way flights from any origination city. Fractional providers usually offer both purchase and lease options.
- **Jet card/bulk charter:** A family purchases flight time in twenty-five-hour increments from a fractional program to be used within an annual time frame. In addition, numerous traditional charter companies offer comparable block charter products designed to compete with the jet card programs.
- **On-demand charter:** A family contracts with a Part 135 air carrier (i.e., a charter operator) to conduct a flight or series of flights on an ad hoc basis, where costs are quoted by the charter operator specific to a proposed flight itinerary and type of aircraft requested.

Analysis of any business aviation alternative requires a basic understanding of the fixed and variable/direct costs of owning and operating a business jet. An overall operating budget should be prepared for each method of air transportation services discussed here. However, with respect to full or shared ownership, assumptions are necessary to varying degrees, resulting in some level of financial risk relative to the other methods of accessing air transportation services.

FIXED COSTS Fixed costs are those that the family office is committed to paying regardless of the number of hours the aircraft will be flown. Fixed costs are typically determined as annual costs and allocated to the aircraft on an hourly basis according to the number of hours the aircraft is flown. Generally, the four largest fixed costs are (1) aircraft financing (direct or implied), (2) crew labor expenses (salaries and benefits for the pilots and flight attendants), (3) calendar-based maintenance and maintenance service contracts with minimums, and (4) connectivity services.

In addition to these costs, the following fixed costs are those associated with aircraft overhead and ongoing investment in personnel:

- Hangar and office expenses
- Aircraft insurance
- Crew training
- Flight planning services and other subscription services
- Management fees, if applicable

VARIABLE COSTS   Variable costs are those directly attributed to the operation of an aircraft and are incurred only as a result of flying the aircraft. Fuel costs represent the majority of the variable operating costs, typically accounting for 50 to 75 percent of the total.

The other key component of variable costs is associated with hourly and cycle-based maintenance, unexpected maintenance events, and routine maintenance of the aircraft. The most expensive maintenance costs are typically jet engine overhauls and inspections required on a periodic interval mandated by the engine manufacturer. Because both aircraft and engine maintenance costs are typically billed and calculated according to hours of aircraft operation, these can be calculated as hourly variable costs as well. Other variable costs include per diem–based backup pilot support, crew overnight and per diem food costs, landing fees, catering, cleaning, aircraft modernization, modification and refurbishment, and numerous other smaller costs.

When utilizing product type options such as fractional programs, jet cards, block charter, and on-demand charter, additional charges may be levied, such as fuel surcharges, meaning that the quoted price includes a base cost of fuel per gallon and a surcharge levied to reflect the differential between the actual fuel cost and the base number. Be aware of the fact that the base number varies among industry providers. Other costs include repositioning costs (i.e., when the plane must be relocated as a result of a flight), minimum flight time costs, overnight charges, and federal taxes.

Comparing the Costs of Flying Privately

The choice of form of accessing air transportation services depends in large part on two factors: annual aircraft usage and budgeting. If usage is fewer than 100 hours per year, it is uneconomical to consider full ownership, but all other options are available. Note that shared ownership is not a market product; it is generally a unique set of circumstances whereby a family identifies another family to share in the purchase of the aircraft. With respect to all options, a general rule of thumb is that the per-hour cost or shared ownership will be the least costly per flight hour, followed by full ownership (provided that sufficient hours are being flown), closely followed by on-demand charter, block charter, fractional ownership, and jet cards, in descending order. Results may deviate based on actual market depreciation and financing costs combined with ultimate annual usage with respect to any of the ownership options. Of course, convenience of use is always an important nonmonetary consideration.

Table 5.1 presents a matrix showing the conversion of anticipated fixed annual costs to hourly fixed costs for a six-passenger seat, midsize jet.

TABLE 5.1
Costs to fly private aircraft

	Full aircraft ownership	Managed/ shared ownership	Fractional ownership	Jet charter/ card
Annual fixed costs	$1.2 million	$1 million*	$745,000*	N/A
Typical annual usage (hours used for calculation)	250–400 hours	150–200 hours	100–200 hours	25–100 hours
Hourly fixed costs (Annual Fixed Costs + Annual Usage)	$3,000/hour	$4,000/hour	$3,725/hour	No cost
Variable operating costs per hour	$1,900/hour	$1,900/hour	$3,600/hour	$8,750/hour
Total hourly aircraft cost (Fixed + Variable Costs)	$4,900/hour	$5,900/hour	$7,325/hour	$8,750/hour

* Includes management fees

Source: Igojet, LLC, "A Primer on the Business Aviation Industry," 2010.

Acquiring Aircraft

Regardless of the method of accessing air transportation services, it is advisable to engage experts such as aviation lawyers or other consultants who can advise on the various options and provide industry referrals. An aviation lawyer or consultant should be objective and unbiased. Keep in mind that business aviation is generally practiced by boutique law and consulting firms (as opposed to airline-type work, which is handled by larger firms). The National Business Aviation Association (NBAA) provides many resources about prospective aviation advisers, and attendance at an NBAA conference or virtual event will allow the family office manager to connect directly to the best of the best advisers.

Certainly, there are numerous other "advisers" who have deep knowledge of and a range of diverse opinions within private aviation. A team approach is recommended for a successful decision and acquisition.

The following information will provide a time line to the acquisition of a whole or shared aircraft. The time line associated with the acquisition of a jet card, a block charter product, or a fractional program ownership or lease product is vastly shortened and can be accomplished in a week or so if necessary. However, despite the shortened time frame to accomplish the acquisition, tax and organizational planning, discussed next, may still be relevant and should be factored into the time line.

Steps in Acquiring Business Aircraft

The decision to purchase a business aircraft may evolve over time for a first-time buyer, or it may be made rather quickly for those trading up from an existing aircraft. Either way, once the determination to purchase an aircraft is made, the most common next step is to contact an aircraft broker. The aircraft broker then works to identify the most suitable aircraft and generate a letter of intent. Next, an aviation attorney is hired to prepare a purchase agreement. Either concurrent with the negotiation of the purchase agreement or after execution thereof, additional parties are contacted, such as prospective lenders and management companies.

While the foregoing approach will work, it is not ideal. The best practice approach to acquiring a business aircraft is discussed next.

When financing is a component of an aircraft acquisition transaction, the financing will generally be the longest lead-time item. In the typical transaction, working with the lender becomes a fire drill because the process begins late in the game. Ideally, contact with prospective lenders should be initiated as soon as the decision is made to finance the aircraft purchase. It is common for several lenders to submit financing proposals, and it typically takes two to four weeks to select the lender and refine the chosen proposal. While some lenders require specific make, model, and serial number of the aircraft to submit a proposal, it is possible to provide the lender with a close approximation of the desired aircraft type and cost and then to proceed on a nonbinding basis. Once a lender is selected, it can take a week or longer for the borrower to submit complete financial and other data, thereby allowing the lender to obtain credit committee approval and commit to financing the transaction. Thereafter, it can take a week or two to obtain draft loan documentation. Clearly, the entire process is lengthy, so getting an early start is ideal.

Concurrent with initiating contact with a lender, it is generally preferable to contact an aviation tax attorney. If the attorney is contacted prior to the lender, they can provide referrals to lenders that will fit the client profile. If the attorney is contacted later, they can still provide referrals to aircraft brokers, management companies, escrow companies, and any other party transaction participants. In addition, many aviation attorneys are skilled at both Federal Aviation Administration (FAA) and tax matters, as well as mainstream transactional and commercial issues, allowing the completion of all state and federal tax planning and the formation of a special-purpose entity to take title, if appropriate. With the planning completed early in the process, the transaction will proceed more smoothly from the perspective of having a coordinated letter of intent and purchase agreement, forming the acquiring entity, identifying states where the aircraft can be delivered, and other important matters.

Once ownership structuring has been conducted and the loan process initiated, it is time to contact an aircraft broker. Commonly, an aircraft broker will expeditiously select an aircraft make and model that meets the client's mission and other requirements and recommend available aircraft in the marketplace.

Most aircraft brokers will also have a template letter of intent available from prior transactions. While using a template may be tempting from the perspective of timeliness and cost, a good aviation tax attorney should be able to prepare the letter of intent on the day needed, and for minimal cost. Unequivocally, a letter of intent prepared by an aviation tax attorney will be comprehensive and unambiguous, and it will dovetail with the definitive purchase agreement.

On average, negotiations of the letter of intent should take one week, factoring in reaching agreement on the purchase price. Once executed, the attorney will prepare and negotiate the purchase agreement over a period of roughly two weeks. Of course, these are simply approximations. The time line may move more slowly or quickly.

Concurrent with completing the purchase agreement negotiations, all financial and other due diligence matters should be completed with the lender. After contract execution, it is normal for the aircraft to immediately undergo a prepurchase inspection, which, depending on the size of the aircraft, can take anywhere from one to three weeks. During the inspection, the lender should be preparing loan documents and circulating them for review and negotiation, which should take one week (or possibly longer).

In the event that external aircraft management is desirable, the selection of an aircraft management company should commence while the purchase agreement is being negotiated. Once selected, it is customary to allow one or two weeks for the preparation and negotiation of management documentation. In some transactions, it is necessary to execute such documentation prior to closing. For example, in some states, sales tax planning will rely on a common carrier exemption, which requires the aircraft to be leased to a common carrier (aka a "charter company") at the time of title transfer. While it is not always part of an aircraft transaction, it is advisable to have one or two preclosing conference calls, time permitting, to ensure that all items on the closing checklist are timely completed.

Implicit in the steps given here is the requirement for several phone calls to complete all acquisition structuring and tax planning; to work through preclosing requirements, including registration of the acquiring entity as a sales tax vendor, if appropriate; to complete sales tax exemption and other relevant forms; to obtain board

approval; and to complete various other items identified on the closing checklist.

Importance of a Team Approach

When acquiring an aircraft, it is important that the principals of the
family or the family office ensures that the team of tax and legal
advisers, brokers, and/or consultants work together seamlessly. With
respect to each of these professionals, it is also important to ensure that
(1) the tax and legal advisers are experts at private aviation; (2) if
brokers are used, that there is clarity about conflicts of interest; and
(3) any consultants employed are experienced at acquiring the class of
aircraft being sought.

Tax Issues

While tax issues are relevant to all forms of accessing air transportation
services, more complex issues arise where there is more flexibility on
structuring (i.e., whole or shared ownership). Because the other forms
of accessing air transportation services are products, the structure is
somewhat rigid. Nonetheless, as mentioned next, certain tax issues are
germane to all forms.

Tax planning is essentially a melting pot of issues. Compromises
may have to be made, as optimal planning in one area may lead to less
optimal planning in another. The starting place for any tax planning
is state sales and use tax. State sales and use tax is typically a onetime
tax, and failure to plan properly can result in the tax being due. Optimal planning can result in deferral or elimination of the tax. Because
state sales and use tax planning is "form over substance," the planning
needs to be done first in order to identify the structure that is needed
to meet the state law requirements.

Despite normal expectations, because aircraft is moveable personal
property, it is very possible to create a connection to more than one
state with the aircraft, thereby creating liability for taxes in more than one
state. This is particularly problematic if the planning produces a result
of zero liability in the primary state, inasmuch as there won't be any
opportunity to gain a credit in another state. As a general rule of thumb,
it is very difficult, if not impossible, to escape a connection with the state
where the aircraft is principally hangered. This is true regardless of where

the aircraft is located at the time that title transfers, and regardless of the state of formation of the entity that takes title (e.g., Delaware).

After state sales and use tax planning is completed, federal income and excise tax planning should be conducted. While this planning is "substance over form," the taxpayer is generally held to the form of the structure, so it is necessary to structure correctly. There are numerous tax code sections that are unique to aircraft, or have special interpretation as they relate to aircraft. It is absolutely advisable to have an aviation tax lawyer or accountant conduct this research and advise on the ideal structuring. Keep in mind that the structuring needs to be reconciled with the state sales and use tax structuring.

In addition, the FAA has a variety of rules under Part 91 (private aviation) that pertain to structuring and cash flow. The tax advisers should be fully familiar with FAA regulations or else they may easily make mistakes. Also, all structuring should factor in cash flow objectives, liability protection planning objectives, shareholder concerns, and public filings (e.g., securities law) issues. The melting pot will be evident once the planning is discussed and completed.

Management, Operations, and Staffing

In addition to numerous other issues that wealthy families must address when acquiring private aircraft, determining how best to manage, operate, and staff (i.e., pilots and support) these expensive and complex assets is critical. There are typically two ways to do this: hire an aircraft management company to manage the aircraft, provide maintenance, and staff the pilots and related support personnel; or create a flight department that employs pilots and any required support professionals such as schedulers and flight attendants. In either case, there is a role for a regional airport to hanger the aircraft and provide needed fueling, maintenance, and related services at the direction of either the fixed-base operator (FBO) or dedicated flight department.

For most owners who are just starting to acquire private aircraft, or those who do not have multiple planes or extensive needs in terms of flight hours, using a management company is typically the best choice. This is also typically the case when the owner would like to charter the plane out to third parties.

FIXED-BASE OPERATORS At most major regional, national, and international airports, there are one or more FBOs, whose business it is to assist aircraft owners with fueling, hangaring, maintenance, and similar services. Families who own planes invariably work with FBOs, either directly or through aircraft management companies.

AIRCRAFT MANAGEMENT COMPANIES Aircraft management companies help owners oversee some of or all the management of their private aircraft. With charter aircraft management, the management company simply provides opportunities for the owner to charter the aircraft out to others for a fee. In these cases, the owner maintains responsibility and control over the operations of the aircraft.

Management companies can also provide what is known as "turn-key aircraft management," in which they take care of maintenance and repairs, hiring and paying crews, training, handling security, ensuring compliance with FAA rules and regulations, and other duties. With turnkey management, the owner transfers operational responsibility to the management company.

Hiring an aircraft management company is usually one of the first things that new owners do to ensure that all the operational, staffing, maintenance, and FAA requirements are being met. This approach will help get the family, and often its family office, up to speed on all these issues. Over time, the family may decide to take over some of or all these responsibilities, including creating a flight department.

FLIGHT DEPARTMENTS Families with substantial wealth, significant private travel needs, or both have the option to establish their own flight departments, where they formally employ pilots and support staff. In these cases, the pilots handle many of the responsibilities otherwise conducted by the aircraft management company or FBO, although there is typically some role for a local airport in terms of hangering the plane, providing light maintenance that does not require sending the aircraft to a dedicated maintenance company, installing upgrades, and other tasks.

As with other services conducted in house by a family office, overseeing a flight department introduces numerous responsibilities and challenges. These include finding, hiring, and managing pilots; being responsible for related needs, such as scheduling and flight attendants (whether done in house or with external vendors); providing proper training and licensing; and ensuring strict compliance with FAA rules and documentation.

It is worth mentioning that finding, hiring, and managing pilots can be a distinct challenge for family offices (not because they are family offices, but because of industry challenges). Pilots are professionals who have aligned their passion with their vocation and are not necessarily motivated by many of the same things as other employees within a family office. As a result, managing a flight department requires the family office to be attuned to these nuances. Further, pilots may not be experienced in many of the business management needs that come with overseeing staff, preparing and maintaining budgets, and other responsibilities. If this is the case, the family office will need to work with the flight departments to provide support and training in these areas.

OTHER CONSIDERATIONS Similar to concierge service providers within a family office, pilots tend to interact with the principals and their family members in a direct and recurring manner. This can introduce certain challenges in the management of the family, particularly by senior managers who normally manage communication between principals and the various service providers. While this is not necessarily a bad thing, it does mean that principals will experience directly the quality of people and services being provided by the flight departments in a way that might not exist with other functions.[4]

ASSESSMENT AND ISSUES SURFACED

What Did We Learn?

Solving the complexity challenges that come with substantial wealth is one of the primary roles of a family office. In the case of John's family, the complexity has to do with their daily lifestyle needs, the numerous residences that John and Sofia own, and the planes that John would like to purchase. The challenge for wealthy families is not just the breadth of these needs, but that, for many of them, they are new challenges, and they do not know how or from whom to get help. The family office must be able to anticipate when investing to solve incremental needs is warranted and how to go about doing this, either internally or externally.

Case Questions

- What are the key new service or advisory areas where John and Sofia need help?
- What are the specific job responsibilities across each of the areas, and what should be conducted in house versus outsourced?
- How does the family office identify new personnel and/or external resources, and what should they look for?
- How can Michael help John with his decision to buy the two planes?
- What questions should Michael be asking both John and external advisers regarding the planes?

RECOMMENDED SOLUTIONS

Responses to Case Questions

What are the key new service or advisory areas where John and Sofia need help?

John and Sofia have expressed a need for more help in what would be considered concierge services (e.g., lifestyle, travel, or events); estate management (overseeing the ranch and numerous residences); and private aviation. These are all niche service areas, with dedicated professionals and third-party vendors increasingly available to fill them. For family offices that outsource both the oversight and delivery of these services, the responsibility for finding the right external provider and ensuring the proper delivery of services falls on the CFO and their staff. For larger family offices with more expansive needs, they might create separate roles for a chief of staff, concierge, estate manager, or chief pilot.

What are the specific job responsibilities across each of the areas, and what should be conducted in house versus outsourced?

It is important to note that the roles that Jason is looking to fill are professionals who can coordinate the delivery of services by mostly third-party providers (as opposed to providing the services with internal family office staff). The reasons for outsourcing these activities focus on the geographic dispersion of the assets (e.g., estate management), the specialized nature of the advice and services needed (e.g., pilots), and the need for external information and capabilities not available to the family office (e.g., travel and concierge).

A key responsibility for Jason and professionals in his position is knowing the vendors in each of the various service areas and being able to assess which ones will be the best fit for the family. In the area of estate management, there are a limited number of providers with experience dealing with family offices. However, for lifestyle, concierge, and event assistance, there are numerous types of providers and vendors ranging from credit card concierge services, to small boutiques and individual providers, to large, multinational travel and related services. For the aircraft, considerations should include the extent of dedicated flight support needed (i.e., how many hours a year John and his family will be flying) and whether John wants to manage a dedicated flight department, and economics (i.e., does he want to make his planes available to others for charter, thereby reducing the costs of ownership and achieving certain tax benefits).

How does the family office identify new personnel and/or external resources, and what should they look for?

This is an important role, and one that requires particular attention to staff. Despite the fact that in this particular case, the role is largely to ensure the coordination of services delivered by third parties, Jason will have to find someone who is knowledgeable about the various areas and has an understanding of the unique issues and dynamics of working for a wealthy family. Many families rely on existing staff to perform these functions, such as the CFO or a personal assistant. For smaller, less complex family offices, this arrangement can be functional because these professionals have a familiarity with the family and the needs of the job are neither too specialized nor time consuming. However, for a family office the size of Left Seat Management, and given the breadth of the family's needs across multiple areas, hiring a dedicated operations manager is likely the right solution for John and Sofia. Fortunately, as the number of wealthy families has increased, an industry that supports family offices has developed, with both experienced professionals and specialty service providers in each of these areas. Jason should look for assistance in conducting this search by consulting his peers at other family offices, using a recruiting firm, or both.

How can Michael help John with his decision to buy the two planes?

Michael should speak with an aviation attorney about the options, issues, and process for buying and operating private aircraft. It will be important for him to become familiar with many of the legal, tax, regulatory, operational, and budgetary issues that apply to private planes. For this particular assignment, it will also be important for Michael to remember that John is very knowledgeable about the space and will play a more active role than he normally does in many other things that he asks of the family office.

What questions should Michael be asking both John and external advisers regarding the planes?

Having gotten up to speed on the options, issues, and process, Michael should meet with John to discuss what he has in mind, particularly with respect to the management of the aircraft. Questions that are relevant are:

- Will John want to employ his own pilots?
- Does John want to allow one or both of his planes to be chartered?
- How much is he willing to spend on the planes and their ongoing operational costs (for both acquisition and annual maintenance)?

Moreover, Michael should make sure that both he and John are aware of the various tax implications of John's choices around owning and managing the aircraft.

CHAPTER SIX

Investments

CASE STUDY

Summary

- Eighteen months after the creation of the Left Seat Management family office
- Regulatory issues
- Approaches to managing investments
- Specific investment areas

Key Words/Concepts

- Regulatory issues
- Investment management
- Direct investing
- Venture investing
- Social impact investing
- Art and collectibles

Challenge

It was Sunday morning, and John finally had time to get away and find some peace and quiet in his personal library and home office. This was his sanctuary from calls and meetings, where he could spend time reading books that he never had time to get to when he was building his business. This was also the place that John could be alone and focus on matters that he wanted to catch up on.

One of the things that he was looking forward to reading was the financial package he received monthly from his family office team. These financials covered his entire family enterprise, and the team knew that he was meticulous in his review of the materials, often sending detailed questions back to them for clarification. John really liked finding "mistakes" in the financials, partially to keep his team on their toes and partially to show that he wanted to run the family office with the same level of detail with which he ran his operating company.

John fondly remembered what his financial reviews had been like before the sale of Rybat Manufacturing. He got buried in the day-to-day details of running the company and had very little time to sit down to pore over the scattered statements and disorganized investor updates that made up his investment portfolio. He would make regular attempts to catch up on his financials, but these sessions were often done by phone or on a golf course with his broker and bankers. For John, investment proposals were often discussed at the clubhouse in an unstructured manner, with him taking ad hoc meetings based on whoever could get his attention that week.

Investing changed dramatically for John after his liquidity event. At first, he was a bit apprehensive to make any dramatic changes to his investment strategy. He didn't really think that he had a strategy at that point in his life anyway. After some vanity and long-delayed purchases (e.g., a new house, a classic car, a luxury family vacation in the Seychelles), he knew that he needed to put more thought into what to do with his new level of wealth.

John initially spent a couple of months learning as much as he could from peers who had gone through similar company sales, as well as from his current lineup of financial advisers. These meetings led to interesting new connections and even more new ideas of how wealthy families approached their own investing strategies. The problem for John was that there were so many types of approaches that it became impossible for him to get a sense of the best solution for him. During this period, he felt that he was spending too much time hearing about niche investment strategies and too little about big picture approaches to managing his wealth. He also made a few angel investments during this period, which he thought he understood well because they were in his sphere of industry experience. However, most of those investments did poorly in the end. John was quickly realizing that it was very different being a business investor than his previous vast experience as a business operator.

Luckily, John was able to turn to Michael, his trusted adviser and the head of his family office, to develop a comprehensive investment strategy for his liquid investments and, increasingly, his private ones as well. John and Michael used a number of banks, brokerage firms, and asset managers to execute the investment strategy for the family. Michael also helped John upgrade his investment advisers while still maintaining long-term relationships that he valued strongly.

However, John was noticing that these outside experts didn't always agree on the best approaches to investing. Some advocated taking or increasing exposure to certain asset classes or strategies, while others advised against it. This was frustrating to John and delayed his decision-making, as it invariably required him to evaluate the different investment views by comparing notes across both the outside advisers and his network.

At John's request, the family office also started to dabble in impact investing. Michael advised John that he had worked with many wealthy families to incorporate this type of investing as a way to not only assist John and Sofia in their desire to contribute to society beyond their philanthropy, but also to engage the children in investing, promote family unity, and involve them in general family office matters. At some point, John wanted to expand the family's impact investing, but he was wary about it because he didn't know much about the space and did not know when and how best to get the children more deeply involved.

In addition, there was the increasing amount of time and money Sofia and he were "investing" on finding and acquiring art and collectibles related to their involvement with museums; purchases of artwork, sculptures, and antique furniture for their new homes; and John's classic car collection. It was becoming clear to John that he needed to develop a better way for both Sofia and him to manage and engage in these various pursuits.

John also found that he was particularly interested in direct investing. To date, he had made a number of small investments on the advice of his friends, peers, and other wealthy families, although he did so largely without a formal strategy. Typically, he made decisions based on the relationship he had with the person who brought the deal to him, as well as whether the investment thesis and expected returns made logical sense to him.

Despite not having a background in private investing, John found that he enjoyed seeing and evaluating deal flow, employing his experience and network to assess deals, and having the opportunity to engage with other families. These activities reminded him of his days building Rybat Manufacturing. He believed that his insights into the manufacturing industry could be of great value to him, and potentially to other families who were less well connected or knowledgeable in the space. John was also attracted to the investment returns that private deals offered and the ability to access unique opportunities in a host of other areas not otherwise available to traditional investors. He committed to making direct investing a more significant part of the overall investment portfolio and enlisting Michael and the family office to assist him.

BACKGROUND INFORMATION

Regulatory Issues

In the course of managing the finances and investments of a family, a family office frequently provides advice related to the family's investments in securities.[1] This activity would ordinarily subject the family office to regulation under the Investment Advisers Act of 1940 (Advisers Act). The Act defines an "investment adviser" as anyone who provides advice regarding securities, is engaged in the business of providing such services, and does so for compensation. As it clearly falls within this particularly broad definition of "investment adviser," the family office would be required to register with the Securities and Exchange Commission (SEC) unless it can find an exemption.

In 2011, pursuant to a directive in the Dodd-Frank Act, the SEC adopted a rule in the Advisers Act codified as Rule 202(a)(11)(G)-1, more commonly referred to as the "Family Office Rule," which effectively excludes family offices from the broad definition of "investment adviser." The adoption of the Family Office Rule was largely driven by the fact that families who have set up family offices to manage their wealth are financially sophisticated and less in need of the protections that the Advisers Act was intended to provide to typical investors.

Satisfying the requirements of the Family Office Rule allows a family office not only to escape the burdens associated with registration under the Advisers Act, but also to completely avoid the Act's other numerous provisions, as well as any additional state or licensing requirements applicable to investment advisers. In contrast, an investment adviser who is able to meet an *exemption* from registration (but not an *exclusion* from the "investment adviser" definition, such as the Family Office Rule) still remains subject to the other provisions. As a result, understanding the requirements and intricacies of the Family Office Rule is critical to successful family office compliance.

The Family Office Rule

The Family Office Rule sets forth three requirements that the family office must meet to qualify for exclusion from regulation under the Advisers Act. In addition, the rule supplements these requirements with complex definitions that further limit the availability of the exclusion.

Fundamentally, a family office is a company, and it includes its directors, partners, members, managers, trustees, and employees acting within the scope of their employment. To be considered a family office that qualifies for the exclusion, it must (1) provide investment advice only to "family clients"; (2) be wholly owned by family clients and exclusively controlled by family members and other family entities; and (3) not hold itself out to the public as an investment adviser.

Also, the SEC has explicitly indicated that the Family Office Rule exclusion does not extend to family offices serving multiple families such as multi-family offices (MFOs)—it is available only for single-family offices (SFOs). For instance, family offices should be aware that the Family Office Rule does not provide any exclusion in a situation in which several families have established separate family offices but have staffed their family offices with the same (or substantially the same) employees.

FAMILY CLIENTS While the last two elements of the Family Office Rule are relatively straightforward, the first requirement, that the family office is limited to only "family clients," is far more complex. It encompasses a multifaceted definition that is further broken into the following subcategories of defined terms: current and former family members, current and former key employees, the estates of such persons, a company owned and controlled by such persons, and affiliated trusts and nonprofit organizations meeting certain requirements.

FAMILY MEMBERS The first subcategory included in the definition of "family client" is "family members," which generally includes all lineal descendants up to ten generations removed from a common ancestor. The definition is relatively expansive, as it recognizes adopted children, stepchildren, and foster children, as well as spouses and spousal equivalents of such family members. In addition, the "family client" definition covers individuals designated as former family members, meaning a spouse, spousal equivalent, or stepchild who was a family member at one time, but is no longer part of the family due to divorce or another similar event. With regard to such former family members, the rule does not place any limitation as to the time frame after such an event in which the former family member can continue to take part in the family office, nor does it restrict the person's ability to make new investments, as it does with former key employees, as discussed in the next section.

It is important to note, however, that because the basis of the definition is linked to a common ancestor, the term "family member" does not extend to the in-laws of family members. Thus, any investment by in-laws made through the family office may cause the family office to no longer be eligible for the Family Office Rule exclusion.

In addition, the "family member" definition is rather flexible in several other respects because the designated common ancestor can be either living or deceased, and such a designation is not permanent; rather, it can be changed as the family office evolves over time.

KEY EMPLOYEES "Key employees" of the family office, their estates, and certain entities through which they may invest are also included in the definition of "family clients." This allows the family office to attract talent by offering investment opportunities provided by the family office, while at the same time aligning key employees' interests with the family without disqualifying the office from the Family Office Rule exclusion.

As with the definition of "family members," the definition of "key employees" is also quite complex. The term encompasses an employee of the family office or its affiliated family office who (1) is an executive officer, director, trustee, or general partner, or is serving in a similar capacity; or (2) in connection with their regular duties, participates in the investment activities of the family office (excluding those who are solely clerical, secretarial, or administrative employees and those who have participated for less than twelve months).

The complexity of the "key employees" definition is offset by its flexibility. First, it recognizes that some families may have more than one family office due to any number of structuring preferences or for business or tax reasons. The rule, therefore, extends the definition to cover the key employees of an "affiliated family office," which is defined as a separate family office that (1) is wholly owned by family clients of the other family office; (2) is controlled by family members and family entities of the other family office; and (3) has no clients other than family clients of the other family office. Second, the definition further includes trusts where a key employee is the sole contributor and decision-maker. Third, it also includes such key employees' spouses or spousal equivalents, but only to the extent that they hold a joint, community interest in the investment property.

That being said, it is important to note that this flexibility does not extend to key employees of family companies other than the family office or its affiliated family office. Therefore, investment by such other key employees may cause the family office not to qualify for the Family Office Rule exclusion.

Finally, just as with former family members, the rule recognizes former key employees—defined as individuals who were key employees at one time, but are no longer—and it allows them to keep their preexisting investments under the family office's management. However, in contrast to former family members, the rule limits former key employees from making additional investments after their employment has ended.

ESTATES AND TRUSTS To accommodate common estate-planning activities for testamentary and charitable giving purposes, the Family Office Rule's definition of "family client" also includes any estates of current and former family members, as well as those of current and former key employees. This has the effect of allowing the family office to advise the executor of such an estate, even if the estate ultimately will be distributed to nonfamily members.

Furthermore, trusts are included in the definition, but the rule places certain limitations that are particularly dependent on the circumstances. Any revocable trusts that have one or more family clients as their grantors are included as family clients (their beneficiaries can be nonfamily clients and still qualify under the rule). In contrast, irrevocable trusts are also included, but only if the current beneficiaries are also family clients.

NONPROFIT ORGANIZATIONS   The definition of "family client" further includes any nonprofit organization, charitable foundation, charitable trust, or other charitable organization that is funded exclusively by one or more other family clients. While such charitable organizations are permitted to be originally established by nonfamily members, all the funds that they currently hold must have come solely from family members, and any funding received from persons other than family members will disqualify such organizations from the Family Office Rule exclusion.

OTHER FAMILY ENTITIES   To facilitate the family office's ability to conduct their activities through the use of typical investment structures, including pooled investment vehicles, the rule also extends the definition of "family client" to include "any company, wholly owned (directly or indirectly) exclusively by, and operated for the sole benefit of, one or more other family clients." This means that any investment in the company by a nonfamily client disqualifies it from receiving investment advisory services through the family office.

Wholly Owned by Family Clients and Controlled by Family Members

The second element of the Family Office Rule requires that a family office be (1) wholly owned by family clients and (2) exclusively controlled by family members and family entities. This means that while any family client (including key employees) may hold an ownership interest in the family office, control must remain exclusively with family members and family entities, not with its key employees or their affiliated entities or trusts. "Control" is defined as "the power to exercise a controlling influence over the management or policies of a company, unless such power is solely the result of being an officer of such company."

No Holding out of the Family Office as an Investment Adviser

The final requirement of the Family Office Rule is that the family office must not hold itself out to the public as an investment adviser. This restriction has been interpreted broadly and prohibits any behavior suggesting that the family office is attempting to enter into a traditional investment adviser relationship with nonfamily clients. Unsurprisingly, if a family office engages in this type of behavior, it must register as an investment adviser under the Advisers Act.

Family offices may not be aware that, as a result of giving investment advice, they fall within the purview of the Advisers Act and thus must fit their ownership and investment processes within the parameters of the Family Office Rule to avoid the registration requirements of the Advisers Act. Family offices that do not satisfy the requirements of the Family Office Rule may need to restructure themselves to qualify for the exclusion, analyze whether they qualify under an applicable exemption, apply for a specific exemptive order from the SEC, or register as an investment adviser. Family offices that are currently in compliance with the Family Office Rule must remain vigilant and have policies in place to ensure that there is no inadvertent disqualification from the exclusion.

Investing Generally

The range of investment activities for which a family office is responsible is extensive and varied. They include overseeing liquid assets, alternative assets (e.g., real estate, hedge funds, and private equity funds), single-stock positions, direct investments in private companies, and impact investing such as in environmental, social, and governance (ESG) and socially responsible investment (SRI) funds. There are also considerable differences in how wealthy families go about overseeing investments. Some families will manage all their investments in house, while others are more delegatory, choosing to outsource some of or all the investment functions.

For these reasons, sharing universal best practices for investment management across family offices is not within the purview of this chapter. However, there are broadly distinctive ways in which family offices structure the management of their investments, which overlap somewhat with both the organizational and behavioral types of family offices that were described earlier. In addition, there are specific investment activities that warrant discussion because of similarities, challenges, and best practices within them, including direct investing, venture investing, social impact investing, and art and collectibles investing. Each of these is discussed in detail later in this chapter.

Different Ways That Family Offices Invest

DELEGATORY Many family offices, regardless of the magnitude of their wealth, choose to outsource the management of their portfolio entirely to third parties. This outsourcing tends to stem from the fundamental view or preference by the principals, the family office senior executives, or both. Interestingly, the decision to outsource does not necessarily depend on the family's level of sophistication or resources. Families that choose to outsource some of or all their investment activities are comfortable relying on others for investment advice and strategy execution and farm out these responsibilities to banks, brokerage firms, asset managers, or investment consultants (or often a combination of the four).

One common variation on this approach is when the family office is responsible for asset allocation, which is usually conducted by the chief investment officer, who develops the overall strategy around the asset classes that the family should own, the relative allocation for each, and when and by how much to rebalance periodically. These duties are often done in conjunction with one or more of the outside providers who have the resources, technology, and experience with other significant investors to help them.

ACTIVE-CONTROLLING With the tremendous growth in wealth accumulated by financial services firms and the founders and other professionals involved with them, it is not uncommon to see family offices being created by former hedge fund managers, private equity principals, and finance executives. These principals are very familiar with investing, the markets, and the various execution partners and platforms (both internal and external) available to assist them. Family offices overseen by these types of principals often establish their own investing businesses within the office and actively trade their portfolios, particularly in those markets or asset classes in which they have expertise.

While less common, there are also those principals who, despite not having grown up professionally as an investor or finance professional, decide to bring in house the lion's share of investing responsibilities. In these cases, the family office is staffed similar to an investment management firm or hedge fund with a senior and experienced chief investment officer, active traders, and portfolio managers. These types of investors may still delegate the execution of some of their strategies to third parties. However, it is the controlling nature over a significant portion of their investable assets that distinguishes these family offices from others.

THE HYBRID APPROACH   Some family offices take a hybrid approach to how they invest money on behalf of their principals and family members. These family offices may be active-controlling with respect to a particular strategy or asset class, and outsource other investment management needs to banks, brokerage firms, asset managers, or investment consultants. Many principals, as well as the senior executives they hire, have a penchant for certain types of investing and therefore decide to conduct these activities themselves. Investing directly in private companies, often called "direct investing," is a primary example of an investment type that principals choose to get involved with based on a specific interest. Moreover, family offices, often dictated by their size, may also internally manage the cash and short-duration, fixed-income portions of their portfolio, believing that they can do so as well, and at less cost, than outsourcing to a third party.

Finally, there are those family offices that prefer to actively trade a particular asset class or strategy. In some cases, they do so to develop a performance track record that they, or the team they hire, can market to other investors down the road as a separate asset management business.

Why Is This Important?

It is important for principals, family office executives, and those who provide advice and services to these various types of investors to understand these distinctions. For principals, it helps them better understand whom they should hire and appreciate that there are numerous ways that their portfolio can be overseen—all done in a way that satisfies their desire for control or ability to be more actively involved in certain investment activities. For family office executives, this understanding can help them better assess how to staff for the investment function and where to focus their time, often in those areas where the principal has expressed a desire to be actively involved, whether individually or via the family office's investment team. Finally, for service providers, understanding both what the family is doing with their investment capital and how they are doing it, can help them better assess the advice and services they should be providing. For more delegatory families, this may mean broad support in areas such as asset allocation, manager search and selection, and reporting. For more active-controlling family offices, it means serving as an execution partner in one or more asset classes or for select strategies.

Investing in Private Companies

Private investing, also referred to as "direct investing" (figure 6.1), is where a wealthy family makes an investment into a company directly instead of through an intermediary such as a private equity fund. Direct investments are almost invariably illiquid, and the investment focus in this chapter is on such illiquid assets: real estate, infrastructure equity, private equity, and emerging alternatives (including infrastructure debt). Illiquid assets are the largest portion of assets commonly referred to as "alternative investments." Hedge funds are ignored because investments in these funds are generally more liquid.

Many family offices reduced their exposure to traditional investment strategies after the financial crisis of 2007–2009.[2] Such strategies often rely heavily on portfolio allocations to public securities such as stocks and bonds. Instead, they turned increasingly to nonpublic (i.e., private) investment markets, and as a group, family offices have since become major players in the financing of private companies. They are now an important source of capital for start-ups, middle-stage financings, and other private deals of all sorts, including the high-flying financing market for private companies with $1 billion-plus valuations known as "unicorns."

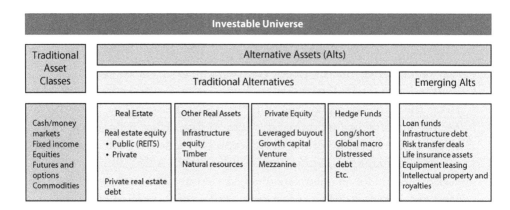

Figure 6.1 Private investing–direct investing *Source*: World Economic Forum, "Direct Investing by Institutional Investors: Implications for Investors and Policy-Makers," 2014.

At the same time, family offices also turned away from traditional private equity funds in favor of making direct private equity investments on their own. These direct investments avoid the fees, absence of control, and limited transparency that go with investing in a private equity fund. True, direct investments also lack liquidity, but they may be no worse in that regard than private equity funds with long-term lock-up requirements for investors. Indeed, despite the lack of liquidity, many families are comfortable buying and operating businesses, whether on their own or with other families as partners. Direct investing may be ingrained in their DNA. For those who became wealthy by successfully building and monetizing a business, this level of concentration and "all hands on deck" approach to investing is natural, and often preferred.

To be sure, direct investing is not a new phenomenon. Family offices have always done it to some extent or other. For example, direct investment in commercial real estate is a longtime favorite and can be found in many family office portfolios. What's new is the willingness of family offices to become active investors and repeat deal-makers, sometimes with high visibility in the marketplace, in order to take advantage of the often-greater returns in the burgeoning private capital marketplace.

Family offices that invest directly in private companies do so for a number of reasons, including the following:

- Comfort and familiarity with private investing by the principals, given their prior investing experience or because it is how they made their money
- An effort by the family (or the family office) to garner greater returns than in public markets
- A desire for greater control over investments, relative to investing through private equity funds, in terms of which investments to make and when and how to enter and exit
- A belief that they can invest at a lower cost by avoiding the standard 2 percent management and 20 percent carried interest fees charged by private equity firms

Approaches to Direct Investing

Direct investments by family offices typically follow one of these three approaches: by partnering with other family offices or a private equity firm, through coinvestments with other family offices or private equity firms, and/or by investing on their own. Table 6.1 gives a brief summary of each option and its perceived benefits.

Investment Resources and Capabilities

There are a number of constraints faced by family offices interested in direct investing, including scale, skills, management, and talent. A family office needs to have sufficient resources to afford the required staffing and related infrastructure needed to make direct investments (i.e., scale and skills). And it must have a governance framework that is robust enough to manage the downside risks and operational potholes of running acquired businesses (i.e., management and talent). Also required are family buy-in to the direct investing strategy and a structure of institutional processes to make investment decisions.

What follows is a list of important questions that each family should ask themselves before embarking on a robust direct investing program or deciding which of the abovementioned models makes the most sense for them (figure 6.2).

Table 6.1
Direct investing approaches

Method	Description	Potential benefits
Partnering with others	The family joins with other families or private equity firms in select investments.	It permits families to leverage the expertise, deal flow, talent, and/ or financial resources of another investment partner.
Coinvesting with others	The family coinvests directly in specific deals brought to them as part of a fund in which they are an investor. In these cases, the family's coinvestment usually is not charged a management or carried interest fee.	It enables a family to use its investment in a fund sponsored by another family or private equity firm (see the benefits of the "partnering with others" option) to increase its exposure to select deals only.
Investing directly on their own	The family sources, evaluates, invests, and manages a private company investment on their own (outside of investing in a private equity fund, in partnership with others, or as a coinvestment).	It provides a family with the greatest amount of control over all aspects of direct investing.

Alternatives to Investing in Private Equity Firms

While family offices are inundated with opportunities to invest, and selectively coinvest, with private equity firms, many families are biased against these types of financial sponsors. The reasons have to do with the perception by family offices (rightly or wrongly) that many of these funds are structured and priced for ultra-high-net-worth (UHNW) investors that otherwise cannot gain access to direct deal flow or focus on the needs of institutional investors that do not have many of the same investment objectives, cash-flow considerations, or tax

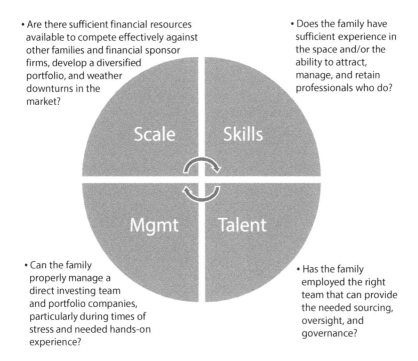

• Are there sufficient financial resources available to compete effectively against other families and financial sponsor firms, develop a diversified portfolio, and weather downturns in the market?

• Does the family have sufficient experience in the space and/or the ability to attract, manage, and retain professionals who do?

• Can the family properly manage a direct investing team and portfolio companies, particularly during times of stress and needed hands-on experience?

• Has the family employed the right team that can provide the needed sourcing, oversight, and governance?

Figure 6.2 Important questions that each family should ask before embarking on a robust direct investing program

considerations, with embedded conflicts of interest and shorter time horizons than most family offices would like.

Consequently, family offices that desire to invest in private markets and are comfortable (and able) to do so themselves, and would like to invite other families to invest with them for the reasons mentioned here, are developing partnership and coinvestment approaches themselves. These solutions provide the investment benefits listed in table 6.1, while at the same time avoiding or mitigating the challenges of more traditional private equity funds.

How Families Invest and Partner with Each Other

Family offices have been partnering and coinvesting with others as long as they have been private investors.[3] Over the years, these experiences have taught them how best to conduct this form of direct investing, in which they can enjoy the advantages while mitigating the challenges. While family offices also partner and coinvest with private equity managers, it tends to be rare and often limited to only the largest family offices.

There are a number of benefits to partnering and coinvesting with other significant pools of capital, including family offices and private equity funds. These include access to more deals; using the skills, insights, and deal flow of another family; and more available capital for doing larger deals.

However, as with any partnership, there can be inequalities with respect to the relative contribution by each partner. These issues tend to manifest themselves the most with family office investment partnerships in which the families expect to participate with equal economics despite significant differences in relative contribution. Of course, family offices can be great partners despite their significant differences and what they contribute. This tends to be true when each partner understands what is expected of them and economics are tied to what each has or can provide.

The most effective partnerships between wealthy families occur when both sides have a willingness to partner and a capacity to contribute (see figure 6.3).[4] Instances where this is not the case include the following:

- When families want the opportunity to partner but do not have other important attributes to contribute (e.g., deal flow, expertise) and do not want to pay management fees or carry to the other partner
- Families that have experience, capital, access to deal flow, and other important elements but are not particularly looking for partners other than for a unilateral benefit, such as to enhance returns or to reduce portfolio risk

As a result of these experiences, family offices have started to evolve their approach to partnering with others such that the relative relationship and contributions are more explicitly balanced economically. In many respects, this is a natural professionalization of the family office partnership model. These evolutions include allowing families to participate on a deal-by-deal basis (so-called club deals) coupled with a minimum amount of capital contributed via a committed fund structure.

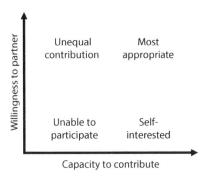

Figure 6.3 A matrix illustrating the elements of effective partnership in direct investing *Source*: H. E. "Bud" Scruggs, the Cynosure Group, 2020.

In club deals, families are part of a preexisting and defined group that agrees to review and contribute capital to select investment opportunities made available to them by the sponsor family or private equity firm.

Committed Club Structures

A number of sponsoring family offices are modifying their partnership and coinvestment structures to reduce the limitations of pure partnership or coinvestment models, while retaining many of the advantages.[5] These are increasingly being called "committed club structures." Under these structures, many of the attractive attributes of traditional private equity funds and club deals are combined. Specifically, a sponsoring family office (usually one with a successful track record in private investing) establishes a "fund" and obtains capital commitments from both institutional and family offices. However, the fund is structured in a manner that provides investors with many of the attributes that come with partnering and coinvesting, such as the following:

- A level of committed capital such that the sponsoring family office has enough "dry powder" to do deals and compete against both financial sponsor firms and strategic buyers
- Much longer fund terms, which allow investors to indirectly own portfolio investments via the fund for a longer period of time than with traditional private equity funds

- The right for investors to coinvest in deals done by the fund based on their own additional underwriting (usually with no additional management fee or carry)
- Reduced administrative and oversight fees because fund investments are made as part of a pooled vehicle
- Flexibility around the timing and taxation of exits because certain investors own a portion of the underlying portfolio companies directly
- The ability to attract sellers that are interested in family office investors

Committed club structures formally combine the characteristics of private investing among family offices (i.e., a comingled single fund structure, with clublike coinvestment opportunities, predominantly for family office investors). In addition, the term of the fund is much longer than typical private equity funds thereby tapping into the desire by family offices to be more permanent investors (so-called patient capital).

Regulatory Issues Specific to Direct Investing

While coinvestments with other family offices or private equity funds may make financial and business sense, family offices and private equity funds that partake in those activities should be mindful of the risks associated with pooling capital with others.[6] The first set of issues to consider are the regulatory issues related to wheeling and dealing in the private capital space. Any person or entity that is in the business of raising capital generally needs to be registered as a "broker-dealer" with the SEC or applicable state agency or else be exempted from those registration requirements. While private equity funds can raise capital for their own funds by relying upon Rule 506(b) of Regulation D of the Securities Act of 1933, that exemption doesn't necessarily allow them to help raise money for other companies. To the extent that a private equity fund manager regularly solicits others to coinvest along with their fund, they may be required to register as broker-dealers. The same is true for a family office that regularly solicits other family offices to make coinvestments.

The rules that require registration as a broker-dealer are broad and encompass anything that is "engaged in the business of effecting transactions in securities." Unfortunately, there is not a lot of clear-cut guidance on what it means to be engaged in the business of effecting transactions in securities. Registration issues for private equity funds, however, have continued to surface over the last decade as a result of the SEC's enforcement against private equity firms.

In addition to the broker-dealer registration issues, family offices need to be concerned about maintaining their family office exemption if they want to remain exempt from the SEC's Investment Adviser registration requirements. If a family office engages in a transaction where they pool money with other families and further take the lead on managing that money, they might lose their exemption as a family office because they are now managing other people's money. While family offices may like to control their underlying coinvestments, they need to assess whether that control would destroy their family office exemption.

In addition to the regulatory issues, family offices need to be concerned about the antifraud provisions of federal securities laws. All securities transactions, even exempt private ones between families and private equity funds, are subject to the antifraud provisions. Any false or misleading statement in connection with the sale of a security is subject to civil and criminal liability. That liability is typically assessed on the one promoting or selling the security if the deal should go south. If a family office promoted a proposition and solicited other family offices to join it by making false or misleading statements, they could be the one held liable. In general, people go after the entity that sold them the security or lured them into the deal.

For these reasons, family offices engaged in direct investing, particularly when it involves partnerships or coinvestments with other wealthy families, should consult with appropriate legal counsel with experience in securities laws and registration rules and regulations for broker-dealers and registered investment advisers.

Investing in Venture Capital

The fundamental model of venture capital is based on investors financially backing, supporting, and adding unique value to businesses in the early and late stages of growth.[7] Financial backing is provided with capital by investors so that the business that is receiving funding can accelerate to deliver on expected milestones, revenue multiples, and increases in valuation.

Supporting businesses and adding value are achieved in a number of ways, including the following:

- Introduction to additional capital
- Strategic relationships
- Subject matter expertise in a certain industry
- Hands-on support in technology development
- Candid feedback
- Dedicated mentoring and education

Venture capital has evolved to provide support during various stages in the funding life cycle and food chain. Some general examples of the venture capital stages are early stage, growth stage, and late stage.

EARLY STAGE   Early-stage opportunities are usually broken into two categories, called preseed and seed. Preseed investments typically offer an opportunity for a team that has developed a very initial concept or low-fidelity tech solution. Preseed companies can usually use "friends and family" funding or an incubator to help validate an idea by using lean start-up approaches and customer insights to achieve a viable technology solution. An "incubator" is an organization that will mentor very early-stage ideas and concepts and help them grow into more defined businesses. Some incubators are also available at college tech transfer offices, where groundbreaking technologies are developed in labs. These initial concepts still need to be commercialized with the support of the incubator.

Seed-stage investments are normally consistent with teams that have developed a more advanced prototype and solution, ideally with revenue or validated customers in the pipeline. Accelerators help seed-stage start-ups get traction as fast as possible. There is normally a selection process of premier start-ups that are part of a cohort of start-ups during a fixed time, which provide resources, capital, and introductions to investors to prepare for the next round of funding. The earlier the investment stage, the higher the potential to achieve a large multiple in returns. Along with the return potential opportunities of the early stage comes the risk of the company failing. In addition, early investors' shares could be diluted by other investors in future rounds.

Early-stage investors are able to mitigate the impact of dilution by exercising pro rata rights, which provide the right to reinvest during the next round for a certain amount that will allow the investor to maintain the same percentage of ownership. When due diligence is performed for investments in companies at this stage, little financial or market data is publicly available to support these decisions. This is a significant difference when comparing investment research to public markets that are readily available in research terminals, news, and filings. It is also difficult to determine the level of parity between projections and future realities in the early stage. As a result, investors are making a large bet on the abilities of the founding team, their conviction on how big the market will be, how big the exit will be, and how the liquidity event will come to fruition, whether it is through a strategic acquisition, a mergers and acquisitions (M&A) deal, or an initial public offering (IPO).

GROWTH STAGE The growth stage, also known to be allocated to companies as "growth capital," is considered to be the more mature stage of a company, in which capital can be deployed to accelerate the company further to advance technology, expand to new sectors and regions, and increase revenue quickly. Often, two contending factors when a company matures are growth versus profitability. Founders of companies need to decide whether it is more important to be profitable now or grow quickly at the cost of getting further from being profitable. There are pros and cons to both. The benefit of growing quickly without being profitable is taking over market share, which could give the company an advantage over competitors and allow it to be more profitable later.

LATE STAGE A late-stage venture usually has the lowest multiple in returns, but it also offers more favorable terms for downside protection, the lowest risk, and the least amount of time to an exit. Senior debt issued in the late stage has a higher priority to be paid first during a liquidity event, should one occur. Most important, this capital generally has a larger magnitude, which often justifies the lower multiple.

Ways to Invest in Venture Capital

VENTURE CAPITAL FUNDS When it comes to allocating to venture capital, family offices have a few options. One method is to follow the selection process used by institutional investors, where they research potential managers and funds for investment. Through this similar approach, family offices can assess the quality of the manager and understand their investment thesis, investment strategy, unique edge, and track record. This initial approach also assists in generating an early assessment in preparation for the more robust phase of diligence.

Venture capital fund structures include a number of innovations, including dedicated angel networks, which write larger checks; seed investors, which focus on being "lead only"; and family office networks, which make special syndicated deals available. The traditional seven- to ten-year venture capital fund, with a 2 percent management fee and 20 percent carried interest, has also evolved into new structures, including those that simply issue venture debt or use special-purpose vehicles (SPVs) to invest directly in deals with more favorable terms regarding carry and management fees. In addition, a rolling fund structure has offered innovations in asset allocation, where new emerging funds can acquire capital that renews every quarter from a network of investors.

INVESTING DIRECTLY INTO A COMPANY'S CAPITALIZATION TABLE Another method of getting access to venture deals is to invest directly in a company through its capitalization table (cap table). Many family offices build their own venture investment teams, which are tasked with getting access to, and investing in, the best deals. This approach gives the family more control over their portfolio, including being able to choose the companies included in it and how it is constructed. Venture capital managed internally as an asset class is attractive to family offices because their capital can be handled with a patient approach and is not constrained as to the terms, deals, and time horizon of venture funds.

Another benefit with direct investing in venture companies is the ability to avoid paying carry and management fees. However, there are times where the fees and carry charges levied by venture funds are justified, given their access to highly exclusive deals that are limited to a small pool of select investors. In these instances, syndicated investments among a network of qualified investors and family offices are valuable. A significant benefit of participating in syndicated deals is the opportunity for a wealthy family or the family office to build a community among like-minded and connected investors that have greater access to exclusive deal flow.

Best Practices for Family Offices That Invest in Venture Capital

ATTEND THE RIGHT INDUSTRY EVENTS AND NETWORKS
Close-knit events, as well as the networks they can span, provide family offices with a way to develop a community and foster collaboration, although it is important to curate groups continuously. It is prudent to understand the reputation of the event organizer and the quality of both the attendees and the deal flow before spending time on attending. Many of the larger events consist of service providers that are primarily using the platform to sell services and products. Regardless, family offices should constantly build their community and have frequent touchpoints with respect to potential deals on which they can collaborate.

CONDUCT DUE DILIGENCE SPECIFIC TO THE ASSET CLASS
When performing due diligence, it is important for family offices to develop a thorough checklist of items to consider for various types of asset classes. The type of due diligence required for a real estate deal might be very different than that needed for a venture deal. It is also a great idea to share deals with peers and get additional data points from other family offices. This will help the family office synthesize data and make better-informed investment decisions. Reference checks from various levels of customers, investors, partners, vendors, and channel partners are also important.

DEVELOP IMPORTANT RELATIONSHIPS The venture capital business relies heavily on investing in friendships and relationships before business is done. This is invaluable because of information asymmetry in the industry, in which a small group of investors can have unique and exclusive knowledge that gives them access to better deal flow.

A frequent mistake occurs when an investor heavily focuses on transactions rather than on building meaningful connections. When this happens, the potential for valuable long-term relationships and partnership diminishes. However, when this is done effectively and genuinely, a wealth of opportunities come to fruition in the form of lifelong bonds, trust, and world-class deal flow.

For example, one best practice is to attract the interest of both parties before sharing deal flow or introductions. When introductions are not done appropriately, confidence among important potential partners might be lost because the introduction might be viewed as an imposition or a waste of time.

FOCUS ON EMOTIONAL INTELLIGENCE A skill that is constantly being exercised is emotional intelligence. Venture investing involves a close-knit community with varying levels of experience, reputation, and skills across its many participants. It is, therefore, important for industry professionals to be aware of their own strengths, weaknesses, and development. Doing so will help tailor their collaboration style to work best with strategic partners, as well as build empathy for others that might be less experienced in the space.

ENGAGE THE NEXT GENERATION Often, the next generation of a wealthy family struggles with maintaining the family legacy, while embracing change and modern investment opportunities. Venture capital provides the next generation, and by extension the family, with access to new technologies and founders who will innovate. Millennials and Gen-Zs, who often have access to new and emerging technologies, will eventually mature into the older generation, which will accumulate wealth that amounts to much more than what the currently wealthy generation possesses.

PARTNER TO FIND GREAT EMERGING MANAGERS Another form of manager selection, which is seen more frequently in Silicon Valley than in other sectors, is where successful tech entrepreneurs have formed family offices that invest in new fund managers who have a certain belief, theme, or tech focus. Employing the family's network, including the interest and access provided by the next generation, to invest in these tech entrepreneurs can prove to be very advantageous. Furthermore, there are wealthy individuals who altruistically want to support and mentor new managers, which can also result in early-seed funding of these emerging managers via a "fund of funds" model or a traditional limited-partnership structure.

Investing for Impact

What Is Impact Investing?

Family offices around the world have been increasingly moving toward impact investing as a way to steward their wealth and deploy capital aligned with their values.[8] "Impact investing" involves investments that are intended to have an impact as well as gaining a financial return, with the definition of what counts as "impact" based on the perspective of the investor. Impact investments range across a spectrum of social and environmental outcomes and financial targets and take on traditional investment forms and vehicles. In line with a philosophy of "doing well by doing good," impact investors intend to create a benefit to society by making investment decisions that take into consideration factors beyond financial gain. Through impact investing, family offices have the ability to manage their wealth in a way that aligns with their values and beliefs and leads to long-term growth.

The evolution toward ethical and responsible investing and the eventual formalization of the practice of impact investing have led to the growth of an industry. There are many examples throughout history of families, religious institutions, and governments investing capital to promote social good. Around 2007, the term "impact investing" was coined to capture the surge of investors, philanthropists, government institutions, and entrepreneurs intentionally shifting their perspective on why and how they deploy capital, and the rise of impact products and strategies that followed.

As an industry, impact investing and the opportunities that exist within it are growing. This growth is driven both by an increasing number of family offices incorporating impact investing into asset management and the larger portion of capital committed for those already engaged. With a substantial amount of intergenerational wealth transfer expected to occur over the next few decades, there is great potential for significant changes in the dynamics of wealth ownership, decision-making, and investment power. Women and Millennials are expected to reap much of the benefits of this wealth transfer. As a group, these investors are generally more inclined to invest their capital in financial opportunities that align with their values (as opposed to focusing strictly on returns).

Why Is Impact Investing Relevant for Family Offices?

There are numerous motivations behind family offices opting for what is known as "double bottom line" or "triple bottom line" investments, seeking to unlock the impact of their capital and find value over and above the financial dollar. One factor is that impact investing allows family offices to create a legacy derived from their investments in addition to their philanthropic or business efforts. When done with intention, capital investments across the portfolio spectrum have the potential to influence the environment, change social policy, and affect global change. Family offices seeking to promote a positive legacy focused on a particular societal issue or core value can use impact investing as a means to do so.

The process of developing an impact investing strategy and executing it is empowering in itself. It provides the opportunity to build cohesion and engage family members in the leadership and management of the family office. Given the autonomy and flexibility that family offices possess, they are in a unique position to reflect on the purpose of their capital and either seek out or build investments that they find meaningful. Many investors find that the practice of reflecting on their relationships to money is empowering and inspires family members to become more active in taking control of their wealth. Focusing and catalyzing capital toward a societal or global issue provide the family with a shared sense of purpose and renewed identity.

What Does Impact Investing for Family Offices Look Like?

There is no standard picture of what impact investing looks like. This provides a unique opportunity for family offices to design and craft customized impact portfolios that cater to their own individual needs and interests. That being said, there are several frameworks and organizations that provide guidelines and models for incorporating impact across asset classes.

The Global Impact Investing Network (GIIN), for example, is a nonprofit organization that focuses on reducing barriers to impact investment so that more investors can allocate capital to fund solutions to the world's most intractable challenges. The United Nations Sustainable Development Goals provide a blueprint of seventeen goals to help promote global peace and prosperity. These frameworks provide investors with impactful themes, such as empowering women, fighting climate change, and reducing poverty, to consider when making their investment decisions. It is a best practice for family offices to consider the range of models for impact that currently exist and adapt the elements that fit with what they are trying to do.

Some family offices have chosen to move all their investable assets to impact investing, while others carve out a specific subset of their portfolio for the purpose. Whether a family decides to take a total portfolio approach or is experimenting with only a small portion of their wealth, distinct techniques and tools can be applied to manage for impact in each asset class.

Within public markets, positive and negative screens can be applied to rule out bad actors while investing in companies that align with the family's impact goals. These strategies are often referred to as "ESG investing" or "responsible investing." For private equity and debt investments, a number of organizations have emerged to provide resources for validating and certifying impact funds. Within real estate, some impact investors focus on particular geographies and developments, including "opportunity zones," which are areas designed to spur economic development and job creation in distressed communities while providing tax benefits to investors. Others have looked at investing in affordable housing opportunities that lead to positive impacts and financial returns.

Family offices that consider impact investing from the philanthropic angle may deploy mission-related investments (MRIs) and program-related investments (PRIs) from their charitable foundations or endowments. Both MRIs and PRIs can take the form of equity, debt, or a guarantee, differing only in their expectations of return. MRIs are evaluated to be at market rate, while PRIs have below-market expectations and are treated like grants. From zero and low-interest loans to equity investments in high-risk venture deals, charitable foundations can catalyze their capital, thereby creating incentives for businesses and other enterprises besides the traditional nonprofits to meet certain impact goals and missions.

How Can a Family Office Start Integrating Impact Investing Practices into Its Portfolio?

It is one thing to talk about impact, and quite another to start moving capital toward it. For many families, the uncharted territory can be intimidating, although those who have embarked on the process tend to find it extremely rewarding. It is important to engage with trusted professionals and advisers who can provide objective support for and guidance on developing the appropriate strategy for incorporating impact into asset management.

Some of the first steps in building an impact portfolio begin with taking the time to articulate family values and understand the family's shared vision about what impact means. It is often helpful to create or update an investment policy statement, which includes impact themes and goals. Once all this has been done, the family office can begin to consider and select impact metrics that they find relevant, in addition to frameworks and systems for measuring and evaluating impact performance. Joining networks, researching, and attending industry events can help families better understand the current resources and opportunities that exist. Through practice and discussion, family offices can uncover the ways in which impact has and will be a driving force behind their wealth management strategy.

Challenges in Implementing an Impact Investing Framework

Many family offices face a number of common challenges and barriers when implementing an impact-investing strategy. One issue that often arises is difficulty getting family buy-in and encouraging family members to become engaged in the impact-investing process. Furthermore, not all financial advisers and asset managers have the necessary knowledge or awareness of the impact-investing products available on the market. Myths and other misconceptions (e.g., that socially responsible investing will always cause a trade-off in financial terms) prevent many from engaging in the viable opportunities that can come from impact investing.

Disagreement on how impact can be properly attributed and measured also often arises as a source of conflict. As a result, third-party organizations have arisen to help provide guidelines and certifications for how to select metrics and measure for impact. Working with advisers that can help craft a methodology for impact investing that aligns with the goals of the family office can help resolve many of these issues.

Despite these challenges, incorporating an impact investing strategy can both reap financial reward and empower the family office with a deep sense of purpose. With an impact-investing strategy, family assets can be deployed with meaning, creating long lasting value and a distinctive legacy.

Investing in Art and Collectibles

With substantially wealthy individuals, what begins as a passion and a personal connection to artworks and collectibles often turns into an important investment.[9] As such, it needs to be monitored and continuously evaluated along with other significant asset classes, such as real estate holdings. When doing so, family office executives should focus on the following key elements:

- Determining family goals (i.e., whether to hold art for aesthetic or investment value—or both)
- Starting strategic and tax planning early once a decision is made to invest in art as a collector or investor
- Managing art holdings as an investment

Any item in this genre can be classified as fine art, a collectible, or an antique. Here are some general guidelines for these categories:

- **Fine art:** Flat or three-dimensional visual art, comprising paintings, prints, posters, photographs, drawings, other artworks on paper, and sculpture. The category may also include conceptual art, to the extent that there is a tangible component. Some increasingly use the term "fine art" to include three-dimensional, tangible personal property such as twentieth-century furniture and other objects, but these are normally considered "decorative art." The word "fine" does not denote a greater value than "decorative"; these are just terms that differentiate between the two areas of collecting.
- **Collectibles:** This includes decorative art such as Hollywood and sports memorabilia, stamps, coins, books, pens, classic cars, wine, whiskey, couture and accessories, minerals, fossils, and other categories. A collectible does not necessarily have to be valuable or antique.
- **Antiques:** This classification includes decorative art such as furniture, objects, and other mostly three-dimensional items that were created at least 100 years ago, although exact dating is flexible.

The Art Market

Global sales of artworks and antiques reached an estimated $64.1 billion in 2019. Less liquid than the traditional equities market, the art market has nonetheless solidified as a distinct asset class, with major auctions traditionally occurring in the spring and winter of each year, therefore determining changes in levels of pricing every six months. The market is divided between dealer/private transactions and auction transactions, with over 50 percent of sales occurring in the dealer/private platform, and the remainder at auction. Transactions in contemporary and modern fine art currently drive the art market in overall turnover, and because auction results are publicly recorded, it is those prices that are used most often to gauge the vibrancy of various sectors of the market, with art fair results adding to the data points.

With auctions, online sales, as opposed to live auctions, are becoming increasingly prevalent and accepted in the art market, with an unprecedented $70+ million online bids being recorded in July 2020, exponentially above the approximately $1.3 million online sale record that was recorded earlier that spring. Given that the art market remains the least regulated of the major asset classes in transactional matters and appraisers of tangible personal property are not required to be licensed in the United States, the art market is an opaque economy, and whether buying or selling, extra due diligence must be undertaken in this area.

Art has a tendency to transcend generations. According to a survey of art collectors, over three-quarters indicated plans to leave their collections to heirs rather than sell them. Notwithstanding this intention, a little more than half had educated their heirs on how to manage their collections, including having appraisals performed.

Given the market opaqueness, lack of regulation, and complexity, family office executives with financial responsibilities should become knowledgeable about art investment concepts and take part in the process of making decisions about family office art transactions.

Family office executives need to focus on the following key elements when art is included in the investment portfolio:

- Determining family goals (i.e., holding art for aesthetic reasons as opposed to investment value)
- Starting strategic and tax planning early once a decision is made to invest in art as a collection or investment
- Managing art as an investment

Artworks and Collectibles as an Investment

As in managing other asset classes, family office executives should consider undertaking specific actions in the following areas: art valuation, risk management, legal and art stewardship, art lending, and strategies for wealth preservation and estate planning. (Tax considerations are as important in art as in other asset classes, but they are beyond the scope of this book and will not be included in this discussion.)

Art Valuation

Family offices should use the expertise of internal and external teams to assess economic conditions, financial and art market dynamics, and other variables that may influence the price, activity, availability of supply, and future attractiveness of opportunities for investment. These opportunities are generated by the underlying dynamic of the art market, which is inefficient and illiquid, lacks price transparency, and has highly differentiated products. Similar to private equity, a family office not only must engage in the right transaction at the right time and at the right price, but also must enhance the value of each artwork through a variety of curatorial and marketing practices commonly practiced by successful collectors.

Because the art market is ever-changing and unexpected life events such as death or divorce can occur, it is best to be prepared and thereby avert any additional stress being placed on the family.

Such trigger events cause valuation to be examined for the following reasons:

- Income tax purposes if the art is transferred during life to a charitable beneficiary
- Gift tax purposes if the art is transferred during life to a noncharitable beneficiary
- Estate tax purposes if the art is owned at death
- Insurance purposes if the art is maintained during life

Risk Management

Families may not be ready to make decisions on art due to other business or personal priorities. At a minimum, a general disposition in the will provides flexibility and direction from the collector as to where and with whom the collection would reside. It is highly recommended that a succession plan be developed, which involves establishing legal structures to own and retain the art.

Taking an annual physical inventory of art and keeping insurance records current are best practices that are highly recommended. Fair market valuations are required for tax purposes, whereas replacement value (or retail value) is required for insurance purposes. Therefore, independent art appraisers should be involved with the valuation process. An appraisal should be performed and certified by a qualified appraiser. It is important to note that an appraisal for purposes such as transfer to a limited liability company (LLC), estate tax filings, or making charitable donations must be performed and certified by a qualified appraiser, which is defined as a vetted member, in good standing, of one of the three major appraisal organizations; being compliant with up-to-date Uniform Standards of Professional Appraisal Practice (USPAP) standards and methodology, a set of congressionally sanctioned standards for professional appraisal practice; and has not been disqualified by the Internal Revenue Service (IRS) from preparing appraisals for federal tax purposes. The Appraisers Association of America (AAA) is a nonprofit association exclusively of personal-property appraisers and is a reliable source for selecting appraisers with appropriate expertise in specific categories of art, antiques, and collectibles and can confirm the credentials of an appraiser. Members of the AAA must adhere to a strict code of ethics and be current with USPAP, which includes standards for competency, ethics, objectivity, report writing, and record keeping. Members are also required to keep up to date with connoisseurship, art market trends, and legal issues pertaining to the field.

Family office finance and administrative staff should keep thorough records of recipients, invoices, and other details in their inventory records, such as

- Name of artist
- Description of artwork
- Location
- Cost basis
- Insurance value
- Fair market value
- Name of purchaser
- Name of seller

This type of documentation also supports provenance, which is important to confirm the authenticity of artworks. Provenance is proved by documentation on ownership beginning with the creator to current seller; it includes the involvement of art experts to protect against fraud.

Legal and Art Stewardship

Owning art well is important both for practical reasons and to prevent emotional distress within the family upon the collector's death. Establishing a succession plan requires advisers to determine appropriate legal structures to own the art and devise a mechanism for funding taxes upon death.

Use of an art LLC is a common legal strategy that allows the collector to simply transfer ownership of a collection to the LLC. The LLC owns the art, and the collector owns the LLC. Family members may receive an interest in the LLC to alleviate any concerns about the exact designation of pieces of art to the various family members. Benefits include the ability to do the following:

- Legally safeguard the asset and collector, especially in transporting pieces globally
- Move value in a collection through shares in an LLC
- Maintain ownership privacy

Trust structures may be established for significant gifts of art or LLC interests. There can be trade-offs for the financial and tax benefits received because owning art in a trust differs from owning art outright. Art held in trust may be required to be stored away and not be available to be enjoyed personally by the collector or trust beneficiaries, or even be loaned to museums. Obtaining competent tax and legal advice in this area is important.

Art Lending

Loans on secured art may provide flexibility and liquidity to satisfy unexpected cash needs, make other investments, avoid significant transaction costs and taxes associated with the sale of art, or pay gift or estate taxes.

Using art as collateral for borrowing rather than selling it outright allows the collector to retain ownership of the art for enjoyment purposes, as well as retaining the potential future appreciation of value.

Borrowing also helps avoid a potential public sale, thus preserving confidentiality.

Strategies for Wealth Preservation/Estate Planning

Strategies for managing and protecting the value of an art investment portfolio may include engaging in art financial transactions or seeking tax benefits. From a charitable perspective, this can be accomplished by donating the art to a charitable beneficiary or creating a private museum. Family offices should consider transparency with family members when developing these strategies with their advisers.

Family offices should consider art as more than a personal interest; rather, they should treat it as an investment. Candid conversations about whether family members share the same passion for any art pieces acquired by the collector are beneficial for effective planning and cohesion. Prioritizing this discussion will help families make the right strategic planning decisions to protect or maximize valuation and minimize the tax consequences.

ASSESSMENT AND ISSUES SURFACED

What Did We Learn?

The family office is starting to take form in terms of overseeing their finances and managing personal assets. These were priorities, given that they were all things that had to be done, and indeed had been done or overseen, by John, Sofia, and/or Janina. Hiring for these duties initially was easier for them to do, therefore, because they had some familiarity with what was required and the solutions, in terms of who to hire and what they needed to do, were similar to John's business.

Investments, however, was a different animal. While John certainly was familiar with investing, his experience was limited by the amounts, the opportunities, and, candidly, the time that he spent on it. He also suspected that his current providers might not be the right ones for him going forward. John hired Michael, in part, because of his background in financial services and his experience with how wealthier clients managed their portfolios. Working with Michael, John now had an investment strategy in place.

Case Questions

- What are the pros and cons of the investment strategy developed by John and Michael relative to other potential approaches?
- Working with outside investment advisers can present a number of challenges. What are these and how can Michael help mitigate them?
- How can Michael help the family promote their interests in various social and environmental causes?
- Are there specific things the family office can do to help John and Sofia with their expanding portfolio of art and collectibles?
- What challenges does John face with respect to his direct investing activities?

RECOMMENDED SOLUTIONS

Responses to Case Questions

What are the pros and cons of the investment strategy developed by John and Michael relative to other potential approaches?

While wealthy families can oversee their investments in numerous ways, one of the primary drivers of this decision is the level of control they want to exercise over strategy, execution, or both. Strategy, in the context of investments, is the development of an asset allocation and the ranges within which they would like to permit their portfolio to be exposed to various asset classes. Execution of that investment strategy involves how the family should gain access to the various asset class exposures, with whom, and/or with which strategies to engage. The manner in which families do so ranges from active-controlling to delegatory, as discussed in this chapter.

In John's case, he has made a conscious decision to take a hybrid approach by hiring Michael, who also has a background in investments, as his CEO. He also could have hired a formal chief investment officer. This approach has the benefits of allowing him to develop and control the strategy, with or without the help of outside advisers, but to rely on others for implementing this strategy. As previously discussed, this is a hybrid approach between doing it all himself through the family office and outsourcing it completely.

Bringing the vast majority of investment strategy and execution plans into the family office provides greater control and flexibility, but it also would require finding, hiring, and managing a large investment team. This is something that neither John nor Michael has expressed any interest in. As an alternative, John could have outsourced both the strategy and execution to a third party such as an investment consulting firm. This requires less involvement by the family office, but it also distances John and Michael from those aspects of investing in which they are interested: strategy and portfolio design.

> *Working with outside investment advisers can present*
> *a number of challenges. What are these and how can*
> *Michael help mitigate them?*

This is a common challenge faced by families who use third parties to develop an executive investment strategy. While having multiple investment execution partners provides the family with access to a broader array of investment ideas and execution strengths, this arrangement must be managed to avoid a number of understandable and predictable issues. These include (1) having "too many cooks in the kitchen," as each adviser provides advice and opinions about how best to allocate and invest; and (2) creating a "horse race" of sorts among the advisers as they jockey past each other for position in the hopes of gaining a greater share of John's investment business for themselves (thereby creating an incentive for them to take more risks with the portfolio).

Michael can help mitigate these issues by adopting formal governance procedures for overseeing the investment portfolio, including establishing an investment committee and developing an investment policy statement. An investment committee provides a formal process by which asset allocation and strategy execution recommendations can be received, assessed, and decided upon. The investment policy statement would also clearly delineate the roles and responsibilities of the various managers and establish the mechanisms by which they are evaluated. It also allows John and Michael to receive advice from industry professionals and trusted colleagues that are not connected with the recommendations.

*How can Michael help the family promote their interests
in various social and environmental causes?*

Developing an impact investing program requires a significant commitment of time to develop the family's strategy, identify causes, select partners, choose investment vehicles, and establish ways to measure success. As a result, Michael can help John and Sofia by first engaging with other family offices and established impact investing programs to help him better understand the space. This will allow Michael to learn best practices that can help the family build their own impact-investing vision. He should also consider hiring a consultant that can help the family develop their areas of interest and consider how their investment activities can promote or support these areas.

*Are there specific things the family office can do to help
John and Sofia with their expanding portfolio
of art and collectibles?*

Specialized fields like art and collectibles require the involvement of experts in numerous areas, including procurement, valuation, acquisition, ownership, storage, and insurance. It is therefore important for the family office to locate and hire these specialists and to involve them early in the process. This not only helps John and Sofia appropriately find, acquire, own, and protect their collections, it educates and engages them with their various passions. As with many other responsibilities, professionals within the family office can locate appropriate specialists by networking with their peers and asking their advisers who work with other wealthy families.

*What challenges does John face with respect
to his direct investing activities?*

John is already somewhat active in direct investing. However, his level of involvement has been modest, which presents a number of challenges. A significant potential pitfall is lack of a formal process for evaluating deals and a lack of network to help locate high-quality deals. Adverse selection around the quality deal flow is a common problem for family offices, especially those new to direct investing. John should consider developing an overall strategy for his direct investing, including (1) determining the relative percentage of his portfolio that he will commit to it, (2) identifying the industries that he would like to gain exposure to, (3) assessing what he is looking for in an investment partner, and (4) considering what he can offer in return. John should also discuss with Michael his various commitments to private equity funds to see if there are coinvestment opportunities available to him. This would be a way for him to use the investments that he is already making with selective financial sponsors to access incremental private investing opportunities, often in areas and industries in which he would not otherwise have access or expertise.

CHAPTER SEVEN

Risk Management

CASE STUDY

Summary

- Two years after the creation of the Left Seat Management family office
- Personal and digital security
- Healthcare-related issues
- Mitigating financial risks
- Obtaining legal advice

Key Words/Concepts

- Security
- Healthcare
- Insurance
- Legal

Challenge

Just after Memorial Day, the Thorne family's highly anticipated Russian visas arrived in the mail. They were excited to receive them, as this was one of the final items on their checklist for their upcoming summer vacation, a fifteen-day trip on the Trans-Siberian Railroad. John had dreamed of doing such a trip for a long time, as his mother grew up in Poland under communist rule and this sparked a strong interest in Cold War history in him. While he had visited many countries in Eastern Europe, he had never traveled to Russia. What better way to finally see Russia than on a luxury train trip with his family?

John's wife, Sofia, was also excited about this trip because of her work on the board of a boutique art gallery with locations in Minneapolis and New York that focused on art from central Asia and Russia. Sofia also enjoyed an entertaining and expensive hobby: buying art for her personal collection from local artists on their family vacations. Her personal art collection was impressive and had received public acclaim. For instance, she was recently featured in the style section of a widely distributed Chicago newspaper, and some rare pieces of her collection were recently loaned out to a prominent art museum in the Midwest. John collected memorabilia from World War I's American Expeditionary Force (in North Russia and Siberia), and he hoped that he could see some local artifacts related to the Polar Bear Expedition on this trip.

Their daughters were already bragging to their friends about the upcoming trip, with the exception of the youngest, Emilia. She wasn't excited about being off the grid, with only sporadic Internet access available to keep in touch with her friends. Sofia had assured her that according to the tour company, they would have sufficient reliable Internet access for texting and sometimes for video calls. Their oldest, Olivia, had picked up photography as a hobby during her frequent travels to participate in horse shows over the years, and she was excited to post new pictures to her many social media channels.

Summer was here. John was more than ready for a vacation. He was exhausted from having to deal with a recent staffing problem at his family office. Jason, the family office's chief financial officer (CFO), had hired an analyst named Katya to help lighten some of his workload, but it turned out that this employee had a checkered past with the family office she had previously worked at. John was approached by the principal of that family office and learned that she left under negative circumstances due to difficulties working with others in a small office. In light of this news, John decided to let the analyst go, and he spent the last two weeks with his lawyer and Jason to create a smooth transition of this new employee out of the family office.

There were also other issues with the family. Sofia's mother, Gabriella, who lived in Los Angeles, had been having health problems and couldn't seem to get the medical attention she needed through her current healthcare providers. This was starting to take a toll on Sofia, who reasoned that with their resources and connections, including at the Children's Hospital, they should be able to find someone who could provide Gabriella with better care.

The Thornes flew their Challenger 350 to Vladivostok, stopping in Anchorage for two days on the way over. After a day of touring around Vladivostok, the family began their fifteen-day journey to Moscow.

Reliable cell phone coverage turned out to be more challenging than originally described, and Internet coverage was poor unless the train was near one of the major cities and towns on the route. Irkutsk was one of those places, and the family arrived there early that morning. Given the town's reputation as the "Siberian Paris," Sofia had booked a custom tour of some local art galleries and studios before their arrival and was off on the hunt to add to her growing personal collection as the first thing she did that day.

Her tour guide brought Sofia and her daughter Isabella to a charming art gallery located just off of Karl Marx Street. Sofia found some pieces that she just had to have, including a relatively rare piece from an artist she was particularly fond of. The total bill came to around $150,000—too much for her to put on her credit card. Sofia put down a cash deposit and then e-mailed and texted the family office to set up the wire transaction so that they could have the art shipped back home the next day. She received a call from Janina, the family office administrative assistant, a few minutes later.

Janina congratulated her on the order and said that she must be having a great time—this was the second day in a row she was wiring the office money for art purchases. Sofia was puzzled by the comment because this was her first big purchase on the entire trip. Janina explained that she had received a similar e-mail from her yesterday, in which she asked for money to be transferred urgently to buy some art pieces, and Jason had wired $72,000 to a different art gallery in

Irkutsk. Sofia knew there was a problem and asked Jason to call her immediately. John and Sofia had just become victims of wire fraud, and some panic set in at the family office.

Jason indicated to John and Sofia that he had processed a wire transfer based on an e-mail request, similar to what Sofia had often done in the past. Jason knew that the family was traveling in Russia at the time and that Sofia regularly made these kinds of requests while on vacation, so he didn't view this as out of the ordinary. The Thorne family's commercial bank had an established callback verification procedure for any wire over $50,000. Because Jason had power of attorney on their accounts, he received the callback and verified the accuracy and legitimacy of the $72,000 request. Jason then processed the wire transfer and sent Sofia an e-mail confirming that the wire had been processed to "SA Capital Bank." However, Sofia didn't get the e-mail because of the poor Internet connection while in transit to Irkutsk overnight. Moreover, upon further investigation, the e-mail requesting the fraudulent wire came from a different e-mail address than Sofia's true e-mail. Sofia's real e-mail address was art.collector21@freeemailproviderz.com, while the fraudsters reached out to Jason using art.collecter21@freeemailproviderz.com.

John, Sofia, and the family office were at a loss of what to do about this situation. They contacted their commercial bank and let them know that the wire request was fraudulent, which started an internal investigation at the bank. However, they learned that nothing could be done at this point to stop the transfer because the money had likely moved between several locations. Jason contacted their local police, who indicated that there was little they could do beyond filing an official report of the crime, although they ultimately determined that the fraud was perpetrated by hackers located on a farm outside of Seattle. John reached out to his professional adviser network to see if he could find a resource to help with this situation.

John and Jason grew frustrated and felt increasingly helpless as they tried to find someone to help them with this major problem. The cybersecurity landscape was confusing and loaded with buzzwords and point solutions. John was finally referred to a security consultant who specialized in dealing with risk management for small and medium-sized enterprises (SMEs) and family offices. The family hired the consultant to examine this particular case and their overall risk exposure.

Just after this incident, Sofia contacted the family office attorney to determine what, if anything, could be done to recover the funds from this wire fraud. Given Sofia's legal background, and because the family office's legal requirements didn't warrant the expense to have full-time legal counsel, legal services remained outsourced to Natalia, a senior corporate lawyer at a global law firm.

The only major legal risk-planning the family office had done prior to the wire fraud was around family office employment agreements and nondisclosure agreements (NDAs) related to investments. The cybercrime incident and subsequent wire fraud opened John's and Sofia's eyes to looking at their legal exposure in a more strategic manner. When Sofia discussed the wire fraud, Natalia suggested a review of their current insurance policies as a way to mitigate future exposures. Up to that point, the family had done insurance planning on an ad hoc basis with an insurance agent with whom they had worked since Rybat Manufacturing was started.

Shortly after the incident, Michael received an irate call from John. John asked Michael to see what could be recovered for the wire fraud from the family office's insurance policies. Michael wasn't sure whether any of the policies covered a business e-mail compromise (BEC) wire fraud like what had occurred. John was upset to hear that news and asked Michael to do a complete review of all the office's insurance policies to see what else might not be covered.

BACKGROUND INFORMATION

Introduction to Risk Management

The risk and threat landscape for family offices continues to evolve and present new challenges. In particular, COVID-19 created new risk issues for families to consider and manage, but a pandemic is only one dimension of the increasingly complex threats that family offices face.

While some family offices were more prepared to deal with this health crisis, no family was completely immune from the shock to the global economic system and the operational problems that soon followed. Many family offices were forced to go all or partially virtual in short order, which led to numerous types of disruptions.

Figure 7.1 Dimensions of risk

Risks to wealthy families are nothing new. John D. Rockefeller and other magnates of his era used family offices to oversee their vast fortunes. However, the Rockefeller family office never had to deal with ransomware attacks or privacy breaches stemming from the social media accounts of his children.

The evolving landscape of how family office risk and threat management systems can be breached has made the task so much harder. Executives continue to struggle to find effective ways to deal with these multifaceted threats (physical, financial, health, cyber, and privacy-related).

Moreover, the understandable desire by family office professionals to be accommodating of, and responsive to, any and all requests by principals and family members, coupled with the broad access they have to sensitive information, opens this group up to specialized problems. Vendors and families alike have seen this disconnect manifest itself in (1) an underestimation and overlooking of threats, (2) frustration and perplexity concerning effective protective measures, and (3) a reactionary mindset of the family office, constantly putting out operational fires but not being proactive about preventing them.[1]

This chapter provides a guide and frameworks that family offices can consider as part of developing a comprehensive risk and threat management system across the dimensions of issues they face. Figure 7.1 illustrates the various dimensions of risk that family offices encounter.

Ensuring Safety

Due to the growing levels of publicity and the inability of families to truly ever get off the grid, high-net-worth families and their associated family offices are increasingly challenged by both physical and cyber-security issues.[2] Family offices are attractive targets not only because they manage significant financial assets, but also due to their interconnectivity with operating companies and the personal activities of the family. Meanwhile, increased geopolitical tension, rapid technological changes, and greater sophistication of malicious actors all enhance the likelihood and severity of potential family office impacts.

This chapter discusses how family offices can become more informed about these evolving risks and potential mitigation strategies, with a focus on physical and investigative security and cybersecurity. It begins with a high-level assessment of the family office risk profile integrated across physical, cyber, and converged threats, and then explores in greater detail the physical and cyber domains individually (figure 7.2).

Physical security and cybersecurity best practices ground security programs in the identification of high-value assets. In the family office context, risk assessment should start by identifying key business

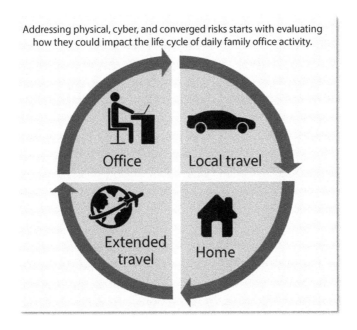

Figure 7.2 Types of risk. *Source*: Chad Sweet, "Family Office Risk Management Practices," The Chertoff Group, 2019.

TABLE 7.1
Threat types and consequences

Physical safety and security threats	Information security threats
• Property intrusion • Stalking • Retribution • Vandalism • Burglary/theft • Natural disasters (e.g., fire, earthquake, flooding) • Target kidnapping and/or ransom • Health emergencies	• Compromise of sensitive data • Stolen credentials allowing access to family office networks, as well as counterparty systems (e.g., financial service online applications) • Disclosure of personal and/or location-specific information on social media • Denial-of-service attack inhibiting family office operations • Ransomware locking all data and files

Converged threats

• Travel security–related threats
• Insider threats from a trusted employee or contractor
• Internet of Things (IoT) threats

Potential consequences

• Loss of life or safety
• Property damage
• Loss of confidentiality resulting in disclosure of sensitive information (investment data, tax returns, business or private e-mail content)
• Loss of data integrity, resulting in corruption of financial data or proprietary processing functions
• Loss of network availability, resulting in operational impacts
• Reputational damage
• Compliance and regulatory penalties

Source: Chad Sweet, "Family Office Risk Management Practices," The Chertoff Group, 2019.

processes and patterns of life, as well as how these factors periodically change, and then seeking to determine the consequences that could result from those risks. Risk itself is generally considered a function of threat, vulnerability, and consequence. For family offices, threats and consequences across the physical and cyber vectors might include the items listed in table 7.1.

Physical and Investigative Advisory Security

Vulnerabilities to the physical infrastructure of family offices can present significant risks. These risks are particularly acute where offices are collocated with family businesses, making families and their employees more vulnerable to physical threats, including natural disasters.

A critical aspect to securing family offices is borne out of the physical and investigative advisory security (P&IAS) practices. Businesses face these issues as they scale their size, footprint, and complexity. From screening potential new employees, to due diligence when making deals, to ensuring that cameras and locks are installed, P&IAS services are critical to ensuring the safety of their assets and employees. As a family's wealth grows, these services become more important, and it is the responsibility of the family office to understand how best to protect the family and their assets.

It is very rare that a family office will keep many P&IAS services in house because of the sheer cost and complexity of providing these services and technologies. Typically, family offices associated with a family business or the principal's operating company will borrow resources and then hire third parties to fill in the gaps. Hiring a full-time P&IAS security director is usually limited to families with a significant net worth, a high public profile, or issues related to their location or travel needs.

THREATS Figure 7.3 reflects a number of common threats to a family office from a physical and investigative standpoint.

SOLUTIONS The P&IAS firms provide a wide range of services, including the following:

- Comprehensive threat assessments
- Mergers and acquisitions (M&A) due diligence
- Principal protective details (local needs and international travel)
- Residential and commercial facility security
- Threat intelligence
- Kidnapping and terrorism threat management and training
- Intrusion detection (red team/blue team)
- Maritime security
- Workplace threat management and training
- Collectibles and high-value-item security and logistical support

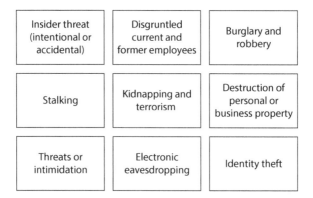

Figure 7.3 Types of threats. *Source*: Chad Sweet, "Family Office Risk Management Practices," The Chertoff Group, 2019.

- Personal security awareness training
- Investigations
- Psychological profiling
- Technical security countermeasures
- 24/7 watch centers

Physical Security

As previously discussed, family offices are attractive targets to malicious actors, and they face increasingly complex physical security risks. Significantly, family office physical infrastructure vulnerabilities can present significant risks that span across other security domains as well. For example, physical intrusions are a means that adversaries use to conduct cyberattacks, which can wreak havoc on a family's reputation and business operations and expose sensitive personal and business-related information.

Family offices should consider four physical risk domains as part of a comprehensive physical security plan: home, local travel, office, and extended travel. While complete risk elimination is not attainable, family offices can greatly reduce their risk across these domains by building a 360-degree physical security program that assesses risk gaps, actively monitors for threats, and responds to threats through carefully planned and coordinated activities (figure 7.4).

Figure 7.4 360-degree security program. *Source*: Chad Sweet, "Family Office Risk Management Practices," The Chertoff Group, 2019.

PHYSICAL THREAT ASSESSMENT Family offices should initially take a threat inventory consisting of exposures, business processes, life patterns of principals, and high-value assets. After threats have been recorded, family offices should outline the potential consequences of these threats.

Effective threat assessments employ open-source and proprietary information and intelligence sources to identify gaps and potential consequences. Typical information and intelligence sources that are gathered and then analyzed include the following:

- Social media outlets, news reports, and blogs
- Commercial database mining on principals, family members, and operating businesses
- Assessments and interviews of family office staff and other employees with access to sensitive information
- Vulnerability assessments of homes, offices, commuting routes, and life habits
- War-gaming exercises to identify worst-case threat scenarios, actors, and potential tactics

PHYSICAL SECURITY BEST PRACTICES The following are a number of best practices that family offices should consider when developing a physical monitoring program:

- Conduct an annual physical security risk assessment of residences, offices, and transportation practices.
- Develop and implement a visitor management system and protocols to ensure the safety of residences, offices, and operating companies.
- Develop mailroom and parcel screening guidelines to prevent the entry of hazards into a family office.
- Develop and train employees in a workplace violence prevention and response program.
- Use Crime Prevention Through Environment Design (CFTED) principles to build physical security into all elements of a family office.
- Research potential threats carefully prior to international travel.
- Develop a customized executive protection program that is consistent with the family office principals' risk tolerance and patterns of daily activities.
- Secure infrastructure at all residences and offices with intrusion detection systems, closed-circuit television (CCTV) coverage, security lighting, fencing, and other elements.
- Develop and implement a key and access credential policy.
- Develop a continuity-of-business plan to react to natural disasters.

MONITORING FOR PHYSICAL SECURITY Family office physical security programs should consistently reinforce effectiveness through continuous monitoring, training, and validation. Weaknesses in control implementation or unintentional modifications can undermine security programs when staff and principals ad lib instead of following an agreed-upon set of protocols. Principals, extended family members, and family office staff should be trained on threats and tested regularly to help create so-called muscle memory. Family offices should consider hiring consultants to simulate physical security events and instill confidence within them about how to act during real-life incidents. Successful family offices use this type of training to build a security culture with all employees that support a family. Basic precepts such as "If you see something, say something" can help principals and executives identify potential problems before they manifest themselves into a physical security incident.

RESPONSE Physical security is considered important by principals and family office staff; however, given the service and convenience orientation of family offices, security protocols are very often overlooked, especially if a family hasn't experienced a serious threat before. However, developing and adhering to a set of security response plans can help a family cope effectively with physical security issues when they arise. Family offices should also consider hosting an all-hands, "lessons learned" session after physical security events occur so that principals and executives can incorporate these experiences to help avoid future problems.

International travel is a common area where family offices are asked to support. Family offices can build templates to help plan and respond. Figure 7.5 presents an example of a travel preparation template that can be customized according to a family's needs.

Know destination risks associated with your destination	• Health, criminal, and cultural attitudes
Enroll in the State Department's Smart Traveler Enrollment Program	• Provides real-time safety and security updates from the local U.S. Embassy; helps the U.S. Embassy contact you in an emergency, whether natural disaster, civil unrest, or family emergency
Avoid social media activity of principals and family members	• If you do engage in social media activity, disable locations settings and post after travel is complete
Pack an emergency medical kit	• Cold remedies, first aid, prescription medicine
Print & maintain multiple color copies of your passport	• Electronic copies on cell phones are convenient but present other vulnerabilities
Avoid public transportation when possible	• Use established taxi companies and ride sharing firms and avoid drivers in unaffiliated or unmarked cars
Know the location and route to your country's nearest embassy, local hospitals, and police stations	• Print and maintain digital and physical copies for each family member
Avoid leaving laptops and other electronic devices unattended in hotel rooms	• These devices are attractive targets for thieves and other nefarious actors
Avoid large crowds, protests, and public gatherings	• These events run a high risk of violence
Vary routes, travel time, and parking location	• This makes it harder for bad actors to plan attacks

Figure 7.5 Travel preparation list *Source*: Chad Sweet, "Family Office Risk Management Practices," The Chertoff Group, 2019.

IN PRACTICE Employing physical security presents challenges to family offices because the industry tends to be fragmented and because of the use of confusing jargon. Many firms in this space specialize in point solutions (e.g., guards, drivers, CCTV experts, electronic countermeasure experts) for family offices. On the other side of the spectrum, family offices have access to comprehensive physical security consulting firms that help them with complete physical programs ranging from building strategic plans and conducting vulnerability tests to hiring the drivers in a foreign country.

To get started on physical security, family offices should consider hiring a comprehensive consulting firm to conduct an initial assessment and provide recommendations for building a plan. Because small to midsized family offices tend to outsource physical security resources, engaging a comprehensive security firm tends to be a good fit and can help manage and control overall spending in this area. Regardless of how robust they are, physical security programs and initiatives should be understood and embraced by all the stakeholders of a family.

Cybersecurity

Family offices are particularly attractive cybertargets not only because they manage significant financial assets, but also due to their interconnectivity with both the underlying family-owned business and the personal activities of the family (including extended family members). A successful intrusion into family office or business information technology (IT) systems could release sensitive information, damage the family's reputation, disrupt the family's business operations, undermine wealth preservation, and enable surveillance of a family member for follow-on threat objectives. Cyberthreats to family offices that may give rise to these damaging consequences, and therefore must be defended against, include the compromise of sensitive data, stolen credentials, disclosure of personal and/or location-specific information, denial of service attacks with the potential to inhibit operations, and ransomware locking of data and files.

Furthermore, high-net-worth families and family offices are facing increasingly complex security risks amid the rise of social media. For example, social media exploitation and social engineering enable hackers to gain unauthorized access to family networks and e-mail or other online entities such as online banking accounts. Information derived from social media is often even sufficient to permit a malicious actor to steal someone's identity, and perpetrators may use accidentally leaked or voluntarily provided personal information for extortion—indeed, the actual and threatened release of leaked information represents one of the fastest-growing segments of social media misuse. Finally, malicious actors often use "patterns of life" information obtained via social media to engage in theft, burglary, or other physical attacks—here, online hygiene awareness has significant implications on the physical security of high-net-worth families and their members. Evidently, growing publicity and social media sharing, as well as the combination of poor cyber hygiene and the ease with which adversaries exploit social media information, represent clear threats to families' personal safety, reputations, and financial and physical security and ought to be considered as part of a family office security program.

CYBERTHREAT ASSESSMENT   Importantly, threat assessments that leverage open-source and proprietary information and intelligence sources—included as part of a physical threat assessment, as mentioned previously—may also yield insightful information on threat actors interested in using IT-related vectors to infiltrate a family office. Specifically, an open-source intelligence (OSINT) scan may identify sensitive family office data on the web, including on social media platforms. OSINT can be complemented by deep web/dark web monitoring to identify potentially compromised credentials, personal identifiable information (PII), or other sensitive data regarding the family office and its members, including any other relevant postings on discussion sites or bulletin boards. It is common for family offices to underappreciate the intent of threat actors to target the high-net-worth individuals themselves as well as family office employees, independent advisers, and household staff; however, more robust threat discovery efforts as part of an overall cybersecurity strategy can raise awareness of threat activity and inform decision-making.

In addition, family offices should employ a pathways analysis that considers reasonably plausible scenarios for the pathway that an adversary could take to infiltrate a family office, including the following elements:

- **Reconnaissance:** Explores the sources (i.e., social media) that an attacker may use to collect information about the intended target within the family office
- **Initial entry:** Maps how an attacker would gain initial entry inside the target's network perimeter, such as through phishing,

a watering hole attack, credential subversion, or a hardware-based attack
- **Establishment of communications with an external attack controller:** Highlights the methods that an attacker would use to establish communications with an external attack controller
- **Lateral movement and privilege escalation:** Reveals how an attacker could traverse a network, escalate privileges, and identify critical information assets to ultimately compromise the confidentiality, integrity, or availability of key data systems

A threat pathways analysis ultimately highlights a family office's potential cyber vulnerabilities, providing the office with a fuller picture of the risks to its environment. Given the range of threats that any organization—including family offices—may face, eliminating risk is not feasible; however, focusing on high-value assets and reasonably foreseeable scenarios for how those assets could be compromised helps build defensible priorities.

As previously noted, physical intrusions are also a means that adversaries use to conduct cyberattacks, making the implementation of an effective physical security program a critical component of reducing cyber risks in a family office environment. However, there are also a number of cyber-specific mitigation measures that family offices and their members can reasonably take to improve their cyber posture. Next, we highlight a number of cybersecurity best practices for family offices, first offering governance-related recommendations, followed by technical recommendations that, if implemented, can reduce the risk of dire consequences such as the disclosure of sensitive information, corruption of financial data, loss of network availability, and reputational damage.

GOVERNANCE BEST PRACTICES **Governance and risk management:** Family offices should consider establishing a comprehensive security strategy and the associated road map for all aspects of family office staff security requirements. Where there is overlap and integration, this process may require close coordination with security leadership at larger family offices. A robust governance and risk management program would include periodic security assessments—including risk assessments and audits—and methods for tracking and remediating findings and progress. Furthermore, any device connected to the family office's network is a potential opportunity for hackers. Without a comprehensive understanding of these connections, it is difficult to define the risk surface or understand where to place key controls, raising the imperative for a robust and thorough asset management capability.

Security policies and procedures: A fundamental step for family offices is often to create a specific set of information security policies, standards, and procedures, which provides a minimum baseline to allow for compliance testing across the organization. Without clearly documented policies and procedures, family members and family office employees lack proper guidance and cannot be held accountable for their actions. Given the increasing risks associated with social media, security policies and procedures should also outline guidance for social media use, including for both during company time and when outside the office. Family office employees must be made aware of the risks associated with oversharing on social media and noncompliance with broader cyber hygiene measures both to the family members themselves and the office's sensitive information and reputation.

Training and awareness: Cyberattackers often rely on an organization's own employees to gain initial entry into an organization's network, such as through phishing, credential compromises, or watering hole attacks. Employees poorly trained in cyber hygiene can put the family office's sensitive data at heightened risk of compromise. Within family offices, implementation of a robust cyber awareness and training program is key. While firewalls, antivirus software, and secure e-mail programs reduce the technological vulnerabilities of a family office from cyberattacks, effective cybersecurity also requires mitigation of the human impact of cyber risk. Without all these, expensive tools and investments may be rendered useless.

Highly applicable to the nature of family offices, business, travel, and remote work create an additional set of cyber risks. In addition to reinforcing in-office cybersecurity guidance such as password security and spear phishing prevention, security awareness and training for family offices ought to include guidance for remote work, such as using a virtual private network (VPN) or a mobile hot spot in lieu of public Wi-Fi and ensuring that all devices are password protected and never left unattended. All guidance reinforced to employees and family members through training and awareness should be clearly documented in family office security policies and procedures.

Incident response: Because total risk elimination is impossible, it is crucial for family offices to be prepared for a cyber incident that may affect business operations. Developing an incident response plan, associated incident scenarios, and related procedures should address family and staff response responsibilities, internal and external communications during the incident, and continuity of business operations. "Tabletop" exercises modeled after likely threat scenarios can enhance cyber preparedness in the event of an incident and should be used to test the effectiveness and understanding of the family office's incident response plan.

Personnel screening and insider threat: While zero-day vulnerabilities, ransomware, and unpatched software continue to pose significant threats themselves, a potentially more dangerous threat continues to grow within businesses—namely, an organization's own employees. Instituting robust background investigations as part of the onboarding process for new employees and employing periodic reinvestigations for employees and staff with access to sensitive family office information can provide a family office with the necessary insight into the insider risks it may face and allow leadership to take action when needed.

TECHNICAL BEST PRACTICES **Access control:** Weak access and authentication mechanisms leave family offices vulnerable to attackers who are adept at exploiting weak passwords and inadequate access security. Password protecting all devices with strong, unique passwords and working to include multifactor authentication across all systems and applications used can significantly enhance a family office's cybersecurity posture. Also included in the organization's security policies and procedures should be a requirement for mandatory password changes on a regular basis for all family members, employees, household staff, and third parties for all accounts and applications. To more easily facilitate the creation, storage, and refreshing of unique passwords across all accounts, family offices should consider implementing a password management platform.

Manage privileged access to sensitive data: Closely related to access control, a critical tenant of a cybersecurity program is auditing roles, responsibilities, and access permissions regularly to control access to sensitive information on an as-needed basis. As is reflected by a threat pathways approach, compromise of network administrative privileges is a primary method for attackers to gain access to valuable data by escalating privileges within the network. Limiting administrative privileges only to those who critically need access to perform their job functions reduces the attack surface of a family office or business.

Equip all residence and office computers with updated antivirus and antispyware software: Without antivirus software, computers are at risk of becoming infected with malware, which can lead to data compromise and other severe impacts to business objectives. Spyware is software that, without a user's knowledge, monitors and gathers information about a user from their Internet connection—mined information may even include account credentials and credit card numbers, posing a significant risk to individuals and the family office writ large. Similar to antivirus software, antispyware can detect spyware activity and either delete such programs automatically or alert users of their presence.

Data security: Given the highly sensitive nature of the data that family offices regularly handle, data security is one of the most critical aspects of a cybersecurity program and must be addressed for both data at rest and data in transit. Data security should start with confining storage to approved corporate sites and systems, disallowing the transfer of all family office–related information to personal devices, flash drives, or unauthorized cloud storage providers. Furthermore, sensitive documents shared electronically with other employees, family members, staff, or third parties should be password protected; alternatively, employing a single, enterprisewide, cloud-based file storage and information sharing platform is a secure and convenient way to facilitate data sharing, which can be further enhanced via robust passwords, multifactor authentication, and privileged access. These recommendations should be documented clearly in security policies and procedures and be reinforced consistently through security training and awareness. Finally, family offices should strongly consider using encryption for sensitive business information—if an attacker successfully infiltrates the network, strong encryption, if correctly implemented, can prevent access to and exposure of sensitive data.

Wireless security: Attackers can observe communications and breach your perimeter by identifying and accessing an unprotected wireless network, making strong wireless security measures a critical aspect of overall cybersecurity. First, it is a fundamental best practice for any organization's Wi-Fi network to feature a robust, unique password, changed from the default router administrator credentials provided by the manufacturer that can readily be found on the manufacturer's website. It is critical to change the name of the router—referred to as the "service set identifier (SSID)"—so that it does not contain any self-identifying information (i.e., business name or address). If feasible, it is also strongly encouraged to establish a media access control (MAC) whitelist for the wireless network, a method of authorizing only specific, approved devices to connect to the corporate network. MAC whitelisting should be implemented by IT, but first it requires insight into how many devices are currently connected, whether or not they reasonably should be, and the MAC address for each—information that ideally should be readily available if an asset management program is in place. Finally, family offices should establish a distinct wireless network for guests, separate and segmented from the official business network that is relied upon by employees and family members. This network should require its own unique password, which is changed periodically in accordance with password security best practices.

The family members themselves—the ripest targets of malicious actors, as well as any employee who regularly works from home, should also employ these best practices outside the office. As mentioned in the security training and awareness guidance, employees should be required and consistently reminded to avoid using public Wi-Fi networks, which are unsecured, and therefore a viable avenue for bad actors to observe network traffic and acquire sensitive information quite easily. Instead, when working remotely, family members and employees should rely on VPNs, which create an encrypted tunnel between your device and the VPN service to protect against nearby hackers; mobile hot spots provisioned by IT are also a secure alternative to public Wi-Fi.

Keep software updated and patched: Attackers exploit software vulnerabilities to gain network access, and unpatched and legacy software feature known security vulnerabilities that bad actors can easily target. Patching operating systems and applications before bad actors can exploit them is a fundamental technical mitigation measure. Employees, family members, and other staff should also be required to restart their machines periodically to process updates and install patches as soon as they become available, preventing prolonged exposure to known threats that can compromise family office security.

MONITORING As with physical security programs, cybersecurity programs must consistently reinforce effectiveness throughout continuous monitoring, training, and validation. For example, training and awareness programs must consistently be repeated subsequent to the initial onboarding process and should be further reinforced with social engineering tests that use realistic scenarios to put employees in believable situations where they must exercise their judgment accordingly.

For a cybersecurity program to be effective in the long term, it is critical that family office leadership advocate for the creation of a strong security culture by setting a precedent that permeates the organization. Where necessary, leadership should begin to hold employees accountable for their security posture through both positive incentives and negative reinforcements, drawing on documented policies and procedures to track compliance. Family offices should also consider hiring consultants to simulate cybersecurity events and instill confidence in family members and employees about how to act during real incidents based on defined roles and responsibilities.

RESPONSE Cybersecurity is often recognized as important, particularly given the increase in high-profile cyberbreaches that have had both reputational and financial impacts on businesses and individuals; however, given a common gap in technical acumen and a propensity to favor convenience, security protocols are often overlooked in small office settings, especially if a serious breach has not yet occurred. Even if a breach has not yet happened in the family office environment, developing and adhering to a set of security response plans can help a family cope effectively with cybersecurity issues when they do arise. Given the critical and sensitive nature of the data that family offices rely on, full and incremental backups of data should be made regularly. If an incident were to occur, family offices should consider hosting an all-hands, "lessons learned" session to reflect on the experience and coordinate improvements to processes, procedures, and technologies in the future. Finally, in addition to mitigating and avoiding risks, family offices may consider transferring risks through the use of cyber insurance, which can complement the governance and technical best practices described throughout this chapter.

Managing Healthcare

Healthcare has become an increasingly important component of family life organization for affluent families.[3] Family offices often are charged with the responsibility of managing the healthcare needs of their principals and family members, along with their already complex traditional responsibilities.

Within the context of how quickly healthcare is changing, and in turn how quickly the health status of the family members can change, it is no wonder that family offices view the healthcare responsibility with some trepidation. The healthcare theme is large and expansive—and it is an extremely complicated landscape. Objective, authoritative information on medical strategy, access, price, and quality is very difficult to find.

There is also the added complication that affluent families generally have homes and businesses in more than one location and therefore travel extensively throughout the globe. These realities lead, in many cases, to a reactive rather than proactive approach to managing the family's healthcare needs. Unfortunately, reactive mode is nearly always suboptimal. When organized and accessed properly, modern healthcare is truly a miracle. It can add years of productive life and can save a life when illness occurs.

It is certainly no secret that affluent individuals and their families routinely seek the finest physicians and healthcare facilities, and that it is really difficult for laypeople to understand exactly what quality healthcare is—it is a subject of much debate even among experts. This is why an effective family office can be of great value to both the principal and their family.

Healthcare Advisory and Advocacy

Specialization abounds in virtually every major business category, but none more so than in the healthcare industry. For example, in years past, an individual might see an orthopedist for a wide range of knee, hip, shoulder, and spine issues. Today, at some top hospitals, a patient may be referred to a specific physician based on what *part* of the knee needs treatment! Healthcare advisory firms provide the navigational and organizational specialization that is required to partner with a family office to build a successful preventative and interventional platform for principals and their families.

What are the essential elements of a healthcare advisory firm? Top healthcare advisory firms have a cadre of professionals who can leverage their deep domain knowledge of healthcare in all forms. They enjoy close relationships with the physicians, scientists, and administrators that truly matter in the healthcare industry, resulting in an ability to provide clients with ready access to exclusive, closed practices. They have invested heavily in an intelligence-gathering capability that can provide expert advice on the diagnosis and optimal treatment for any medical issue. Investment in intelligence also allows the advisory firm to span geographies via a network of top specialists and facilities throughout the world. They have a planning function that synthesizes emerging diagnostic and treatment technologies with the immediate and long-term needs of their clients.

The following is a review of the typical healthcare needs of an affluent family as viewed through the lens of a competent health advisory firm:

- Preferred, expedited access to top physicians, hospitals, and allied/ancillary services.
- A formal design for preventative healthcare services that meets the immediate and long-term objectives of the principal. This includes the expert selection of the physician cadre, the specific logic behind those selections, and the strategy and logic behind the recommended diagnostic regimen.
- An expert case management capability in place and ready to be deployed should a family member experience a major health crisis or chronic illness. Over time, no family can escape the reality that at some time, a loved one will become seriously ill. A knowledgeable health advisory firm can immediately research the medical issue and clearly communicate the options available to properly diagnose and treat a disease. A top advisory firm will offer second and even third opinions from world-class institutions to ensure that the optimal care pathway will be pursued. This also gives the client the opportunity to assess multiple treatment philosophies and treatment options. Once a decision is made, the adviser can ruthlessly assemble a world-class care team across multiple campuses, faculties, and geographies that best organizes and deploys state-of-the-science care.
- Coordination of routine and emergency healthcare services on a 24/7/365 basis in any location. Provide advanced contingency planning to access healthcare services, when needed, in parts of the world that are frequently visited.

- Secure coordination and management of patient medical records across multiple providers, platforms, and locales.
- A single, unified, and comprehensive medical record and coordination of medical information among all providers. The utility of this feature should not be underestimated. A common medical record platform among one's health providers fosters clear communication, prevents mishaps like drug interactions or duplicate diagnostic services, and allows the immediate deployment of one's complete medical history to emergency providers. In an emergency, a treatment team has only two options—treat generically in the absence of critical information, or treat more precisely based on a comprehensive medical record. Upon notification, a private health adviser can immediately forward the medical record. It is not difficult to guess in which scenarios the outcomes would be better.
- Create clear, secure, and effective lines of communication between the healthcare system, family members, and the family office. Arrange "need to know" access to patient information that is compliant with the Health Insurance Portability and Accountability Act (HIPAA).

Healthy Principles for Affluent Families

CATALOG HEALTHCARE INFORMATION   Understanding and cataloging the precise healthcare status and needs of each family member are essential to building an effective family office for healthcare. Trust becomes a very important issue. While nearly every confidential detail of the family's financial life is catalogued and managed by the family office, the family's confidential medical information may indeed have been off limits. However, it is critical for anyone managing the family's healthcare needs to be fully informed, have a complete and comprehensive medical record of each family, and have formal, HIPAA-approved access to vital healthcare records. The potential for great healthcare is defeated in so many instances by disparate data. Physicians, labs, and hospitals do not have a unified health information system—there are literally thousands of individual islands of systems and databases, and chances are they cannot talk to one another. This is a great function for the family office, as it is essential to have a secure, organized, and central repository of all medical records of family members. The cornerstone of a sensible approach to an effective long-term program is preventive; we believe that the best medical outcomes are achieved by altogether avoiding the need for catastrophic care, particularly when families are distributed across the globe in the pursuit of business, personal, or other endeavors.

ANTICIPATE AND PLAN FOR EMERGENCY NEEDS GLOB-ALLY No matter what we do, though, the nature of medical and surgical illness is unpredictable. Even those with the best and most regular access to primary and preventative care can experience unanticipated illness, at any time and at any age, by virtue of injury, accident, or a medical event that arises without warning. We further recognize the geographic constraints created by the global mobility of affluent families, as well as the often-limited healthcare infrastructure in many of the countries where principals travel and reside.

The global mobility of families creates another problem that needs to be solved: the healthcare experiences of successful families—from the common cold to orthopedic injuries to unexpected hospitalizations—are typically scattered across the globe in an uncoordinated fashion.

GET THE BEST MEDICAL TEAM The cutting edge of modern medical science and technology is ultrasophisticated and advanced to the extent that the difference between the very best care and merely adequate care can literally be the difference between life and death, recovery or disability. As a result, individuals and families with sufficient personal resources to secure access to the best medical services are strongly advised to do so. Expertly matching provider capability to a specific medical condition requires a deep intelligence capability that is generally the exclusive domain of top healthcare advisory firms. Moreover, top physicians have no or very limited excess capacity—their ability to take on new patients is severely strained. Therefore, gaining access to the very best specialists, essential for achieving the best outcomes, requires the strong, long-term relationships that are the hallmark of top advisory firms.

ENSURE ACCESS TO A BROAD SET OF SPECIALISTS Modern medicine is superspecialized, often with dozens of distinct subdisciplines within each field. In this environment, a one-doctor, one-hospital or single-clinic solution cannot deliver the best care across the healthcare continuum. This highlights a major defect of the concierge medicine model, which generally relies on a single, local physician. Ensuring truly elite care demands access to a broad spectrum of specialists and hospitals, including leading academic medical centers and specialized clinics.

FOCUS ON PREVENTION AND PLANNING With the rapid advance of technology, diagnostic screening and preventative healthcare planning have become among the most sophisticated fields of medicine. Today, we are able to assess every vital system of the human body, screening down to the level of genetic markers. Yet this proven path to optimal health risk management, well-being, and longevity is commonly overlooked. Every sound health risk management plan must begin with a comprehensive, state-of-the-science medical evaluation, repeated annually, as well as developing and maintaining a long-term individual healthcare plan.

DIGITIZE VITAL DATA Less than 5 percent of the population has a unified, secure, and immediately available electronic health record, but neglecting this resource often comes at great cost to the patient. Medical data and records must be stored securely and with absolute confidentiality (i.e., HIPAA-compliant), maintained and updated continually, globally accessible to authorized caregivers on a 24/7/365 basis, and used as an essential tool in a personal health strategy.

Family office executives can mitigate healthcare's risks and uncertainties while simultaneously building an effective global healthcare platform for their principals and families by partnering effectively with a top healthcare advisory firm.

International Travel Medical Needs

For individuals and families who travel globally—whether for professional or personal reasons—medical concierge offices that offer medical advice and coverage to people who are travelling can be life-saving.[4] These are specialty practices whose doctors are trained in emergency medicine and have expert knowledge of diseases endemic to different parts of the world. They can be invaluable by helping local physicians treat medical conditions under their direction with supplies and prescriptions that they provide. These specialist medical professionals can also give directions as to where to seek appropriate medical attention.

Travel medicine professionals are usually internal medicine practitioners or infectious disease specialists. They have a wealth of knowledge about the complexities and risks of international illnesses. The concierge doctor can also be invaluable upon the patient's return from travel as they conduct follow-up care.

It's best for the family and/or family office to enlist professional medical advice from these specialist physicians at least six months in advance of travel. They can provide invaluable information, depending upon the destination, about issues and risks regarding travel during a particular time of year or altitude. Certain destinations outside the United States pose particular health risks, such as food safety, environment, sanitation, and rare diseases. An expert travel medicine physician can ensure that patients have the correct immunizations, preventative medicines, and local medical risk advice.

EVACUATION INSURANCE Evacuation insurance is often overlooked. It typically covers the cost of medical transport from international or national locations if the medical capabilities of the treating facility are not sufficient to meet the current medical needs. The cost of this insurance can be as little as $200 to $300 a year. Without this coverage, air ambulance expenses can run anywhere from $30,000 to $200,000, depending on the location and the severity of the medical emergency.

Many families are tempted to use private aviation as the quickest means of returning home. However, this could prove dangerous and be analogous to taking a taxi to the hospital rather than using an ambulance. Depending on the medical emergency, this can be a serious mistake.

In addition, it's important to understand the fine details of any evacuation policy. Not all policies cover preexisting conditions, pregnancy, mental health issues, alcohol-related or other substance abuse–related illness or injury, or extreme sports, like parasailing or all-terrain vehicle excursions (whether practiced domestically or globally). Many of the policies do not take effect until a patient is already in a hospital.

A policy that can offer evacuation protection regardless of where the sick or injured patient is can be vital. Some evacuation companies only transfer the patient to the nearest hospital that they deem capable of addressing their needs. Others may offer the added benefit of evacuating the patient back to a home hospital. It is advisable for most families to obtain a policy that covers the latter scenario.

Medical record summaries can be an essential part of preparing a family member or family office professional for travel. If a medical emergency occurs, it's vital to have a copy of the patient's history, summarizing even simple medical conditions. Summaries that offer endless, static electronic copies of prior records as a traditional medical practice may be cumbersome to sift through while finding the relevant information. Organizations that offer intelligent, pertinent summaries are an excellent option in addition to the concierge practice itself.

Insuring against Risks

One of the more important responsibilities for a family office is determining, mitigating, and (as needed) insuring the family against the risks that naturally come with substantial wealth. These include protecting the value of various assets (including business interests), reducing health and safety risks related to travel (particularly abroad), limiting exposures to cybercrime, protecting the family's reputation and privacy, and mitigating financial exposures that come with various roles and responsibilities.

While insurance is a topic with which principals are quite familiar, incremental insurance needs in areas pertinent to the assets, activities, and associations inherent to families that have the wealth to warrant a family office require a dedicated focus and significant professional advice and guidance. For these reasons, it is a best practice for someone within the family office to be designated a risk manager who will spend time periodically assessing a family's areas of risk exposure, determining ways to mitigate or insure against these risks, and working with outside consultants to obtain and structure appropriate solutions, whether in areas such as policies and procedures, employee and family education and training, agreements, and insurance.

Types of Insurable Risks

Generally, risks can be identified based on three broad categories that apply to family members, family office staff, or both (table 7.2).
Types of coverage for the various categories include the following:

- Homes
- Automobiles

TABLE 7.2
Three broad categories of risk

Assets	Activities	Associations
• Homes • Automobiles • Aircraft and watercraft • Fine art and collectibles • Ranches • Horses	• Traveling (international) • Staffing • Electronic communications • Business pursuits	• Serving on boards • Hiring independent contractors • Engaging in business partnerships

- Air and watercraft
- Ranches and livestock
- Equestrian
- Fine art and collectibles
- Excess liability
- Fiduciary liability
- Travel insurance
- Cybersecurity
- Kidnapping and ransom
- Project completion risks
- Workers' compensation
- Employment practices
- Directors and officers (D&O)
- Errors and omissions

Risk Management Process

While risk management processes follow the same general steps, they naturally need to be tailored to the unique needs, activities, and issues of the family, employees, and various external investment, business, and philanthropic activities (figure 7.6). The steps are as follows:

Step 1: Identify the risk—Uncover, recognize, and describe the risks that might affect the family, assets, employees, and various business interests. Reviewing exposures across the three domains mentioned previously (assets, activities, and associations) is a helpful approach to employ.

Figure 7.6 Risk management process

Step 2: Analyze the risk—Once risks are identified, it is important to determine the likelihood and broad consequences of each risk. The natural consequences could be financial, physical, or reputational.

Step 3: Evaluate or rank the risk—Evaluate or rank the risk by determining its magnitude, which is the combination of likelihood and consequence. This will help determine whether risks are significant enough to warrant efforts to avoid or mitigate them.

Step 4: Address the risk—Develop a plan to address each of the identified risks to achieve acceptable risk levels. For some risks, the family may be willing to self-insure through policies and procedures, family member and employee training, outsourcing functions to third parties, or setting limits as to financial exposure. For other risks, the consequences might be so dire or unable to be insured that the family chooses to avoid, reduce, or abandon an asset, activity, or association. In addition, mitigation strategies should be developed for all risks identified and addressed.

Step 5: Monitor and review the risk—A periodic review should be conducted to monitor and review risks, including assessing changes in the family's overall risk profile that would warrant following steps 1 through 4 again.

Prudent risk management is as much about properly resourcing and staffing a risk management function as it is about following a disciplined process. It is also important to work with appropriate experts in the various fields, including family office–experienced insurance brokers, personal security and cybersecurity vendors, specialty asset consultants, and legal teams.

Obtaining Legal Advice

As is the case with any sophisticated business enterprise, a family office will have a variety of legal needs to address in the course of its operations and will need a wide range of specific legal expertise.[5] The family office legal counsel will need to be cognizant of, if not well versed in, a number of specific legal disciplines, including corporate, securities, fund and portfolio company investments, labor, tax, estate and trust planning, and philanthropy. The legal services required by the family office will include the following:

- Structuring and organizing the family office
- Determining how the family office and ongoing expenses will be funded initially and over time
- Structuring the optimal way of hiring and compensating family office executives and staff
- Addressing family office governance and succession planning
- Ensuring compliance with applicable legal and regulatory requirements
- Establishing investment management structures and processes to handle the family office investment portfolio and review of investment documents
- Reviewing technology aspects
- Financial risk management and insurance products
- Coordinating with security advisers to identify and address family, home, travel, and cyber risks
- Tax planning on both the transactional and estate planning levels
- Structures for achieving the family's philanthropic objectives

In-house Counsel versus External Service Providers

As family offices grow in sophistication and complexity, they increasingly face the question long encountered by other business enterprises: what legal functions should be outsourced and what (if any) legal functions can be most efficiently brought in house? The fundamental question as to whether, and to what extent, the legal function should be brought in house is, in essence, no different for a family office than it is for any similar-sized business enterprise. A company considering bringing its legal functions in house typically looks at factors such as the projected fully loaded employment costs (e.g., salary, benefits, overhead) of having in-house counsel compared with the company's current and projected legal expenses for outside lawyers.

For a family office, the analysis starts with the same economic question, but the unique nature of the family office model can make the decision much more difficult in many ways. As the corporate, investment, regulatory, tax, insurance, labor, and other challenges confronting family offices become more complex, it is likely that family offices, even family offices with in-house counsel, will need to rely on outside legal specialists.

Lawyers and the Family Office

In looking at the legal needs of a family office, the family decision-makers need to consider not just the cost analysis described previously, but also the particular legal profile and legal needs of the family.[6] The fundamental analysis—beyond simply whether the family office has the economic scale to make the cost proposition work—is a determination by the family decision-makers of what core legal functions the family anticipates it will need.

As has been discussed throughout this book, no two family offices are exactly the same. The legal needs of a family office that is overseeing the management of one or more family-owned or family-controlled operating businesses will differ widely from a family office that is principally an investor of family wealth. Likewise, a family office serving an immediate family of one or two generations will have a different legal profile, and widely differing legal needs, than one serving multiple generations of a founding family.

Core to the legal needs of almost every family office will be tax advice—income, gift, and estate tax planning. For a family office that is principally involved with the stewardship of a family's investments (rather than the ownership of operating businesses), the necessary tax support will likely extend to robust expertise on partnership tax issues. Beyond taxes, however, a family office implementing a sophisticated alternative investment strategy will need state-of-the-art legal advice regarding transactional matters, including structuring and negotiating private equity investments, coinvestments with other families, debt finance and derivatives transactions, and real estate investments.

Adding to the complexity of those legal needs, all the legal strategies involved in those transactional matters need to be harmonized with, and optimized for, the family entity and trust structures developed through the family's estate and gift tax planning process. This means that a family office's legal team—whether internal or external—needs to provide close working coordination between the tax experts and the transactional lawyers to ensure that the entry by family members or entities into complex transaction structures don't create inadvertent estate or gift tax risks.

Coordination, in this context, means both the technical coordination between transaction structures and estate planning and the coordination of the family's legal strategy at a macro level. This need for coordination requires family leadership to consider what arrangement of counsel (or multiple sets of counsel) will not only provide the ideal mix of top-drawer subject-matter expertise, but will also coordinate the planning of estate and gift tax strategies and entity structures most effectively and efficiently across multiple generations of the family. Any well-functioning relationship between lawyers and their clients will involve a significant element of interpersonal compatibility and fit. In addition, to ensure the coordination of legal strategy and planning across generations, family leadership needs to be mindful of the importance of facilitating the development of those relationships across the succeeding generations.

REGULATORY   For the family office itself, there are important regulatory issues to be considered. If the family office provides investment advice about family investments, absent an exemption, the family office would be required to register as an investment adviser under the Investment Advisers Act of 1940, as amended (the Advisers Act). Since 2011, the Advisers Act recognizes an exemption from registration for family offices that manage their own family's financial portfolio. To be eligible for this exemption, the family office needs to coordinate with legal counsel to confirm compliance with the applicable eligibility and operational requirements. Similarly, family offices that provide investment advice with respect to commodities may obtain "no-action" relief from registration with the U.S. Commodities Futures Trading Commission as a commodity trading adviser if the eligibility requirements are satisfied. If the family office invests in publicly traded securities, legal counsel also needs to ensure that any applicable filings are made in a timely manner with the Securities and Exchange Commission (SEC).

CORPORATE FORMALITIES Apart from the Advisers Act, much as would be the case for the persons responsible for the legal function in a group of companies, the family office needs to ensure that the corporate formalities are observed and maintained for all the legal entities within the family group. The term "corporate formalities" refers broadly to the formal legal steps to be taken by legal entities to substantiate their existence as separate legal entities.

This suite of corporate housekeeping matters typically includes such things as maintaining the good legal standing of each entity through all required state franchise tax or similar filings, the maintenance of separate books and records for each entity, the regular election of directors and officers for each entity, the keeping of separate records of resolutions adopted and actions taken by each entity, and the maintenance of separate bank accounts for each entity. In the corporate context, these steps are important to ensure that the legal separateness of each entity is respected for the purposes of liability limitation and financial responsibility. Those considerations, of course, are equally relevant for family entities. In addition, the maintenance of proper corporate formalities can help provide legal substance for intrafamily transactions and help to mitigate the risk of inadvertent gift tax exposure.

ESTATE AND WEALTH TRANSFERS The operation of the family office will, in most instances, be intertwined with the estate plans of family members, particularly the first generation, and in many cases will involve trust planning. Investments, sales, loans, employment relationships, and other transactions between and among family members, trusts for the benefit of family members, and family-owned entities are common and present special challenges. The family office legal counsel will need to ensure that all such intrafamily transactions are properly documented and do not result in unintended gifts that would be subject to gift tax. Similarly, the family office attorney will be responsible for ensuring that inadvertent actions are not undertaken that risk causing assets that are otherwise excluded from a family member's estate to become includible in the estate. The family office, through the use of family investment vehicles, can also facilitate tax planning, including estate and gift tax valuation discounts.

CONFLICTS OF INTEREST As to the lawyers themselves, whether in-house counsel or external, the family office, with its constellation of entities and individual family members all requiring legal advice, can present a special challenge—the ethical issue of conflicts of interest and the question "Who is the client?" Providing legal advice to multiple generations of family members can present unique challenges to the family lawyer and the family decision-makers, whether senior family members or family office professionals, and the lawyer needs to be alert to potential conflicts of interest. Although written conflict waivers, joint representation agreements, and other structural approaches can be valuable tools for mitigating the potential for ethical conflicts of interest and avoiding intrafamily disputes, it is almost inevitable that circumstances will arise in which the differing interests of family members will make it advisable to retain separate counsel. Identifying those circumstances, when they arise, and managing that process, pose a unique challenge to the family lawyer.

MANAGING RISK A critical responsibility of the family office is to manage risk for family members. Of course, ensuring appropriate levels of property and casualty, life, medical, and long-term care insurance should be a primary focus of the family office. One key item that is often overlooked is directors and officers (D&O) insurance for those individuals who manage the family office. The D&O policy should be carefully reviewed and customized for each family, as the underwriters and brokers often do not fully understand the complex structures of each family and the scope of coverage is often narrower than assumed by family members.

Another area of risk management that the family office should undertake is to ensure that legal contracts and agreements are reviewed with a focus on indemnification and clawback provisions that could adversely affect family members and entities. Similarly, situations in which family members or family entities must guarantee obligations will need to be carefully evaluated from a legal point of view.

Family offices, being a source of substantial wealth, are being confronted with cybersecurity risks with increasing frequency. These threats continue to grow in sophistication and complexity and expose the family to serious financial risk, potential disclosure of confidential personal information, and disruption of computer systems. The family office counsel will need to assist in balancing the critical needs for cybersecurity with the desires of family members for simple, cost-effective, and efficient communications and interface with the family office.

Another area of risk for wealthy families involves maintenance of privacy and confidentiality. Most family offices are good at making sure that they have employees of the family office sign employment agreements and NDAs, but many other family activities require similar documentation. This includes hiring assistants, managers of properties, pilots, and household staff. It will also be important that confidentiality restrictions cover both financial and personal information.

Wealthy families are unfortunately confronted with increased exposure to personal risk. This is especially true for prominent families in the public domain or associated with businesses that publicly report financial information. To protect against these risks, the family office counsel can be instrumental in the engagement of security advisers to assess and develop security plans that encompass cybersecurity; personal security needs, including security plans for residences; due diligence and background investigations on personal staff and service providers (e.g., private airplane pilots, yacht crews, household employees, and family office employees); emergency preparedness; travel safety; and monitoring of negative or concerning public comments for assessment. The family office counsel will be tasked with coordinating with security advisers to develop an appropriate security plan that is compatible with the family's lifestyle and minimizes any disruptions to family culture.

SPECIAL ASSETS   The family office will be confronted with requests of family members to purchase, operate, and otherwise deal with special classes of assets, including aircraft; yachts; artworks; oil, gas, and mineral properties; precious metals; and foreign assets. Contracts with very specific terms that also should be negotiated with respect to those assets include buying; selling; leveraging and leasing aircraft; buying, selling, leveraging, or consigning art from dealers or auction houses; and creating purchase agreements for natural resources or precious metals.

INVESTMENTS It is critical that the family office attorney review and negotiate all investment agreements entered into by a family office to ensure that the fiduciaries understand the terms and risks. A family may not be able to negotiate specific terms in each instance, but understanding the risks in documentation is critical. This review includes managed accounts, fund investments, coinvestments, direct investments, and agreements applicable to leverage. Often, specific structures need to be set up to make entities eligible to invest in funds that have qualified purchaser requirements.

It is becoming commonplace for family office investment portfolios to include an allocation to international assets. International investment funds exist around the globe and cover a multitude of investment asset classes, including hedge funds, private equity funds, venture capital funds, currency, real estate, and manufacturing. The family office counsel will need to be involved to ensure compliance with any applicable non-U.S. laws, as well as assisting with "know your customer" (KYC) requirements.

ENTITY STRUCTURE AND FUNDING Often, family offices set up various structures to provide limitations of liability across various family assets. This acts as an insurance policy to protect cross-liability. Family investment vehicles are an efficient means of managing family wealth and achieving desired objectives. Family investment vehicles also facilitate centralized management and economies of scale through a pooling of assets.

Family offices, as well as any separate entities that own assets, can be established as C Corps, S Corps, or limited liability companies (LLCs), depending on the particular family circumstances. A review of the tax considerations and a determination of the optimal tax structure for the family office should be made.

PRIVATE TRUST COMPANIES For ultra-high-net-worth (UHNW) families with advanced trust planning, consideration should be given to using a private trust company, which provides a vehicle for trusteeship not tied to any one individual trustee and thus minimizes trustee succession issues. Private trust companies can also provide significant tax benefits depending on the jurisdiction. The family office counsel needs to navigate the regulatory requirements for establishing and operating a private trust company, state law requirements applicable to fiduciaries, and applicable tax laws.

PHILANTHROPY The family office will undoubtedly be at the fore-front of implementing the family's philanthropic objectives. The family office attorney needs to ensure that gifts are made to qualified organizations in compliance with applicable tax rules. The family office may also coordinate the establishment of a private family foundation as a means of consolidating the family's gift-giving program. The family office counsel will assist the family office in navigating the complex rules and restrictions that apply to private family foundations to avoid self-dealing and other potential pitfalls.

ASSESSMENT AND ISSUES SURFACED

What Did We Learn?

The Thorne family has an immediate problem to solve around the wire fraud issue that unearthed lapses in digital hygiene and security, wire authorization protocols, and insurance coverage. In addition, an issue surfaced with respect to employee onboarding that fortunately was resolved through the proactive efforts of one of John's peers. Finally, the challenges of how to provide world-class healthcare to Sofia's mother became front and center. In each of these areas, the family office (and the family) realized that they were not as prepared, or as protected, as they thought they were or should be.

Case Questions

- What are reasons why the Thorne family would be more likely to fall victim to fraud and cybercrime than the rest of the general population?
- How was the wire fraud perpetrated?
- What should the family office do in response to this wire fraud?
- What could the family office have done to preempt hiring an employee with a checkered past?
- How can legal services provide risk management?
- Is there an insurance policy that could cover this wire fraud and BEC scheme?
- What are some considerations around risk management that the family should consider in the future?
- How can the family office help Sofia's mother, Gabriella?

RECOMMENDED SOLUTIONS

Responses to Case Questions

*What are reasons why the Thorne family would be
more likely to fall victim to fraud and cybercrime
than the rest of the general population?*

An obvious risk factor for this family is the magnitude of their wealth. The Thornes have been accumulating wealth from their private business for the last two decades, and the sale of their operating company resulted in a very large liquidity event. The family's public profile also lends itself to a large increased risk of fraud and cybercrime, including John's coverage in the newspaper over the years and Sofia's increasingly public philanthropic activities.

Another challenge stems from the informal processes and procedures in the family office itself. Family offices are geared toward convenience and quick responses for the principals. Principals are oriented towards efficient service delivery from the family office versus highly effective risk management structures. In this instance, the quick response to the fake request via e-mail, and without verbal confirmation, allowed the fraud to be perpetrated when it might otherwise have been detected.

How was the wire fraud perpetrated?

This case presents a classic case of a BEC scam. In this scenario, a genuine-looking e-mail was received by someone that normally handles the finances in a family office. The e-mail appeared to come from the principal, the request looked legitimate, and the demand was similar to previous requests. The e-mail also incorporated a sense of urgency by the requestor during a time when the principal was known to be unreachable to confirm its legitimacy.

What should the family office do in response to this wire fraud?

The family should focus on three main areas to shore up their defenses: training and education of staff and family members, establishment of risk management policies and procedures, and upgrade of security technology to support family office operations.

The simple act of writing down what to do when a fraud or information compromise occurs is another powerful tool that the family office should implement. There are many good examples available on the Internet, and the family office should work with a security consultant to customize these policies and procedures and educate the staff and family members about them.

What could the family office have done to preempt hiring an employee with a checkered past?

At a minimum, the family office should have performed a new hire background and reference check. Bad hires or bad "leavers" can be a source of great frustration for family offices. Again, normal business practices often call for more-than-perfunctory background checks of new hires before they join a company. Family offices will sometimes do some light screening with credit and criminal checks, but given the extremely sensitive and personal nature of working in a family office, more than just superficial screening should be considered. Where the position or profile of the family warrants it, family offices should consider working with security and risk specialists to do a deeper dive on candidate backgrounds. Moreover, families should also implement ways to monitor employees after they are hired, as situations may change dramatically and put the family at risk. Families should also consult with an employment law expert when developing these human resource–related policies to ensure compliance with local and national laws.

How can legal services provide risk management?

These typically involve family office employment agreements, NDAs for investments and other purposes, establishing legal structures for asset protection and privacy considerations, and review of insurance policies and proposals (such as crime and cyberloss policies).

Is there an insurance policy that could cover this wire fraud and BEC scheme?

Possibly. Commercial crime and cyberloss policies have a tremendous amount of fine print that family offices need to evaluate to determine if their insurance covers BEC frauds that result in wire fraud. Sometimes the mechanism of how the wire fraud and the intended purpose of the wire will affect whether a claim will be paid. Cybersecurity insurance is a relatively new space in risk management. Cybersecurity underwriting standards and claim evaluations are in their infancy compared to other insurance policies and practices. These factors should be closely evaluated as family offices explore implementing cybersecurity insurance into their overall risk management structure.

What are some considerations around risk management that the family should consider in the future?

As the Thorne family's public profile and number of family members continues to grow, additional risk management issues will surface. Increased exposure can come from a variety of sources: philanthropic work, direct investments in operating companies, marriages, divorces, international travel, political volunteering, seeking public office, to name only a few. The family office should plan to conduct yearly or biannual assessments of the entire enterprise using an external risk management consultant. That way, they can identify gaps on a systematic basis and fill in with solutions that balance convenience, effectiveness, and security.

How can the family office help Sofia's mother, Gabriella?

Knowing where and how to get the best medical care is difficult, and it is the hope that most families will not have to become expert on these issues. However, given the importance of these issues to families when they arise, family office–specialized healthcare advisory and advocacy companies are emerging. These companies provide ongoing consulting and support for family members, ranging from extensive preventative care to treatment of rare and acute illnesses. These firms offer wealthy families access to the top medical professionals in their field and the top medical facilities in the world. Some service providers in this field also specialize in international medical services, such as medical evacuation and remote diagnosis and treatment assistance. The family office can immediately assist Gabriella by working with one of these companies that can also be available for broader health and wellness needs that the family may have in the future.

CHAPTER EIGHT

Philanthropy

CASE STUDY

Summary

- Three years after the creation of the Left Seat Management family office
- Focus on philanthropic ambitions
- Charitable vehicles

Key Words/Concepts

- Family philanthropy
- Donor-advised funds (DAFs)
- Supporting organizations
- Private foundations
- Charitable planning trusts

Challenge

Having grown up in Mexico City, Sofia was unfortunately all too familiar with poverty and the devastating effects that it has on families, particularly the children. She had the good fortune of growing up in a middle-class family with parents who allowed her to pursue her education and ultimately become a lawyer in Chicago, where she met John. She had a blessed life with three healthy children, a husband she loved, and now financial security to boot. Sofia wanted to share her good fortune with others, especially helping children in need.

Her involvement with the local Children's Hospital provided her with this opportunity. Sofia was a great advocate for the research and care that this hospital was famous for. She knew that she could be of particular value to the hospital by giving and helping them raise money. This was an important contribution for her, and Sofia intended to stay involved and continue to help where she could. She also enjoyed spending time at a local art museum, which gave her a chance to learn about art, engage with artists, and help promote John's and her interests in central Asian and Russian art.

However, neither the Children's Hospital nor the art museum allowed her to get intimately involved with their programs, and she began to consider doing something with children directly. Her life experience gave her an appreciation of the benefits of education to help poor and underserved populations elevate themselves out of poverty. As such, she wanted to provide support to these groups in a more tangible and direct manner. Specifically, she wanted to help the children in and around Chicago to get the additional educational resources they needed at an early age so that they could develop the skills and confidence to be successful as they grew older.

Sofia reached out to Michael to ask him to help her based on his experience with other families and to employ the resources of the family office. She also thought that more organizational support by the family office would be of great help to John, who she knew wanted to do more but was never able to make time for it. Her children were also starting to show an interest in helping others, either because of school projects or what they were seeing their friends do.

John was also interested in expanding his philanthropy, although he did not want to run or manage programs. As an engineering student who often struggled to balance his time and financial demands, John wanted to help deserving students where he could. To this end, he was eager to help the school but did not want to be burdened with the management of any assistance programs.

BACKGROUND INFORMATION

Giving as a Family

The family office is likely to play a central role in the family's philanthropic activities, whatever their mission, scale, or scope.[1] For example, foundation administration is a routine task commonly assigned to the family office, and that covers such matters as record keeping, legal compliance, and tax reporting for the family foundation. Increasingly, though, family members are taking a hands-on approach to philanthropy, meaning that they want to be actively involved not just in setting philanthropic strategy and giving policy, but in giving gifts and assessing their impact and effectiveness. These donors want to see where their money is going and what it is achieving.

The more active a family becomes, the more will be expected of the family office to support the extent of their charitable endeavors. Moreover, wealthy families look to their philanthropic activities as a means to create a legacy—a way to be remembered by both family members and the community. Helping to nurture and build that legacy will be another important job for the family office.

For those families who are mostly passive with their giving, they can outsource a number of solutions to manage their grant-making, such as community foundations, commercial donor-advised funds (DAFs), or philanthropic advisory firms. For those who wish to develop their own philanthropic mission and to manage the functions in house, focusing on philanthropy as a business has paramount importance. Andrew Carnegie famously said, "It is more difficult to give money away intelligently than to earn it in the first place." Families looking to manage their philanthropy in house should take this advice to heart, focusing on the areas that they care the most about and considering all the issues that come with active philanthropy.

Getting Started with Philanthropy

While all wealthy families are different, most that give philanthropically will follow certain common steps for deciding what, where, and to whom to give their charitable donations or grants. The following sections describe these basic steps as a suggested practice. Note that the steps listed here are presented in a simple, orderly form, and there is room to be much more thorough and creative within this process.

ARTICULATE A PHILANTHROPY MISSION STATEMENT Just as a family would put thought into any gift they give, it's important to think through how, what, and where they might give philanthropically. By discussing the family's vision for change and shared values, family members can determine the areas or causes on which they wish to focus their giving. A philanthropy mission statement describes this focus and is used to direct giving in the years to come. One way to approach creating a philanthropy mission statement is to find the right balance among the following elements:

- What the family cares about and most wants to change
- The causes to which the family or family office is already giving
- What the community or region of focus needs

SET GUIDELINES FOR GIVING Giving guidelines present an extension of a philanthropy mission statement. It's a lens through which to decide what will be funded and what won't. For example, some countries offer tax advantages for donating to tax-exempt nonprofits, in which case families may want to direct their giving to these types of organizations. Other families may wish to limit their giving to one particular geographic area—a country, city, or town they grew up in.

As part of internal giving guidelines, a family might decide what percentage to allocate to strategic (also called "impact") giving, what percentage to allocate to legacy giving (the family's history of giving), and what percentage to allocate to more fluid, ad hoc giving, such as disaster relief, emergency funds, or family members' discretionary gifts (those that are of interest to individuals and may fall outside the mission statement).

RESEARCH OPPORTUNITIES AND ORGANIZATIONS Once the family knows what it wants to accomplish, the next step is searching for others that can bring the vision and mission to life. This involves locating organizations and projects that are doing the work that the family wants to achieve. At this stage, it can be helpful to consult an expert or adviser in the specific issue area that can educate the family and help determine the needs and gaps. Once the family has narrowed its choices, it's time to look more closely at the organizations, companies, and projects that the family is considering. Due diligence can be a simple or complex process: examples include checking an organization's website, reviewing its financial records, and scheduling a site visit to meet the people actually doing the work.

Supporting Family Philanthropy

Family office professionals can support the family's philanthropy in a number of ways. Typically, these services fall into four categories related to the philanthropic journey: planning, family governance, implementing, and assessing impact. The following describes the activities that fall into these categories.

PLANNING

- Introduce philanthropy into wealth management conversations.
- Explore the family's motivations and objectives for giving.
- Help individuals and families narrow down and designate a chosen area of giving.
- Research the needs in that issue area or community—who is doing what, where the gaps and opportunities to contribute are, and how to make an impact.
- Bring in an adviser or expert on the chosen issue area.
- Make contacts with other donors funding locally or by issue area.
- Provide resources on philanthropy.
- Set up networking opportunities with peers.
- Find out what tax advantages are available.

FAMILY GOVERNANCE

- Help the family articulate their vision, values, mission for philanthropy, and process for making decisions.
- Help the family office principals write or record their donating intent during their lives. This will allow the family to communicate openly about their values and wishes as a family for their philanthropy over the long term.
- Facilitate discussions for how to get the family involved.

- Help set preemptive policies to mitigate unproductive family dynamics.
- Educate the current or next generation on philanthropy (e.g., set up a youth board to teach children or young adults how to make grants, work together, and other philanthropic skills).

IMPLEMENTING

- Set up giving vehicles.
- Identify causes, charities, organizations, and projects to support.
- Conduct due diligence on those organizations, including making site visits.
- Manage and oversee donation and grant agreements.
- Review and advise on current giving portfolio.

ASSESSING IMPACT

- Request reports from recipient organizations.
- Monitor donations and financial reports.
- Survey grant partners and community members to evaluate results.
- Determine the social return on investment.

This is not an exhaustive list, nor is it meant to imply that family offices should engage in all these activities. Rather, it's a starting place to support the family's needs with regard to their philanthropy at any point along the way. Family offices might offer a range of these services either in house or with third parties.

How Philanthropy Adds Value to Families

The following are some ways that family offices can use philanthropy to add value to the families they represent.

PHILANTHROPY SOFTENS DISCUSSIONS ABOUT MORE COMPLEX FAMILY AND GOVERNANCE ISSUES Research has shown that families that prosper from one generation to the next do so because they have robust governance structures in place. A philanthropy conversation with the family could serve as an entry point to other, more potentially contentious discussions, such as family governance, succession, charters, and unproductive dynamics.

PHILANTHROPY TEACHES THE FAMILY TO WORK TOGETHER AND PROMOTES FAMILY UNITY OVER TIME Philanthropy develops collaborative skills. Drawing the family members together around a philanthropic cause teaches new skills, including collaboration, compromise, and shared decision-making. This can bring new layers to relationships and boost the chances for family unity over the long term.

PHILANTHROPY TRAINS THE NEXT GENERATION TO BE GOOD STEWARDS OF THE FAMILY'S WEALTH Across all cultures and regions, philanthropy is seen as an excellent way to educate and ground the next generation. When done well, it can teach the next generation about the family's enterprise, finances, and values and empower them to do something meaningful. It can help younger family members develop their own sense of purpose and give them a lesson in sharing power and responsibility before the stakes get higher.

Philanthropy can help families align their values, create a legacy, and bring the family together in a way that makes a difference in the world. Family offices are uniquely positioned to play a role in helping families achieve these goals.

Involving the Next Generation

Many successful family offices realize that family unity and long-term wealth preservation depend on their ability to prepare the family's younger wealth owners. One of the biggest concerns is how to teach and pass on leadership to younger-generation family members (commonly referred to as the "next generation").

Motivating the next generation can be a challenging task. Older family members may believe that their young adult children enjoy the benefits of wealth and want to have little to do with the accompanying responsibilities. Or they may be waiting to see if or when their children express the interest, skills, or follow-through to engage in the family enterprise.

In spite of their concerns, some families don't do much to ready younger family members for their future roles in managing the family enterprise or working together. The next generation may view the family enterprise as elusive at best, or a burden at worst. They may lack understanding about the family's wealth, business, and philanthropy—and why it's important to be involved in them. There may be uncertainty that the older generation even wants them involved, or if so, what that involvement would entail. Finally, there may be a reluctance to get caught up in family dynamics and conflicts.

Philanthropy is an excellent way to bridge this conflict—teaching the next generation about the family enterprise, finances, and values, and empowering them to do something meaningful. It can help younger family members develop their own sense of purpose and give them a chance to practice good stewardship, take responsibility, and share power.

IDEAS FOR ENGAGING THE NEXT GENERATION   Family offices can use different methods to engage the new generation in the family's business and philanthropy. The following are a few suggestions:

- Invite younger family members to meetings as observers or even participants.
- Talk to the next generation and find out what their interests are.
- Take them on site visits of the family business and/or recipients of family funds.
- Allow younger members an appropriate amount of money that they collectively must decide to give away, facilitating discussions to uncover their motivations and thought processes.
- Provide ongoing professional development through conferences, workshops, and learning and networking events.
- Offer them a chance to serve on advisory committees of the family council or board.
- Encourage them to serve on charitable boards as a training ground for running the family office or family business, and learning about other perspectives.
- Ask them for input on projects that they are interested in or about which they have expertise.
- Establish a next generation fund or philanthropy program to train the younger family members on philanthropy and grow their collaborative skills.
- Encourage the family to share stories about successes and challenges, as research has shown that this builds resilience and confidence in the next generation.

One thing to keep in mind is that philanthropic responsibilities can also impose a burden on children who are either not interested or ill prepared to handle some the responsibilities and pressures. Children of wealth are often burdened by their family name, inasmuch as others may see them as a potential means for their own personal or professional gain. This includes charities that, although well intentioned, often aggressively solicit young adult children for contributions, particularly if they know that they are associated with a family foundation. In so doing, these charities convey a sense of importance and value that some children have a hard time reconciling with, given that it's not really their money.

This phenomenon is unfortunately inevitable to some extent, and it will likely happen regardless of whether a child is active in the family's philanthropy. It is, however, something that both parents and family office professionals should be mindful of, and they should help prepare the children for this situation through wealth education efforts, either directly or via family philanthropy.

Charitable Entities

Wealthy families use a number of types of charitable vehicles, each of which has different benefits, tax considerations, administrative responsibilities, costs, and restrictions. The appropriate charitable vehicle for a family depends on these factors, as well as a number of others, including the family's level of charitable giving, tax circumstances, desired level of control, and philanthropic ambitions. As a result, there is no "right" charitable vehicle for every wealthy family to use, and indeed many families use a combination of them.

The following are common types of philanthropic vehicles used by wealthy families as an alternative, or supplement, to making outright gifts of cash or property to public charities.

Donor-Advised Funds (DAFs)

DAFs are charitable vehicles established and maintained by a public charity, often referred to as the "sponsoring organization." Examples include community foundations, religious organizations, universities, and financial institutions. Their purpose is to allow families to contribute cash or property to a DAF set up by the sponsoring organization, while receiving a charitable deduction at the time of the contribution. Because DAFs are associated with public charities, charitable contributions receive advantageous tax treatment over private foundations.

They also do not have minimum distribution requirements, excise taxes, or other prohibitive rules as private foundations do.

A family can, whether immediately or over time, request that the sponsoring organization disburse money to charitable causes across a broad range of recipients, whether recommended by the sponsoring organization or identified by the family. While the family can recommend that the sponsoring organization make charitable gifts to recipients, such gifts must technically be permitted and approved by the sponsoring organization. This is an important distinction of DAFs as opposed to private foundations. While private foundations have more onerous rules and restrictions, greater administrative burdens and costs, and less favorable tax treatment, families that set up private foundations control how the foundation is run and where permissible charitable distributions are made. On the other hand, while DAFs in practice are quite flexible and afford a great deal of discretion to the families that fund them, they are controlled by the sponsoring organization.

Supporting Organizations

Supporting organizations, while less frequently used by wealthy families than private foundations or DAFs, can be effective charitable vehicles where the family would like to support a specific charitable organization. Examples include hospitals, museums, public charities, and community foundations. As with a DAF, because the "supported organization" is a public charity, charitable contributions to it receive more advantageous tax treatment than those made to a private foundation. In addition, there are fewer restrictions on when and how money or property contributed can be held or dispersed, so long as they are consistent with the charitable mission of the supported organization.

Supporting organizations provide families with the ability to have a greater level of involvement in and governance over their philanthropic vehicles than DAFs do, but only within strict guidelines regarding control, which can be confusing. Supporting organizations must be operated, supervised, or controlled by the supported charity. The actual manner in which these requirements are enforced is based on a number of tests across organizational, operational, control, and relationship guidelines. For example, under one such test, supporting organizations can have family members as part of the board but cannot hold more than 50 percent of the vote or have veto power.

Private Foundations

Private foundations, which are discussed at length in this section, provide wealthy families with the most control of and oversight over their charitable giving. These are charitable entities established, controlled, and managed by the family themselves, with the assistance of the family office or outside professionals. As such, the family has complete control over governance, investments, staffing, grant-making, and other aspects. However, this level of control comes at a cost in terms of administrative complexity, restrictions, costs, and less favorable tax treatment of charitable contributions.

For families with significant philanthropic ambitions, whether financially or based on a desired level of involvement or control, private foundations are often the preferred philanthropic vehicle. Furthermore, while private foundations require more time, effort, and attention than other philanthropic vehicles, these requirements are not overly burdensome and are well within what a wealthy family is able to do, particularly those with family offices.

Charitable Planning Trusts

In addition to the philanthropic vehicles discussed thus far, there are a number of charitable planning trusts used by wealthy families to augment their giving, often with considerable income or estate tax benefits. These include charitable remainder trusts and charitable lead trusts.

While a detailed discussion of these types of charitable vehicles is beyond the scope of this book, they are worth understanding, inasmuch as they can help initiate and facilitate a family's charitable giving. Often, families meaningfully expand their philanthropic activities once they have a liquidity event or engage in robust estate planning. When properly used, charitable planning trusts are an effective means by which to reduce taxes (whether income or estate), while also contributing to the family's philanthropic plans and ambitions, whether immediately or in the future.

As with each of these philanthropic vehicles, families should consider using charitable planning trusts only based on the advice and with the involvement of their legal and tax advisers.

Private Foundations

Private foundations, also known as "family foundations," are used by wealthy families that desire the greatest level of control over their giving. They are also a charitable vehicle that requires a great deal of administration and oversight. For these reasons, private foundations are often overseen by family office professionals, working in whole or in part with family members, dedicated foundation staff, or both.

The discussion that follows[2] provides a broad summary of many of the legal, operational, and tax rules that apply to private foundations as of 2020.[3] Please note, however, that these rules do not consider special provisions that came about as a result of the COVID-19 pandemic—namely, the Coronavirus Aid, Relief, and Economic Security (CARES) Act and related legislation such as the Consolidated Appropriations Act, 2021, which contained a number of additional Covid-19 relief provisions. Readers should consult their tax and legal advisers when considering which philanthropic vehicles make the most sense for a wealthy family or family office, as well as the applicability of any legal, regulatory, operational, and tax rules, including the deductibility of contributions to private foundations and other charitable entities.

Presumption of Private Foundation Status

An organization organized and operated for charitable purposes is presumed to be a private foundation unless it demonstrates that it fits into one of the exceptions listed in the Internal Revenue Code (IRC). If a charitable organization is not a type of public charity described by the IRC, then it is a private foundation.

Private foundations themselves can be divided into two groups: (1) private operating foundations that directly carry out charitable activities and are exempt from certain distribution and other requirements; and (2) private, nonoperating foundations that primarily receive charitable gifts, invest in funds, and make grants to other charitable organizations. Private foundations generally receive their funding from one primary source, such as an individual, family, or corporation. The most common type of private foundation is the nonoperating foundation, and it is the focus of this discussion because it has the most restrictions.

However, families can also establish private operating foundations if the majority of their income is used to provide a charitable service or operate a charitable program. Private operating foundations receive better treatment regarding charitable contribution limits and are subject to slightly more relaxed rules with respect to activities and excise taxes. A brief summary of these rules is included at the end of this chapter.

Advantages of a Private Foundation

The private foundation provides more control to the donor than does a donation to a DAF, community foundation, or supporting organization because the donor has the right to distribute the foundation assets to organizations (public charities) that they prefer and because they can stay in control of the foundation's investments. The foundation often makes the donations for the family. This is efficient for the philanthropic family because it designates one entity to receive all requests for donations. The establishment of grant procedures and reviews of grant applications by the board of directors or a committee designated by the board makes the grant approval process more objective because applications must meet preset criteria. This can alleviate the pressure placed on family members by grant-seeking organizations or individuals. In addition, special drafting of the organizational documents can maintain the family line as members or directors of the foundation. The family foundation can give younger family members an opportunity to participate in a meaningful endeavor and to become familiar with the charitable goals, intentions, and business management philosophy of the foundation's creator.

Organization of a Private Foundation—Form of Entity

The foundation is established by the creation of a nonprofit entity under applicable state law. A corporation is generally the preferred entity for the private foundation because it provides more protection from liability for the organization's officers and directors, but the foundation can also take the form of a charitable trust. The decisions of directors in a corporate structure are usually evaluated according to the business judgment rule, as opposed to the stricter fiduciary standards applicable to trustees. Careful drafting of corporate documents can provide family-line succession as members or directors of the foundation. A trust format can be made very inflexible, which may be advantageous for founders who want the tightest possible control after their death or incapacity.

Operation of a Private Foundation—Restrictions

Private foundations are subject to a number of restrictions that must be monitored closely and adhered to. Failure to do so can subject both the foundation and its managers to taxes and penalties, as follows:

- A tax of 1.39 percent of the net investment income of a private foundation for the taxable year
- Restrictions on acts of self-dealing
- Minimum requirements for distribution of income (typically 5 percent of investment assets), but this does not apply to operating foundations
- Restrictions on the retention of "excess business holdings"
- Restrictions on investing assets in a manner that jeopardizes the carrying-out of the exempt purposes
- Restrictions on certain types of expenditures, referred to as "taxable expenditures"
- Tax upon termination of status as a private foundation unless certain requirements are met
- Prohibitions upon private inurement and private benefit
- Taxes on unrelated business income

Limitations on Donors' Income Tax Charitable Deductions

In addition to the restrictions and excise taxes imposed on private foundations, other rules and limitations regarding private foundations make them less attractive to donors. For gifts of cash and nonappreciated property, a donor's income tax deduction is limited to an amount equal to 30 percent of the donor's adjusted gross income in the taxable year, as opposed to 50 percent (generally) for gifts of cash and other nonappreciated property to public charities and to other foundations that qualify as public charities. Any excess can be carried forward for the next five years.

The deduction may be zero, however, if the donor has contributed capital gains property to public charities in excess of the 30 percent deduction limitation. Corporate contributions are limited to 10 percent of taxable income, with a five-year carry-forward of excess contributions. For gifts of appreciated property, a donor's income tax deduction is limited to 20 percent of the donor's adjusted gross income, as opposed to 30 percent for gifts of appreciated property to public charities. In addition, gifts of appreciated assets are limited to a deduction of only the donor's basis in the asset unless the asset is publicly traded stock. Charitable contributions in excess of these limitations can generally be carried forward by the taxpayer for the next five years subject to certain ordering rules based on the type of contribution and recipient organization, as well as the year(s) in which they were made. The carryover rules are complex and not intuitive and so it is important to receive advice from legal and tax advisers before engaging in charitable giving at levels that might be subject to these limitations.

There is an exception to the deduction rules for gifts to certain private foundations that are treated as pass-through foundations. If a foundation meets certain criteria (i.e., it is considered a pass-through foundation), the donor may receive a deduction as if the gift were made to a public charity. A "pass-through foundation" is defined as any foundation that makes qualifying distributions in an amount equal to 100 percent of the foundation's contributions for the year before the fifteenth day of the third month following the end of the foundation's taxable year. No special election is necessary; the foundation should just make the appropriate qualifying distributions. To substantiate the higher deduction, the donor must obtain adequate records or other sufficient evidence from the foundation showing that the foundation made the appropriate qualifying distributions. Pass-through treatment of a foundation may be an attractive planning tool for founders who are willing to make the required distributions from the foundation during their life to receive the 50 percent deduction, and then further endow the foundation after death.

Private Operating Foundation

To qualify as a private operating foundation, a foundation must demonstrate that the majority of its income is used to provide a charitable service or operate a charitable program. To do this, a foundation must demonstrate to the Internal Revenue Service (IRS) that it passes the income test. To pass this test, it must show that it spends at least 85 percent of its adjusted net income or its minimum investment return (whichever is less) on the active conduct of its exempt activities (not grants). A foundation's minimum investment return is essentially 5 percent of the fair market value of its assets (other than those held or used for direct charitable activities). In addition, the foundation must pass one of the following three tests:

Assets test: A foundation passes this test if at least 65 percent of their assets

- Are used in the active conduct of their exempt activities, a functionally related business, or a combination thereof
- Consist of stock in a corporation that is controlled by the foundation, and at least 85 percent of the assets of that corporation are used in the active conduct of the foundation's activities
- Any combination of the previous two points

Endowment test: A foundation passes this test if their expenditures on the active conduct of their exempt activities is at least two-thirds of their minimum investment return.

Support test: A foundation passes this test if

- 85 percent or more of their support (excluding gross investment income) is normally received from the general public and five or more unrelated, tax-exempt entities
- No single exempt organization contributes more than 25 percent to their support (excluding gross investment income)
- Not more than 50 percent of their support normally comes from gross investment income

Donations to private operating foundations receive the more generous deductibility limits afforded to public charities, which are as follows:

Type of Gift:

- Cash (50 percent of the donor's adjusted gross income)
- Appreciated property (30 percent of the donor's adjusted gross income)

Finally, to become a private operating foundation, a foundation must demonstrate that it passes these tests for any three years of a specified four-year period (with financials for each of the three years considered individually) or that it passes these tests for a four-year period that includes the current tax year and the previous three years (using this method, the financials for the four years are considered in aggregate).

ASSESSMENT AND ISSUES SURFACED

What Did We Learn?

As with many wealthy families, philanthropy has an important place for both John and Sofia. They each want to share their good fortune by giving back to specific programs that are near and dear to their hearts. As with other new ventures, however, active philanthropy, as opposed to simply writing checks, is unfamiliar to them, and they need help to make sure that they conduct this activity in a prudent manner. Engagement with the family's philanthropy is also a great way for John and Sofia to involve their children and begin a process that educates them about the issues and challenges that come with substantial wealth and how best to address and manage these. The family office can be of great help to them, given the experiences of its professionals, its contacts in the community, and the related work it does in other aspects of their lives (e.g., finance, investments, legal, insurance, wealth education, and other areas).

Case Questions

- How might John and Sofia get started with their broader philanthropic ambitions, and what role can the family office play in helping them?
- What is the most appropriate philanthropic vehicle for the Thorne family?
- What are some of the key steps that John and Sofia should take in developing their philanthropic plans?
- What are some of the reasons why John and Sofia would want to include their children in their philanthropy?
- How can the children be integrated into the philanthropic discussions, and what might be their roles and responsibilities?

- What are some issues that might come up down the road as the family develops its philanthropic strategic plan, engages the children, and runs and supports programs?

RECOMMENDED SOLUTIONS

Responses to Case Questions

How might John and Sofia get started with their broader philanthropic ambitions, and what role can the family office play in helping them?

The most important initial role that the family office can play in helping John and Sofia with their philanthropy is to engage with them around strategic planning and, as needed, take the lead. Raising the topic, hosting meetings to discuss issues, and soliciting and synthesizing advice from experts should be the start. As these discussions unfold, the family will better understand what they need to accomplish their goals, the appropriate structures to use, and what potential outside resources to engage. Ultimately, the family office also plays a role in helping implement, report on, and perhaps evaluate the effectiveness of the family's charitable activities.

What is the most appropriate philanthropic vehicle for the Thorne family?

Families conduct their philanthropy through a variety of charitable vehicles, including DAFs, supporting organizations, and public charities. However, the vehicle of choice for most families that have significant philanthropic resources, active ambitions, and a desire for control is the private foundation.

What are some of the key steps that John and Sofia should take in developing their philanthropic plans?

John and Sofia, with the help of the family office, should orient their initial activities around developing a formal or informal strategic plan. This is more of a process than an outcome, although the end document will be an important instrument that the family can rely on in the future. Part of the strategic plan will be decisions that the family must make around giving guidelines, the process for identifying and deciding on programs to support, and decision-making mechanisms. While this is just the beginning of a longer process for the family, and it will evolve and change over time, it is a critically important first step. The plan will help ensure that the resources, activities, decisions, and involvement of the family are appropriate and consistent with what will help the family accomplish their philanthropic goals.

What are some of the reasons why John and Sofia would want to include their children in their philanthropy?

Growing up with substantial wealth can be a significant challenge for children, not only because of the well-known entitlement issues, but because many children must take over the management of their wealth at some point, often in partnership with their siblings. Understanding how to deal with wealth is not an innate trait—it must be learned either through wealth education or (more commonly) by trial and error. Family philanthropy can help acclimate children to these responsibilities by allowing them to oversee and make decisions over philanthropic assets that serve as a proxy for their own future wealth. The process of developing a philanthropic strategic plan, stewarding assets and programs, and working and dealing with others in these pursuits (including navigating conflicts) can create an invaluable learning environment for children.

How can the children be integrated into the philanthropic discussions, and what might be their roles and responsibilities?

Much of the response to this question depends on the age of the children and their expressed interest in participating. For young adults, it can take the form of inviting them to meetings and letting them see how information is received from various professionals, decisions are made, and conflicts are negotiated and resolved. For older children, the family could allocate to each of the children an amount over which they have the direct ability to give within or outside the family's stated philanthropic mandates. Over time, these young adult children could take on formal governance roles with the family's philanthropy and charitable vehicles.

What are some of the issues that might come up down the road
as the family develops its philanthropic strategic plan,
engages the children, and runs and supports programs?

As John and Sofia embark upon conducting their philanthropy in a more strategic and coordinated manner (with their children, the family office, and outside organizations), they may face a number of challenges for which they should be prepared. These include the following issues.

HOW SHOULD THE FAMILY HANDLE SIGNIFICANT DIFFER-ENCES AMONG FAMILY MEMBERS ABOUT WHERE AND HOW TO GIVE? It is not uncommon for even the most close-knit families to have differing views on how best to conduct their philanthropy, the causes to support, and the roles and responsibilities of family members. This is particularly true once the principals start to involve their children in these activities. In these cases, it is possible to allocate charitable resources among family-specific areas of interest (which are agreed to by all and are supported by the family foundation) *and* family member–specific areas of interest (which are not included in the family foundation's charter). In these cases, each family member is allocated an amount that they can use to support their own causes. This helps avoid conflicts where a particular family member wants to support niche causes that are important to that member but not necessarily important to the rest of the family.

IS THE FAMILY OPEN TO PARTNERING WITH OTHER PHI-LANTHROPISTS AND CHARITABLE ORGANIZATIONS, OR ARE THEY MORE INCLINED TO WANT TO DO SOMETHING ON THEIR OWN? While this question may only become clearer over time as families engage in their philanthropy, it is an important initial consideration for them. Many new philanthropists are enthusiastic about what they can do to help right now, and they often want to jump right in and get started. The challenge is that running a philanthropic program is very much like running a business and requires a great deal of time, effort, patience, and resources. While Sofia certainly has the resources, devotion, and time to be successful at building her own early childhood education program, she should know what is required before committing to one particular course of action. She should also know what options are available to her to provide part of the solution while employing existing providers to supply the others. The family office can help make sure that she is aware of these issues, including by enlisting the help of outside philanthropic consultants. These consultants will provide a great deal of research, insights, and expertise that can help Sofia understand how she can best accomplish her goals.

IS THE FAMILY EXPECTING TO BE THE SOLE FUNDING SOURCE FOR UNIQUE PROGRAMS THAT IT DEVELOPS AND RUNS, PARTICULARLY IN EARLY CHILDHOOD EDUCATION, WHERE THERE IS SUBSTANTIAL NEED AND POTENTIALLY ESSENTIAL FUNDING? Related to the question about running her own programs or working with others to do so, Sofia should understand the funding that will be required to achieve her mission. There are obviously a great number of variables that affect this determination, including the number of children helped, the depth and breadth of the programs, the needed involvement of other public, private, or political groups, and whether she partners with other charities. The answers to these questions will influence the type of philanthropic vehicle she chooses to use, whom she hires, and how she conducts the program, including involving other donors. There is a benefit for many charities to received broad-based funding from the community as opposed to a single family despite how wealthy and involved that family may be. It is not uncommon for philanthropists, particularly those who start a program that requires significant financial and broader public institutional support (educational, cultural, vocational, medical, etc.) to at some point incorporate private or public fundraising programs.

CHAPTER NINE

Next Generation

CASE STUDY

Summary

- Five years after the creation of the Left Seat Management family office
- Issues that children face growing up with wealth
- Wealth education
- Financial assistance

Key Words/Concepts

- Wealth education
- Inheritors and acquirers
- Family bank

Challenge

As John poured the last glass from his favorite Barolo at an elegant, rooftop hotel restaurant with an amazing view of Il Vittoriano, he thought about the last time he visited Rome. It was almost forty years earlier, and under very different conditions—an overcrowded, caliginous hostel with a scenic view of a shared bathroom and bottles of Peroni littering the floor. That trip was with two of his friends from college, who eventually joined him in starting Rybat Manufacturing.

John's youngest daughter picked Italy for this family vacation, and he couldn't help but think of some of the changes that he was seeing in her. Unlike her older sisters and her half-brother Philip, Emilia never knew a world without private planes, luxurious accommodations, and a much more relaxed style of life now that her father wasn't working more than eighty hours a week to build Rybat Manufacturing. In contrast to them, she was starting to take for granted her privileged lifestyle. John thought that one of the reasons that Olivia and Isabella were more grounded than Emilia on these issues had to do with their early childhood experiences. Unlike Emilia, Olivia and Isabella had watched John and Sofia struggle and spend countless hours on building Rybat Manufacturing and balance their work with active, hands-on participants in nonprofits that John and Sofia cared about. Over the last more than twenty-five years they were together, John and Sofia made financial sacrifices to create rewarding lives for their children. After the sale of Rybat Manufacturing, things changed dramatically, and John worried that Emilia was starting to manifest behaviors suggesting that she believed that this new and easier life was just how things were in the world. Emilia was more cognizant and desirous of luxury brands, spent a lot of time on social media promoting their lavish lifestyle (flying privately, going on exotic vacations, hanging out with rich and famous friends), and didn't manifest any real passions in her life save for her social and sporting extracurricular activities. Moreover, the streak of entrepreneurialism and grit that was so evident in his other girls wasn't very strong in Emilia.

John knew all the reasons why it was important to worry about this behavior and why he should work to correct it. His friends in similar situations had also expressed this attitude, which became popularly known as "affluenza," as a problem with which they struggled constantly. He was starting to think about how to employ his resources effectively to help with this mission and decided that the family office might be a good starting point, given the work that Michael, the chief executive officer (CEO), had done with many families over the years.

When he returned to the United States, he sat down with Michael to talk about how the family office could be helpful in instilling those values that he and Sofia held dear, and not just with their youngest, but also with the rest of their daughters. Their oldest daughter, Olivia, had graduated at the top of her class from Columbia University, where she majored in economics and mathematics and studied abroad in Paris. Olivia got a job on Wall Street as an analyst in the investment banking division of a prominent bulge bracket bank. She was working too many hours a week, but she loved her job and had ambitions of eventually joining a private equity firm in New York City.

Isabella was finishing college at the Massachusetts Institute of Technology (MIT), getting degrees in computer science and engineering. She had grown up tinkering with computers, building websites, and creating apps. She was the kid who attended coding and math camps in the summer and was an avid chess player. She had developed and sold a niche social media app for high school kids when she was a senior in high school, and had aspirations of getting into the start-up scene in San Francisco after graduation from MIT. Her dream was to start and run her own company in the Valley someday.

Emilia was attending a private high school in the Chicago area. She was an avid tennis player and swimmer with a diverse set of extracurricular activities that at times distracted her from getting the best grades. She also seemed to find a new passion every month, and some of these interests grew more expensive over the years. She wasn't exhibiting the same kind of drive as her sisters. Ski trips to Aspen with her friends and arguing about what kind of car she wanted (or "deserved") were top of her mind these days.

Philip, John's son from a previous marriage, was a teacher in Chicago. He was married for the second time to Song, whom he had met during a teacher's conference in South Korea. Philip grew up with his mother in suburban Detroit and spent summers in Chicago with John. He graduated from the University of Michigan with a degree in industrial and operations engineering. He was married briefly right after college and had one child, David, with his first wife.

Philip had come a long way from the struggles that he had in his youth. After graduating from college, he completely changed course regarding taking an engineering job, dropped everything, and traveled abroad to try to become a photographer. His drinking in college was heavy, but it became even worse after his travels abroad. It culminated in a drunk-driving accident, but thankfully no one was seriously hurt. Philip rolled his car and was lucky to walk away with only a few bumps and bruises. This event helped turn his life back on track. After the accident, he attended an extensive rehab center, moved in with John and Sofia, and went back to graduate school to get a master's degree in education. Philip then started teaching math in a private school outside Chicago. A few years ago, he remarried, and he and his new wife recently had a child.

Michael had gotten to know all the children since coming in to run the family office. In his private banking career, he had worked with many wealthy families over the years and supported the parents through many common issues that came up with their children. There were some good practices in wealth education, and John and Michael spent an afternoon going over a plan to help John and Sofia with their concerns and goals.

BACKGROUND INFORMATION

Wealth Education

It's a common quandary among wealthy parents—perhaps a universal one: what do we tell the kids, and when? As with many tough questions, the likely answer is, "It depends." Some children will be ready to understand at an early age the challenges they will face as future stewards of significant wealth and begin to behave accordingly. Others may never achieve such an understanding. The financial particulars of each family's situation vary, as do the maturity and capacity of each child. Laying it out on the table all at once may overwhelm them. That's why the answer must usually be, "It depends."

The important question is not just what do they know about the family's wealth. Knowing does not do anything and has no behavioral implications; what is wanted is for children not only to know about their wealth, but also to understand their responsibility, expectations, and values about using it. This is a more active stance. Young inheritors have to know what is expected of them and be engaged in a discussion about whether they are committed, willing, and able to abide by the family's rules and support their values. This is a discussion, not a lecture. The family has to not just offer information, but also hold a values discussion and create expectations and rules about how members should behave. Each young person has to learn a role as a steward of wealth, a more active role than being a passive beneficiary.

Yet—the family's financial particulars aside—there is no reason why every person should not begin at an early age to learn about responsibility and stewardship where money is concerned. Will the children be prepared? The answer to that question depends on their parents. But the family office can, and should, be expected to help.[1]

Life Journeys of Wealth

People come into wealth in essentially two ways: they acquire it during their lifetime through effort or chance, or they inherit it from someone else. The way by which a person comes into wealth is an important determinant of how wealth affects their personality and character. There are a number of stages in the development of an individual's wealth identity, ranging from innocence about the power and pain of wealth, to a level of conflict over their own wealth, to the achievement of a sense of reconciliation and integration of the wealth.[2]

Acquired and Inherited Wealth: What's the Difference?

Acquired wealth can be defined as a significant rise in socioeconomic level within one generation. A hallmark of acquired wealth is the psychological and sociological sensation of transition. The individual achieving wealth status travels not across distance, but rather across socioeconomic class, setting out from a blue-collar or middle-class culture toward the promised land of wealth.

A second fundamental point is that acquirers come, in most cases, to their new status having already developed much of their personal identity in the common culture of their birth. This, then, is the significant factor: with acquired wealth, one's identity is partly or wholly established before it occurs.

Inherited wealth, by contrast, describes those of the multigenerational wealth class who are born into their upper socioeconomic level.

Compared to the transition in socioeconomic class that acquirers experience, the experience in multigenerational wealth is of maintenance of one's class. This gives rise to many of the stresses and anxieties reported by heirs. Inheritors may be fortunate enough to improve their wealth status by their own efforts, thereby achieving that rare combination of being both inheritors and acquirers.

The Five Challenges of Wealth Inheritors

Children of wealth must overcome five key challenges to generate a sense of life purpose and a positive and facilitative emotional connection to their money.[3] Each challenge describes an important aspect of the psychological relationship to the saving, spending, and sharing of wealth. To develop a positive wealth identity, children must resolve conflicts and overcome their vulnerabilities in each area.

CHALLENGE 1: FINANCIAL AWARENESS   Many children avoid the issue of their wealth by using it unconsciously, without knowing anything about it. This challenge indicates the degree to which they have actively become aware of money matters: how much they have, how it is invested, and how it is spent and shared. Not knowing about money is a way of denying it or not being responsible for taking care of it. Success in this area indicates that they have a solid hold on their finances, characterized by the feeling of truly "owning" their money.

CHALLENGE 2: LIFESTYLE MANAGEMENT   The element of lifestyle management points to how children get pleasure from using their money, their spending habits, and the nature of their lives. Positive identity is seen in those who get genuine pleasure and satisfaction from spending their money, and who spend in ways that are not ultimately compulsive or self-destructive. They buy things that have meaning, and they also buy things for fun. However, they also practice values-based spending—balancing saving and sharing money with spending it.

CHALLENGE 3: STEWARDSHIP   It is not enough for children with wealth to just consider their own personal satisfaction. Having wealth gives them the opportunity to influence and help others, and studies show that the greatest pleasure and life satisfaction come when one gives both to oneself and to others. A steward views wealth as a multidimensional resource that is preserved and shared for the benefit of both current and future generations. A healthy person wants to look around and think about what can be done for other people and for the future.

CHALLENGE 4: SELF-ESTEEM/PERSONAL SECURITY Money by itself does not make children feel personally secure or good about themselves. In fact, its presence may lead them to feel increased anxiety. This element of self-esteem refers to how much their sense of personal value, self-respect, and personal identity is founded on wealth. Specifically, it means how comfortable and secure they feel in their own skin, which includes their inheritance and the role that it has defined for their lives. Unless children have a strong sense of personal identity, the fear of losing money may lead them to feel continually vulnerable. Strength in this element means that a child has a solid and coherent foundation of self-esteem and personal security that is not primarily dependent on net worth. They feel in charge of their lives, enjoying the advantages of money without feeling that it makes them a better or more worthwhile person—or an evil one either.

CHALLENGE 5: TRUST IN RELATIONSHIPS A child's willingness to trust others in a personal relationship is affected by wealth. The presence of money can make it hard to trust others, even as it attracts them. Wealthy children must learn how to select and trust other people in their interactions, or they will always feel that money undermines the nature of their relationships. People can always wonder if someone likes them for their money or for who they are. A mature person will find ways to make friends who are genuine. When children find that personal comfort zone in handling the impact of money on personal relationships, they are able to trust other people and deal with money issues without poisoning or undermining their relationships.

How the Family Office Can Help

Family offices can assist principals in preparing their children for both growing up with and being responsible for their wealth. While this must be done with the active involvement or tacit approval of the parents, it is an important role of the family office. Indeed, the daily work of a family office, as well as the utilization of various governance structures in conducting this work, can be a valuable training ground for children of appropriate age. The key is for executives of the family office to anticipate this need and to look for ways to include children, particularly if some of the issues discussed previously manifest themselves. The family office can also develop, usually with the help of outside experts, a number of training programs for children across a range of ages.

Family Meetings

A common practice among successful families is to hold regular family meetings. At the end of the day, the families themselves must come together to address many of the issues that come with substantial wealth. Family meetings are such a forum, and they provide a mechanism for sharing information, communicating and promoting important values, providing education and training, and developing mechanisms for conflict resolution. The family office often plays an important role in scheduling and facilitating family meetings, including creating agendas, preparing and presenting information, answering questions, organizing special events, and inviting speakers.

The Family Bank

Another mechanism commonly used by family offices that oversee the affairs of larger families with adult children across multiple generations is the family bank. This is a mechanism by which the family, typically through the assistance of the family office, can provide financial support to family members for things such as large personal expenditures or new business endeavors.

Benefits come from the formality and professionalism by which the family bank should operate. Families with multiple generations often have members whose financial requests and desired investments range considerably. The family bank provides the family, and therefore the family office, with a way to address these needs in a manner that provides some level of equity with respect to how spending and investment decisions are made across family members. It also provides parents a forum through which they can impart their values and expectations, promote entrepreneurialism, and encourage related engagement among the children.

ASSESSMENT AND ISSUES SURFACED

What Did We Learn?

John is reflecting on his children and how Emilia is dealing with growing up never really knowing what life was like without the megawealth her family has created. He is noticing some trends in his youngest daughter that are not appealing and do not reflect his and Sofia's values. He turns to Michael for help with how to address these issues.

Case Questions

- Why is wealth education important?
- What characteristics do wealthy children have if they grow up in a family that is acquiring wealth versus after the wealth was created?
- What can the family office do to support wealth education for the Thorne family?
- What are family meetings, and how can they be used to support wealth education?
- What roles, if any, are there for children within the family office?
- What wealth education issues should the family office consider five to ten years from now?

RECOMMENDED SOLUTIONS

Responses to Case Questions

Why is wealth education important?

Children of wealthy parents regularly struggle with problems of financial literacy, motivation, outsized lifestyles, identity, and trust. A well-designed wealth education program with measured outcomes can be helpful to mitigate some of these common challenges in the following ways:

- Enabling family members to manage their financial affairs independently through a high degree of financial literacy and subsequent healthy habits around investing, spending, and saving

- Fostering a desire by children to use the family's wealth in a manner consistent with the values espoused by the principals
- Establishing lessons learned and frameworks to help children deal with major life events and challenges such as careers, marriages, births, adoptions, divorce, and death
- Promoting entrepreneurial mindsets and healthy risk-taking behaviors

What characteristics do wealthy children have if they grow up in a family that is acquiring wealth versus after the wealth was created?

How children approach wealth and money is greatly influenced by observing their parents as they go from childhood into young adulthood. Children that grow up in families with more humble beginnings that accumulate significant wealth over a relatively long period of time tend to share their parents' attitudes and behaviors toward wealth (although not always). These children are able to experience and observe their parents' struggles and success at obtaining wealth through (1) a hardy work ethic, (2) financial and personal sacrifices during tough times for the family and/or business, (3) a deep passion and dedication to grow an operating business, (4) learning (sometimes painful) lessons and adapting to challenges as they build their fortunes, and (5) using part of their fortune to support causes in line with the family's values.

However, children of established wealthy parents who have not grown up watching their parents engage in broadly healthy behaviors are often challenged in the areas of motivation, financial literacy, drive and purpose, healthy risk-taking, independence, and anxiety about not having enough wealth to maintain their privileged lifestyle. These children may also experience a relentless sense of pressure to succeed, which can come from observing the tremendous success that their parents have achieved or a direct push by their parents to be successful themselves.

What can the family office do to support wealth education for the Thorne family?

The family office can support John and Sofia's wealth education efforts in several meaningful ways. Once they decide, and indeed demonstrate through their actions and decisions that wealth education is an important goal of theirs, then the family office can act as a coordinating agent. For example, it can help build a wealth education strategy, communicate that strategy to the children, and report the results of these efforts back to them. Family office executives such as John and Jason typically have professional experiences and backgrounds that are relevant to provide advice in areas such as investing, business management, and general financial literacy.

One delivery method for wealth education John can suggest is family meetings. The family office can host these meetings and incorporate wealth education topics into the discussions. John and/or others within the family office can deliver the wealth education instruction directly, through breakout sessions, or with professional external facilitators.

What are family meetings, and how can they be used to support wealth education?

Family meetings are gatherings of family members where information is shared, issues are deliberated, and decisions that affect the family are made. Properly employed, family meetings can be a powerful tool for principals and family offices to align stakeholders to a common vision, serve as a "state of the union" check for the family enterprise, encourage and develop deep bonds among family members, educate family members on critical nonfinancial topics (e.g., cybersecurity), and provide an effective and efficient communication platform to discuss complex (and sometimes prickly) topics that affect the family. Family meetings can be informal or formal and sometimes include a yearly family vacation to a destination.

What roles, if any, are there for children within the family office?

Encouraging participation by children in the family office can be an effective way to engage the future generations of the family; however, execution is critical to success. Principals vary widely in terms of what they want to reveal to children about their wealth. Moreover, some children have little to no desire to be involved in the family's financial affairs, and forcing them to work in the family office could be a distraction to operations and a drain on the limited resources of the office.

However, there are particular strategies that help engage the children with the family office. These include philanthropic activities, participation on governance committees, summer internships, etc. By involving the children slowly in age appropriate roles, they can "learn by watching" how (1) family members interact with the family office and outside advisers, (2) business is conducted across a multitude of areas, and (3) conflicts are raised, discussed, and resolved.

What wealth education issues should the family office consider five to ten years from now?

Five to ten years from now, the family will have matured and hopefully benefited from the structures put in place as the family office continues to flourish. Philip's children will be teenagers and young adults. In this case, the family office would have to increase the breadth of their wealth education programs, given the growing number of both younger and older members of the family. In addition, family members will likely seek support for their own entrepreneurial, personal, and philanthropic projects. Therefore, mechanisms to support those projects (e.g., a family bank) could be deployed to assist with these issues. Finally, the children will be of an age where they can take on more direct responsibility for their own financial affairs and decision making. The family office could begin working with them as individual family office "clients" helping them address issues specific to their needs.

Governance

Background Information for Case Studies 10 through 12

Ten years have passed since John created his family office, Left Seat Management. The family and the family office experienced the typical growing pains during those years, although the challenges they experienced became catalysts behind creating additional structures and developing more formal processes. The family office now oversaw over $1 billion in assets, served twelve family members, and had thirty employees (see figures s3.1 and s3.2).

On the family front, John and Sofia were now the parents of adults who had their own careers and, for some, families of their own. John endeavored to assist his children financially, but he had not taken the steps to transfer or give the children access to a significant amount of the family's wealth. All of his children were pursuing their own paths in life and experiencing their own struggles and joys. While this was what John and Sofia wanted, it also meant that they were in less frequent contact with them.

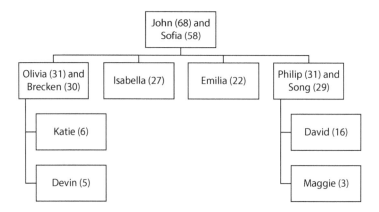

Figure s3.1 The updated Thorne family tree

The family office had become an integral part of all of their lives, albeit to greater and lesser extents. Management of the investment portfolio was increasingly professional, especially with the hiring of a dedicated chief investment officer (CIO), Jack, who oversaw a small team focused on both public securities and private investments. The family office continued to outsource most of their public securities portfolio. They were also very active in direct investing, mostly as minority investors partnering with other families or via private equity funds.

The family was bringing in house much of their increasing amount of legal work by hiring one of their trusted corporate attorneys, Chase, who was supported by a paralegal. John also had decided to establish his own flight department, given his familiarity with private aviation and the challenges of always having to rely on management companies to source pilots. His chief pilot, Henry, had flown with him for years and brought both technical expertise and managerial skills to oversee a function that had become an important part of their lives. Michael also decided to create an Operations Manager role and promoted Veronika to this position to oversee dedicated estate management, concierge, and security personnel.

However, despite this professionalization of the family office, Michael seemed to be dealing continually with staff issues and putting out fires. There were always service and communication breakdowns between family members and the family office that required him to intervene. He also had noted, and was surprised by, the little things

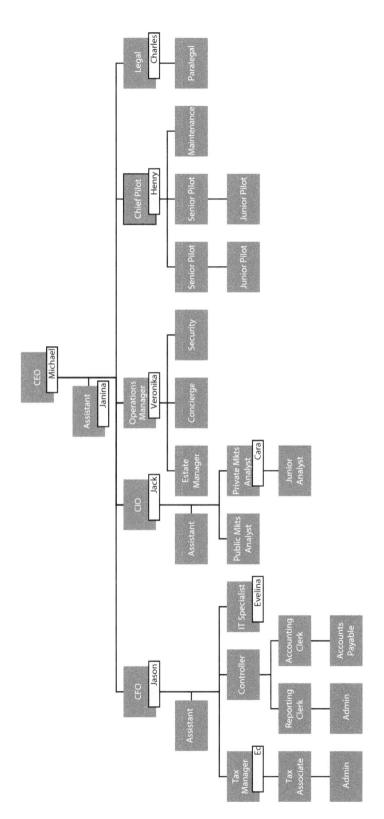

Figure s3.2 The updated Left Seat Management organizational chart

that tended to upset John or Sofia (or both). Based on his experience as a senior executive, he couldn't understand why because all the *major* responsibilities of managing their personal and financial assets were being done well (or, at least no one in the family was complaining about these). Michael was starting to consider whether the family office was focused on all the right things.

As John contemplated his legacy, he was exploring ways that he could creatively get his children more interested and involved in the family office. Their levels of interest varied greatly, and he was growing concerned about how the family office would survive once he and the executives were no longer around. Planning for succession seemed logical, but it was also something he wished he could put off until he was much older. But in just one example, Michael was now sixty-seven and indicating to John that he planned to retire soon.

CHAPTER TEN

Communications and Planning

CASE STUDY

Summary

- Ten years after the creation of the Left Seat Management family office
- Best practices for communications
- Building a sustainable plan

Key Words/Concepts

- Communications
- Strategic planning

Challenge

Michael put the finishing touches on a family newsletter that he had been working on over the last couple of weeks. This newsletter came about after strains in interactions between the family office and the principals regarding services and communication had become all too frequent.

There was also the issue of engagement by the children. Right after the business e-mail compromise fraud that the family experienced during their trip to Russia a number of years ago, the family office hired Evelina, an information technology (IT) specialist, and an outside security consultant who jointly implemented regular training sessions for the family office staff and the family members. At first, attendance at these training seminars was strong because the security event was fresh in everyone's mind. However, over the years, family members less frequently sat in on risk management education sessions. Sometimes the reasons for not attending came from conflicts caused by their increasingly busy personal schedules, although the younger family members simply claimed they "didn't get the message" about the meetings. Michael knew that he was going to have to get creative to make sure that important messages were properly disseminated and understood by the family, and that meetings were attended regularly.

In business environments large or small, miscommunications occur. Family offices are no different and suffer from the same kinds of communication issues. Michael was on top of most things for which the family office was responsible. However, as the scope of services and number of family members grew, Michael noticed that a few things were starting to fall through the cracks. Michael believed that a family newsletter would help him initiate a dialogue around how the family office can better align with John's and his family's service and communication expectations. He also believed that there had to be a better way to organize and execute as the complexity of the family increased.

During this period of time, John was becoming increasingly focused on his passions, which he was able to indulge in more often thanks to his liquidity event. One of those passions was direct investing. John dedicated more of his time on, and worked with Michael to have the family office devote more resources to, supporting his interest in direct investing. John also joined a number of boards and spent time with their management teams to help them expand their businesses. He also increased his personal networking efforts to find new investment opportunities, particularly with other family offices. While John recognized that it was better for him to remain in mostly a minority owner capacity with his direct investments, he missed running a business and having influence over something important to him. He met these desires by taking on leadership roles with one of the charities he generously supported and through focusing on how he could perpetuate his legacy.

The meaning of legacy was evolving for John. He knew what had been important to him when he was building Rybat Manufacturing—namely, managing and growing a company that he built from the bottom up. However, this new chapter of his life was similar in some respects, but very different in others. He had more time to think about his kids and grandkids. How well was he preparing them to live successful lives, and how would they and their children be provided for after both Sofia and he died? What did he define as success, and how did that differ from his children's perspective? Was he going to give the majority of his money away to charity, or should he try to maximize the wealth of his children, grandchildren, and generations of the Thorne family to come?

BACKGROUND INFORMATION

Communications

Family offices may be small and intimate, with few participants all in close proximity to each other. But that doesn't mean they are immune from communications breakdowns. A key imperative for the family office is to develop protocols for communicating with principals and other family members. Communications should be active, outreaching, and engaging, and not limited to formalities like periodic financial reports.

Broadly speaking, family offices should consider a communications plan that evaluates current communications protocols, incorporate family office objectives into it, execute it, and measure its results.

Evaluate Current Communications Protocols

Examining how a family office currently communicates with key stakeholders is a critical step in this process. It will provide both family members and executives with an account of how information is shared, both internally and externally. To make such a survey successful, executives should work with principals to understand their priorities of who should be included (next generation, in-laws, cousins, divorced parties, and others). This will help avoid misunderstandings and ensure alignment with principals. The "who" elements will help answer the "why" and "how" communication questions that follow in this evaluation. Moreover, executives should take this time to evaluate the quality of messages by asking questions such as the following:

- Do the current communications provide adequate information on the financial standing of the family office?
- What happens if the unexpected death of a principal occurs?
- Does the family office's messaging provide inspiration to younger generations of the family to achieve the legacy ambitions of the principals?
- Who in the family office is engaged? Who should be more engaged?
- How do immediate and nonimmediate family members feel about being included in the affairs of the family and the family office?
- Is communication with external advisers/parties adequate (e.g., operating companies, financial/legal/tax advisers, or philanthropic efforts)?
- Are communications transmitted in the right form (e.g., for the next generation) or with the right frequency? Are the right staff supporting these efforts?

These baselines will help all parties ensure that future communications will provide credible messaging with adequate resources.

Incorporate Family Office Objectives

The development of a stronger communications plan can help start or enhance conversations with principals about what they want the family office to do. Executives should incorporate the mission and vision of the principals and help make sure that they fit the SMART paradigm— which means "specific, measurable, attainable, relevant, and time-limited." Doing so will help make sure that communications are aligned and that the principals' goals can actually be met. Taking these steps can help the family office in many ways, including increased family harmony, more transparency about how the family office invests, greater buy-in to the mission and vision of the principals across the family office enterprise, and improved preparation of the next generation to live better lives and take over the reins of the family office.

Execute the Plan and Measure Its Results

Once executives agree on a communications game plan, the hard part of execution begins. Executives should build a project plan that highlights the frequency and mix of messaging across the family office enterprise. Communications methods should be varied, frequent, and tailored to individual stakeholders. These can range from newer technologies (e.g., mobile messages, private family social networks, and videoconferences) to more traditional forms (e.g., hard-copy letters to family members, family meetings and retreats, and a family history book). Examples of deliverables that family offices should consider as they execute a personalized communication plan include the following:

- Regular review of financials in hard copy for principals and digital copies of summarized/minimized financials for next-generation and noncore family principals
- A newsletter that updates the family's foundation efforts and results
- An annual family shareholder letter, written by principals and shared as appropriate
- Congratulations notes to celebrate the accomplishments of family members
- Financial education materials and messaging, such as a monthly blog delivered to next-generation family members
- Economic and geopolitical updates from external advisers

Measuring the results of these activities is easier if goals are defined up front. Executives should start with smaller and less ambitious projects to get some early wins. Families can also consider hiring outside consultants to help facilitate family meetings or manage crisis situations.

In summary, strong communication plans and engagement of principals are critical contributors of success for any family office. Finding the correct communications tempo, messaging, and delivery methods are even more important as the family size grows and operations become more complex. Regardless of the stage or size of the family office, a solid communications plan will help family offices in good times and bad.

Building a Sustainable Plan

No single factor is more important in ensuring the long term "success" of a family across generations than cohesion among family members with respect to certain important objectives, such as a family's vision or mission, desired culture, or legacy.[1] One of the important roles of a family office can be to assist families in determining these objectives and building a sustainable plan that helps them achieve them. To do so effectively, a number of questions need to be asked, including: Is the family willing and able to set up effective governance structures and decision-making processes? Are family dynamics such that comity will prevail over the inevitable misunderstandings? Can major interests across generations be aligned? Is the family committed to working together to determine shared goals, values, and priorities such that they can be articulated into a strategy that will shape its future for another generation or two? A family that can answer "yes" to all those questions exhibits the kind of cohesion that will place it in good stead for a successful future.

It is important to focus here on the last item from this list—namely, developing a strategy that will shape and guide the family for the future. In essence, strategy is a means of implementing a shared vision of things to come. Coalescing around a common vision of the future, and then taking the concrete steps needed to put that vision in place, are prerequisites for a strategic plan. In truth, every organization needs one in some form, from the small charity to the multinational corporation. As the number of stakeholders grows, as complexity increases, and as the planning horizon extends from years to decades, the need for strategic planning becomes more compelling. And that is certainly true of wealthy families.

And yet family offices are not frequently asked by their principals to help with strategic planning, certainly in the first generation, and often beyond. Initially, the founding generation's goals, values, and priorities will take precedence, and whatever strategic plans that might be produced will be in sync with them. If, as is often the case, privacy, control, and service continuity are among the top priorities when the family office is established, they will probably remain so while the founders are still running things. A comprehensive strategic plan for the family's future, including the role of the family office—who needs it? The new family office's initial years will likely be taken up with operational concerns of the moment, such as putting financial and risk controls in place, building and refining an investment approach, and finding the right talent with the necessary expertise. Strategic planning can wait until there's a more pressing need for it.

In contrast, no one would say that a first-generation business doesn't require a strategic plan to chart its course and prosper. A strategic plan can be useful from day one to help the new business retain focus, allocate scarce capital, and respond appropriately to opportunities and unexpected threats. The same is true for wealthy families and the family offices that serve them. Yet, as previously noted, few family offices are asked to take the time to develop and adopt strategic plans for the family or themselves. This seems paradoxical, given that family office principals are often successful business owners who have built their wealth on the basis of strategic business plans. Yet, family and family office strategic plans are still the exception rather than the rule.

Despite this, there are tremendous benefits to the family that come from the family office engaging in a strategic planning process. As a road map, a strategic plan provides the office with direction for short-term challenges, as well as long-term ones. It supplies benchmarks to help the family measure and evaluate both its and the family office's performance towards these plans. And to the extent that the strategic plan both reflects and enhances family cohesion, it can be a powerful bulwark for family sustainability. Strategic plans can help shape the response to adverse or challenging events by guiding decision-making, ensuring that heirs are prepared, and seeing that the family's mission and values are respected.

Those family offices that take the time and effort to help a family engage in a strategic planning process and develop strategic plans find it to be of great benefit. Chief executives of successful family offices are increasingly putting into place strategic management processes modeled after those used in government and business. While strategic planning is most likely adopted by family offices as they mature and develop multigenerational constituencies of family members, it has gained a foothold in the family office world and can be expected to spread as its benefits become more widely recognized.

The Family Office Strategic Planning Process

Family offices can use a strategic planning process to identify requirements and gaps, determine objectives, and develop a feedback mechanism

TABLE 10.1

The family office strategic planning process—defining goals, assessment, and building a road map

Key strategic planning step	Purpose	Success factors
Defining goals	Who are we, and what do we want to become as a family and as an organization?	The initial assessment phase requires articulating both a vision and a mission statement. There are many effective ways that a family can craft these statements. Sometimes using an experienced external facilitator can be helpful.
Assessment	Where are we today in comparison to our goals and objectives?	An assessment helps executives and principals understand the current family office's strategic and operational balance sheet and identify ways to improve, streamline, or jettison existing processes and capabilities. Several methods and tools can be used here, including SWOT and gap analyses.
Building a road map	Where would we like to go, and how will we get there?	A detailed road map to achieve stated goals and objectives can help drive the family office's activities and serve as the blueprint for benchmarks to measure success. Strategic objectives should be well defined, time bound, measurable, distinct, aligned with principals' desires, and clear about the boundaries of the family office's responsibilities.

to monitor the tasks required to complete those objectives while identifying additional areas of improvement.

Tables 10.1 and 10.2 provide an overview of the strategic planning process and success factors that family offices can consider. Customization of this process to fit idiosyncrasies and dynamics within individual families is critical to achieve success in this exercise.

TABLE 10.2

The family office strategic planning process—implementation and tracking

Key strategic planning step	Purpose	Success factors
Implementation	What do we need to do to put the plan into action?	Once a strategy has been developed, family offices should focus on implementation. Here, the family develops a set of action items that support the achievement of goals and allow stakeholders to monitor their progress. Implementation should include the use of a workflow management system to help the family office prioritize, allocate resources, and stay on top of execution. Accountability is key. Those responsible should be identified by project, and projects should be ranked by priority.
Tracking	How are we doing with regard to our plan, and where can (or should) we make adjustments?	Each action item ought to have measurable metrics reported at appropriate intervals, including ownership of action items and progress reports in a format favored by the principals. The monitoring process should be simple and focus on progress and gaps.

BEST PRACTICES Strategic planning can be a rewarding system for families looking to improve direction and operations; however, proper implementation is critical. Family office executives must be careful to design a plan around the desires and needs of the family principals, even if that requires running a less efficient operating model for the family office. Family offices are designed to support the requirements of a family and (typically) not external stakeholders or shareholders. Understanding and operating in this paradigm will help executives with alignment of interests and better relationships with family principals.

Here is a list of best practices that family offices can consider as they build and implement their strategic plans:

- Keep all stakeholders fully informed, with regular communications throughout the process.
- Show quick wins to encourage buy-in and maintain momentum.
- Use an external consultant or professional to design data gathering and communications during the process.
- Monitor projects that support strategic objectives using a robust workflow system.
- Communicate through the media preferred by family members (e.g., electronic versus hard-copy reports).

ASSESSMENT AND ISSUES SURFACED

What Did We Learn?

John's family office has matured, and his family has grown older and larger. John and Michael are starting to feel the predictable growing pains as the family office expands, complexity increases, and the children become more independent. The family office and John are right to focus their efforts on improving family communications, as this will help in the near and long term. Now that the family office has been established for a number of years, John is also well positioned to spend more time on a strategic plan to help Sofia and him achieve their goals.

Case Questions

- What can John and his family office do to improve communications strategies and updates across his entire family enterprise?
- What are some common communications deliverables that family offices produce for principals, and how could John's family office employ them?
- Why should the family office help John and Sofia engage in a strategic planning process?
- How should the family office help John and Sofia develop a strategic plan?

RECOMMENDED SOLUTIONS

Responses to Case Questions

What can John and his family office do to improve communications strategies and updates across his entire family enterprise?

John is experiencing a common issue that principals experience after significant time has passed after a major liquidity event. Life has become more complex, the children are grown and living their own lives, and he is feeling out of touch with them. It is apparent that John is taking some steps to address this by launching his family office newsletter, and there are additional ways that he can use his family office to improve communications for his family.

The first step to fixing issues around communication is developing a formal plan with principals and family office stakeholders. When a family office is in its earliest days, family office professionals are often challenged to create such schemas. Principals create family offices for different reasons, but a common purpose is to make their lives more convenient. As such, they will often skip the chain of command and engage with any and all levels (and employees) within the family office responsible for tasks undertaken to support their lives. This can lead to some communications failures in a family office because additional workflows don't come via a universally accepted method. Family offices will often apply Band-aids to communication issues until major problems arise; principals then tend to lead the charge to find and implement a better strategy.

To kick off a formal communication strategy, John should take stock of who the primary stakeholders are (other principals, family office personnel, outside advisers, extended family members, and others), what messages are currently being delivered, and which ones need to be, how, and at what frequency. Moreover, he should recognize that communication style preferences and methods will vary among individuals, and certainly between generations. Finding ways to make the family meetings and family news updates more interesting and to deliver them in a method tailored to a particular audience's preference will pay dividends.

Finally, to assist with the process, John should work on establishing strong communication feedback loops among the important family office stakeholders so that there is buy-in across the board. He should also make sure that the family office develops a strong project management system, with dashboards and regular reporting to keep items on track and demonstrate progress made (including communicating initial quick "wins" that can be vital to increasing commitment to the process).

What are some common communications deliverables that family offices produce for principals, and how could John's family office employ them?

From the case study, we can see some of the ways that John has addressed communications (e.g., his newsletter, education sessions from external experts, and family meetings), but given the evolving nature of his family, it will be important for John and the family office to customize deliverables to meet the demands of various family members.

Family offices are responsible for a variety of communications-related deliverables, and often the first priority will revolve around consolidated reporting updates to principals. Adapting to the communication preferences around financial reporting presents good lessons for how the family office will need to tailor all the messaging. John should consider utilizing the following typical deliverables:

- A yearly or semiannual "state of the union" letter written by the principal with the help of the family office and delivered throughout the family
- Updates on family philanthropic activities
- Updates on the family bank to appropriate stakeholders
- Wealth education materials for the next generation
- Congratulation notes to members of the family to recognize major accomplishments in their lives
- Training sessions or educational content for family members on topics that affect the entire family (e.g., risk management, health and wellness, business continuity)
- Chronicles of family history
- Maintenance of a variety of family-related chat forums
- Surveys of family members to provide input to support the activities of the family office and the desires of the principals

Why should the family office help John and Sofia engage in a strategic planning process?

At this point in John's life, he is dealing with the issues of how different building and running a family office ecosystem are compared to when he was running his own operating company. The formality of strategic planning and operational execution is typically largely absent in a family office environment. However, that does not mean that John can't employ his family office to build, operate, and (over time) improve its strategic planning process.

A common refrain of family office executives is that they generally feel like they are always putting out operational fires. A rigorous strategic planning process will help family office executives find solutions that move them from feeling that they are constantly jumping from one issue to another while executing a planned and effective business strategy. Family offices that implement a robust strategic planning process are also more equipped to handle additional requirements, such as an expanding number of stakeholders to integrating operating companies. In so doing, they can improve readiness and execution, increase resilience and continuity, advance family harmony, facilitate conflict resolution, and increase cooperation and buy-in across the entire family enterprise.

How should the family office help John and Sofia develop a strategic plan?

Similar to the general idea around improving communication strategies, the family office should work to establish a formal strategic planning process that focuses on obtaining buy-in from John, Sofia, and all other important stakeholders. Given the bespoke and often large degree of variance in both motivations and priorities between principals in a family office, doing so in practice can be a challenge. While families tend to have central figures that yield more influence than others (in this case, John and Sofia), new stakeholders develop as families grow in size and as the family office functions for these family members grow in scope.

There are many established and tested corporate strategic planning frameworks that the family office can modify to fit its preferences and needs. However, a suggested initial design could revolve around a five-step process. In this process, the family office can work with John and Sofia to (1) define their mission and vision, (2) evaluate the current snapshot of the family office, (3) design the future state of the family office and assign goals, (4) manage discrete projects to achieve objectives, and (5) measure and report on progress and course-correct as necessary.

Finally, the family office should consider hiring an expert in the strategic planning field to guide and augment the internal process. There are valuable lessons that can be learned by hearing about how other families have addressed similar issues, needs, and concerns. An independent, and expert, consultant with experience with other families can help make this complex process more effective and efficient for all parties involved.

CHAPTER ELEVEN

Structures

CASE STUDY

Summary

- Ten years after the creation of the Left Seat Management family office
- Governing mechanisms and vehicles
- Regulatory issues

Key Words/Concepts

- Governance structures
- Family businesses and family offices
- Private trust companies (PTCs)

Challenge

John (now sixty-eight), Sofia (now fifty-eight), and the entire extended family were spending the Christmas and New Year holidays in Cabo San Lucas, something they tried to do each year. It was hard to do given the growing size of the family and the busy lives everyone had. The family had grown to twelve members, including two in-laws and four grandchildren.

Philip, who was now forty-one years old, enjoyed being a teacher and had a spunky new baby daughter, Maggie. He also was active in the upbringing and financial support of David, who lived with his mother. John and Sofia helped Philip financially through annual gifts of cash within the gift tax limits. Philip was also the beneficiary of an irrevocable trust that was set up for him many years ago. This trust has accumulated a significant amount of wealth over the years through various gifting strategies John and Sofia employed. With the approval of an independent trustee, Philip was able to take a certain amount of income each year out of the trust. These amounts, when added to his teacher's salary, provided Philip and his family with more than enough to live comfortably.

John and Sofia had done the same for each of their four children. They received the same annual cash gift and could withdraw the same level of income from their trusts once they reached the age of twenty-five.

Olivia, who was now thirty-one, was married to a lovely woman named Brecken, whom she had met while studying abroad in France. Brecken was a fourth-generation family member of one of the country's largest privately held media companies. Olivia and Brecken had stayed in touch after Paris while Olivia worked as an investment banker and Brecken worked in marketing for her family's company. They married three years ago and have adopted two daughters, Devin and Katie. Brecken's family was quite large, with over fifty siblings, cousins, and grandchildren. Brecken involved Olivia with her annual family meetings, inviting her to serve on various family committees, and solicited her opinions and feedback on many of the issues that the family business and family faced. In particular, Olivia was asked to be on the family's investment committee given her background as an investment banker, and the family assembly as an in-law. These experiences gave Olivia a perspective on issues that other families of significant wealth face and how they addressed them, particularly with many more family members across multiple generations.

Isabella, who was now twenty-seven, was enjoying her life in San Francisco. She was working at a start-up and had a long-term, serious boyfriend. Emilia, now twenty-two, was a junior at the University of Colorado Boulder. She indulged her passion for sports by playing tennis. She also took up skiing and became quite good at it. Emilia was focusing on getting a degree in environmental studies but wasn't really sure what she wanted to do after college.

As John looked out over the Sea of Cortez, he thought about his family, particularly his children and grandchildren. He was proud of how they were growing up and, despite understandable sibling conflicts and arguments, seemed to really love and support each other. However, he knew that they were still quite young and had many life challenges ahead of them, some of which were the result of their station in life. John was starting to focus on what he could do to support them after he was no longer around. This need also became clear as he starting hearing from Olivia about what Brecken's family did to help oversee a family business. Her family's company was started 100 years ago and now had to manage a very large business that included siblings and cousins. The business eventually would also have to successfully navigate numerous succession events.

The family office was an obvious means to provide this support to an operating company, although John wasn't sure how or who would do that. As structured and operated today, it dealt with issues as they came up, mostly around managing assets, personal needs, and transactions. Decisions also currently were being made exclusively by John or Michael.

John was interested in how he might involve his children more in the decision-making in the family office, although he never really had a conversation with them about this or their level of interest. He also was concerned about what would happen once both he and Michael were no longer around. Would the children be able to manage the family office? How would they work together? Who else could step in and help?

BACKGROUND INFORMATION

Boards and Committees

There is a great deal of overlap between family offices and the issues and challenges that family businesses face. This is particularly true with respect to the involvement of family members and the benefits and types of various governance institutions. The following is a discussion[1] of various family business governance approaches and structures that apply to select family offices as they grow in size to oversee a larger and diverse group of family members.

The family aspect is what differentiates family companies from their counterparts. This is also true with respect to many family offices, particularly those that have been around a while and oversee the affairs for a number of family members across multiple generations. As a consequence, families can and do play a crucial role in the governance of family offices. This implies different ideas and opinions on how the family office should be run and its strategy set. It becomes mandatory, then, to establish a clear family governance structure that will impose discipline on family members, prevent potential conflicts, and ensure the continuity of the business.

A well-functioning family governance structure will mainly aim at doing the following:

- Communicating the family values, mission, and long-term vision to all family members
- Keeping family members (especially those who are not involved in the family office) informed about major accomplishments, challenges, and strategic directions
- Communicating the rules and decisions that might affect family members' employment, cash flow, and other benefits they usually get from the family office
- Establishing formal communication channels that allow family members to share their ideas, aspirations, and issues
- Allowing the family to come together and make any necessary decisions

Developing such a governance structure will help build trust among family members (especially between those inside and outside the family office) and unify the family, thus increasing the family office's prospects for viability. The major constituents of a family governance structure are

- A family constitution (figure 11.1) that clearly states the family vision, mission, values, and policies regulating family members' relationships with the family office

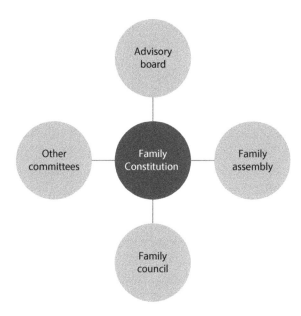

Figure 11.1 The structure of a family constitution

- Family institutions, which can have different forms and purposes (e.g., a family assembly, a family council, and other family committees)

Family Governance Institutions

Family governance institutions help strengthen the family's harmony and relationship with the family office. By allowing family members to get together under one or more organized structures, family institutions increase the communication links between the family and the family office, as well as provide opportunities for family members to network and discuss aspects that can be related to the office. These organized activities help increase understanding and build consensus among family members.

Family members should be well informed about the purpose and activities of any established family governance institutions. This can be achieved by developing written procedures for these institutions and sharing them with all family members.

FAMILY CONSTITUTION The family constitution is also referred to as the family creed, family protocol, statement of family principles, family rules and values, family rules and regulations, or family strategic plan. The family constitution is a statement of the principles that outline the family commitment to the core values, vision, and mission of the family or, as the case may be, the family office. The constitution also defines the roles, compositions, and powers of key governance bodies of the family office, the family members and stakeholders, management, and the board of directors. In addition, the family constitution defines the relationships among the governance bodies and how family members can meaningfully participate in the governance of their family office.

The family constitution is a living document that evolves as the family and its family office continue to evolve. As a consequence, it is necessary to update the constitution regularly to reflect any changes in the family, the family office, or both.

The form and content of family constitutions differ from one family to another depending on the size of the family, its stage of development, and the degree of involvement of family members in the family office. However, a typical family constitution will cover the following elements:

- Family values, a mission statement, and a vision
- Family institutions, including the family assembly, family council, and education committee
- A board of directors (and a board of advisers, if one exists)
- Senior management
- Authority, responsibility, and relationships among the family, the board, and senior management
- Policies regarding important family issues such as family members' employment, transfer of shares, and chief executive officer (CEO) succession.

ADVISORY BOARD The advisory board consists of independent advisers to the principal and senior executives of the family business or family office who typically do not hold voting rights. The board deploys the expertise of its various members to provide guidance on strategic planning, investment policy, and sensitive issues.

The advisory board is a group of experienced and respected individuals that many family offices form when, in the case of a family business, their own boards of directors remain composed only of family members and company senior managers, or, in the case of a family office, when there is no other governing board. In this case, the board or principal might lack expertise and outside perspective in certain strategic areas, such as governance, finance, human resources management, and investment management. Accordingly, the advisory board is then created to compensate for the shortcomings of the principals without the family diluting any control over decision-making or being required to share information with outsiders. The advisory board can also add value to the family office through the business connections that its members might have.

The advisory board is often considered a compromise solution between a family-dominated and a more independent board. Many principals of family offices recognize the need for an independent board but are also uncomfortable with sharing sensitive information (personal or financial) and decision-making power with a group of outsiders. These principals usually opt to create advisory boards as a way of getting outside advice and expertise.

The most practical size for an advisory board is from three to seven members. Keeping the size of the board small helps maintain its effectiveness and makes it possible for its members to clearly communicate their ideas to the rest of the group. Members of the advisory board are usually experts in areas such as finance, management, and investments. They also provide expertise and experience when the family office moves on to new activities. The advisory board usually meets three to four times a year, depending on the family office's size and complexity of operations. The CEO and a few senior managers from the family office can also be part of the advisory board in order to coordinate and orient the meetings' discussions toward the company's/family office's needs.

To ensure the objectivity of the advisory board, the following individuals are typically not part of it:

- Suppliers or vendors to the company or family office
- Friends of the principals with no relevant expertise to offer
- Existing providers of service to the company (e.g., bankers, lawyers, external auditors, consultants), because their advice is already provided in other forms and their objectivity and independence might be questionable because they are working for and being paid by the company

- Individuals who have a conflict of interest with being advisers to the company or family office
- Individuals who are already overcommitted and would not be able to perform their roles as members of the advisory board properly

Table 11.1 summarizes some key advantages and disadvantages of advisory boards.

FAMILY ASSEMBLY The family assembly comprises the universe of family members that is often delineated by major family groups. It is a forum used to educate family members on the family office, family business, philanthropy, or other family undertakings; to provide updates on important events and milestones; and to reinforce the family constitution or mission statement.

Also called the family forum, the family assembly is a formal platform for discussion by all family members about family and related business issues. During the founders stage of the family office, the family assembly is replaced by a more frequent and informal family meeting. These informal meetings allow the founders to communicate family values, generate new ideas, and prepare the next generation of the family office's leaders.

The purpose of the family assembly is to bring family members together to reflect on areas of common interest (family, family office, and family business issues). It allows all the family members to stay informed about these issues and gives them the opportunity to voice their opinions. These assemblies help avoid potential conflicts that might arise among family members because of unequal access to information and other resources. Family assemblies are usually held about once or twice a year to discuss and manage issues of interest to the family. Some of the issues handled by family assemblies include the following:

- Approving any change in the family values and vision
- Educating family members about their rights and responsibilities
- Approving family employment and compensation policies
- Electing family council members (if the council exists)
- Electing other family committees' members
- Dealing with other important family matters

TABLE 11.1
Advantages and disadvantages of advisory boards

Advantages	• Its members have no legal responsibilities, which reduces the company's costs (because insurance is less necessary) and makes it easier to recruit members (because membership is less risky than being part of a board of directors).
	• The board can provide the family office with additional skills, technical expertise, and knowledge that are not available at the current management and board levels.
	• Its advice is usually unbiased.
	• Its members may offer new contacts that can lead to additional insights and opportunities.
Disadvantages	• The advisory board functions like a group of experts whose advice is not systematically followed by the family office. As a consequence, the advisory board might not be taken as seriously as a real board of directors.
	• The advisory board has no authority to request information from the management, so its recommendations can be based only on what management is willing to share with the board members.
	• Advisory board members have little or no influence on the strategy and performance oversight of management.
	• The lack of legal responsibility makes it difficult to hold members of the advisory board accountable for their advice.
	• Some advisory board members might not take their role seriously and put in the necessary preparations and contributions that they would do if they were "real" board members.

Source: International Finance Corporation, *IFC Family Business Governance Handbook* (Washington, DC: World Bank), 2008.

As a general rule, family assemblies are open to all family members. However, some families prefer to set membership restrictions, such as minimum age limits, participation of in-laws, and voting rights during the assembly. The scheduling and chairing of the family assembly are usually handled by the family head or some other respected family figure. In larger families, this task is usually given to the family council, as discussed next.

FAMILY COUNCIL Also called the family supervisory board, the inner council, and the family executive committee, the family council is a working governing body elected by the family assembly among its members to deliberate on family business or family office issues. The council is usually established once the family reaches a critical size (i.e., more than thirty members). In this situation, it becomes very difficult for the family assembly to have meaningful discussions and make prompt and qualified decisions. The family council is established at this point as a representative governance body for the family assembly in coordinating the interests of the family members in their family business or the family office.

The composition, structure, and functioning of family councils differ from one family to another. However, their duties typically include the following:

- Being the primary link between the family, the board, and senior management
- Suggesting and discussing names of candidates for board membership
- Drafting and revising family position papers on its vision, mission, and values
- Drafting and revising family policies such as family employment, compensation, and family shareholding policies
- Dealing with other important matters to the family

Just like any well-functioning committee, the family council should have a manageable size (i.e., five to nine members). These members are usually appointed by the family assembly by considering their qualifications and availability to perform the council's duties. Some families prefer to impose certain restrictions regarding membership in the council, such as age limits and experience requirements and barring the participation of in-laws and family members who also serve on the board or are part of a family company's or family office's senior management. One good practice is to set limited terms for the council's membership to allow more family members to be part of the council and create a feeling of fairness and equal opportunity within the family.

The family council should have a chair, who is also appointed by the family assembly. The chair leads the work of the council and is the main contact person for the family. It is also a good practice to appoint a secretary of the council, who will keep the minutes of meetings and make them available to the family. Depending on the complexity of issues facing the family, the council would meet from two to six times per year. Decisions are usually approved by a majority vote of the council's members.

Table 11.2 outlines the major differences between the family meeting, family assembly, and family council.

Investment Committee

Structuring, implementing, and governing the investment management program for a wealthy family generally benefit from following, over time, the guidelines and approaches adopted by institutional investors. Two of the more important of these approaches is the use of an investment committee and the development of an investment policy statement (IPS).

Family offices of all sizes and stages of development should consider establishing an investment committee to assist in the oversight of their investments, both internally and externally managed.

The objectives of the committee include the following:

- Providing a formal process to manage the family's investable assets
- Developing and implementing investment decisions

The broad responsibilities of the committee include the following:

- Holding regular meetings, typically quarterly
- Developing the IPS
- Selecting and monitoring investments
- Setting reporting guidelines and evaluating performance
- Approving the hiring and firing of advisers and managers
- Documenting any decisions that the committee makes

The investment committee should be made up of both internal and, if possible, external professionals and advisers, although the makeup and diversity of these members tend to evolve over time. Many newer

TABLE 11.2

Family meeting, family council, and family assembly—what's the difference?

	Family meeting	Family assembly	Family council
Stage	Founders	Sibling partnership/ cousin consortium	Sibling partnership/ cousin consortium
Status	Usually informal	Formal	Formal
Membership	Usually open to all family members; additional membership criteria might be set by the founders	Usually open to all family members; additional membership criteria might be set by the family	Family members appointed by the family assembly; selection criteria defined by the family
Size	Small, because family is still in the founders stage; usually six to twelve family members	Depends on the size of the family and membership criteria	Depends on criteria set up for the membership; ideally five to nine members
Number of meetings	Depends on the stage of the family office's development; when the family office is growing fast, can be as frequent as once a week	One to two times a year	Two to six times a year
Main activities	Communication of family values and vision; discussion and generation of new ideas; preparation of the next leaders	Discussion and communication of ideas, disagreements, and vision; approval of major family-related policies and procedures; education of family members on business issues; election of family council and other committees' members	Conflict resolution; development of major family-related policies and procedures; planning; wealth education; coordination of the work with the management and the board

Source: International Finance Corporation, *IFC Family Business Governance Handbook* (Washington, DC: World Bank), 2008.

family offices limit the committee to the principals and senior members of the family office, such as the CEO or chief investment officer (CIO). Principals new to managing money via a committee are often reluctant to invite outsiders to weigh in on investment decisions. It is their money, after all, and they have been making all the decisions in the past and expect to continue to do so in the future. Over time, however, as the family's wealth grows and investment management becomes more complex, or the principals begin transitioning governance to others, receiving independent advice from others becomes more valuable and important.

The chosen membership of the investment committee is of great importance and typically also evolves over time. It is not uncommon for newer committees to include the close friends and peers of the principals. This is understandable and often fine, so long as the committee members bring both valuable expertise and gravitas to the committee. It does no good for any governance committee to be comprised of friends and peers who do not provide expert, balanced views that at times differ from those of the principals.

Other Family Institutions

Families in business or part of a large family office might find it useful to develop other types of institutions that cover areas of particular interest to them. Some of these institutions are the following:

- **Education committee:** This committee is responsible for nurturing the family's human capital and its capacity to collaborate effectively in the tasks of governance. The education committee anticipates the developmental needs of family members and organizes educational events and activities for them. For example, the committee could organize an accounting seminar for family members to help them read and understand the financial statements of their family company or family office.
- **Shares redemption or distributions committee:** This committee is overseen by the family council and manages an established fund for the shareholders of family companies who wish to cash in their stock at a fair price to pursue other activities with this money. The fund is usually built by contributing a percentage of the company's profits to it each year. This committee can also set distribution policies for

family members who are not part of a family company and instead rely on income from a portfolio overseen by the family office.

- **Career planning committee:** This committee serves to establish and oversee entry policies for family members interested in joining the family business or family office. It also helps monitor the careers of family members, offers career mentoring, and keeps shareholders, stakeholders, and the family council informed about their development. The career planning committee can also be very useful for advising family members who choose not to work in the family business or family office about how best to pursue their external careers.
- **Family reunion and recreational committee:** The purpose of this committee is to plan fun events and other activities in order to bring family members together around recreation. The committee also organizes yearly family reunions designed to nurture relationships among family relatives by providing opportunities to come together and enjoy each other's company.

Learning from Family Businesses

In addition to governance structures, there are a number of issues for embedded or related family offices to consider when the family sells their closely held family business. One of them is how the family office should prepare for and manage some of the changes that occur with respect to the roles and responsibilities, family cohesion, individual finances, and mission and vision of the family. These changes will have a material impact on governance because the nature of governance best practices within a family business is often different than for a stand-alone family office.

The following are some observations about the nature of family offices compared with family businesses, as well as some possible implications for family office governance.[2]

THE COHESIVE "GLUE" OF THE BUSINESS IS MISSING For families that own operating businesses, the business itself can act as a cohesive element in keeping them together and focusing on agreed-upon goals for the future. When a family transitions to a primary task of wealth management rather than business management, reasons for staying together may be less clear.

Participants in a family office must think carefully and continually about their reasons for staying together as collaborating owners. While vision and mission are important for business-owning families, the vision and mission for the family office may need to be revisited with greater regularity, and family leaders may need to focus more strongly on managing family cohesiveness.

INDIVIDUAL RIGHTS ARE INHERENT TO OWNERSHIP AND MUST BE RESPECTED The family business typically represents a single entity that should be managed for the benefit of a unified share-holder group. As families grow and family units increase, the benefits of ownership are increasingly distributed among more discrete units (in other words, nuclear families). This can have a further impact on fragmenting ownership vision.

In addition, there are more degrees of freedom with investing than with running a business, so people are free to have more disparity in their financial objectives. The risk, growth, and profit profile of a business is somewhat constrained by the industry in which the business operates, so owners must accept that profile or get out. When it comes to investing, there are many more choices. Family members can choose profiles that fit their needs, which are typically not going to be the same across the group.

Individual ownership units must think carefully through their financial objectives, and a process must be established for them to articulate these objectives and design an investment portfolio that meets their needs. Particularly when individual participants in the office vary considerably in income level and age, the processes of articulating investment objectives and integrating disparate goals become crucial. While a clear investment policy approved by all participants may contribute to the continuity of the family office, recognition of diversity and efforts to accommodate the various perspectives will become increasingly important as the family grows.

The aspiration for a family business is a cohesive ownership group with a consensus on business goals and objectives. By contrast, family office management must be more responsive to individual needs, and processes should be developed to identify and address individual differences and needs.

THE FAMILY CULTURE IS THE BUSINESS CULTURE A key element of family firm governance is the separation of family and business domains. While the family mission, vision, and objectives provide parameters in which the business operates, an independent board, a family employment agreement, and other elements of governance are intended to limit the family's personal influence over business management. In the family office, however, the mission and vision are the family's mission and vision.

The family culture takes on more importance and relevance in the family office context because this culture will form the matrix that gives rise to mission and vision. Well-run family offices recognize these circumstances through a strong and continuing emphasis on shaping a functional family culture, providing financial education, engaging in philanthropic initiatives, and taking an entrepreneurial approach to the creation of new wealth for the family. There should be at least equal emphasis on shaping and nurturing the family culture as on developing structures that support the family office's investment and other activities.

AUTHORITY IS VESTED IN FAMILY OWNERS RATHER THAN THE FAMILY OPERATORS In the family business, business leaders are usually a limited group of family members and nonfamily members whose authority is recognized by family and nonfamily alike. But in the family office, every owner may have a legitimate right to interact with managers. This means there is the potential for a greater number of diverse (and potentially conflicting) authoritative requests being made of managers. This also means that all owners will be responsible for making more decisions in the family office environment than in the family business environment.

Family office managers must be vigilant about the possibility of conflicting messages or requests from family members. Triangulation can be a real threat to the smooth operation of the family office. Executives thus must be clear on their rights, responsibilities, and authority relative to family members. A clear process must be established for managing the flow of requests from the family to the family office staff, and boundaries on what is appropriate to request of the staff must be clearly defined as well. Finally, given the amount of responsibility foisted upon owners in the family office environment, more education of family members with regard to the business of the family office is crucial, whether or not they have a background in the business.

Compared to a family business, family owners in the family office may have considerably more power. Therefore, it is crucial that family office operations be clearly defined with regard to lines of authority and the process of managing family requests to the executives and operators of the office.

FAMILY OFFICES TEND TO OVERSEE A BROAD RANGE OF ENTITIES AND SERVICE PROVIDERS While the family business is often a single entity or a small number of entities, family offices typically manage assets with a broader range of complexity. This may include active management of businesses, majority or minority investments in businesses managed by others, partnerships, or passively managed assets. Such complexity drives increased decision-making requirements for owners and management and a good flow of extensive information so they can make sound decisions. At the same time, even the largest family offices typically outsource a number of their functions, making clarification of accountability and oversight more complicated.

Clear authority and responsibility for oversight of service providers to the family, as well as accountability for service provider performance, are crucial. Also essential to ensure sound decision-making are good information flow and programs that educate family members about the various components of the family investment portfolio. In many ways, the requirements for management accountability, communication with owners, and owner education are similar in the family office and family business contexts.

Is Good Governance Different for Family Offices?

Taken together, these observations suggest that family governance—in the form of vision, mission, role clarity, and next-generation education and development—are at least as important (if not more so) in the family office environment as they are in the family business environment. Family offices differ in their need to recognize and integrate a more powerful role for family owners and to respect and manage individual differences. This points to a requirement for a well-structured organization with articulated policies, plans, and ownership roles that can accommodate the need for ongoing, individually tailored conversations with owners.

Private Trust Companies

Wealthy families create private trust companies (PTCs) to provide a form of governance via privately owned, professionally run trust companies over which the families have some level of control. PTCs are often used when one generation of leadership in a family transitions to another, but that generation is not interested in playing as active a role in the oversight and management of the family's wealth. PTCs are also commonly used where a professional fiduciary is required (or desired) due to tax and estate planning, but where the family wants to retain some level of permitted and appropriate oversight and control.

For families that own family businesses, have active investment family offices, or prefer not to work exclusively through institutional fiduciaries, PTCs offer a unique opportunity to further both their estate planning and family governance schemes. However, they are complex and have substantial operational, legal, tax, and governance issues and requirements that must be understood and followed.

The following discussion provides a brief overview of PTCs and summarizes many of their advantages and disadvantages.[3]

What Is a Private Trust Company?

A PTC is a state-chartered entity designed to provide fiduciary services to members of a family, and as such is prohibited from doing business with the general public. A PTC is distinct from a family office in that it can serve as a fiduciary under state law. They can take on many responsibilities commonly performed by the family office, including investment and financial management, accounting, and recordkeeping. They can also operate separately from the family office, while still relying on it for administrative and back-office support through a service contract.

ADVANTAGES Every family has its own reasons for establishing a PTC, but some of the primary advantages in most cases include:

- A permanent trustee that can adapt to changing family dynamics over time, as opposed to an individual trustee, which often presents succession concerns.
- The consistency and continuity of a trustee that is knowledgeable about the family. Because the PTC serves as a trustee and the board of directors includes several trusted advisers, ideally with differing ages and tenures, it preserves an advantageous institutional memory.
- Enhanced flexibility and control over decision-making. Families can choose board members, draft policies and procedures, structure the

organization to suit their needs, obtain voting power for important decisions, and arrange the distribution process to their liking.

- The ability to contribute to the investment and asset management process through serving on the investment committee of the PTC. In addition, families can be more involved in the drafting of the investment and asset management policies and procedures. This level of involvement is unlike that of a traditional trustee.

- Acting through directors and officers who have errors and omissions insurance provides increased liability protection for decision-makers.

- Better decision-making with respect to closely held and family-owned assets by involving multiple trusted advisers, including lawyers, accountants, investment managers, and others who are intimately familiar with family assets.

- Greater control over trustee fees and costs through ownership, involvement, and decision-making in the PTC.

- Enhanced privacy because the family has more control over the PTC and the disbursement of information. A large institution is not involved in day-to-day administration, and fewer people are privy to family issues and concerns. In addition, some states have laws that reflect this privacy concern.

- The ability to integrate the next generation into the administration of the family enterprise through involvement in board meetings, committees, and decision-making. This level of involvement is unlike that of a traditional trustee situation, in which family involvement can be somewhat limited.

- Families that utilize a family office structure are well equipped to transition to a PTC structure. The families can choose their longtime, trusted advisers to run the family PTC, all while concurrently integrating the next generation into the family's wealth planning and management.

- A PTC can be established in a tax-friendly state that doesn't levy state income or capital gains taxes on trusts.

- A family office may be exempt from registration as a registered investment adviser (RIA) if their PTC is regulated by state law and submits to some level of regulatory oversight.

- It potentially enjoys more flexibility in managing and investing trust assets, such as offering relief from pressure to diversify concentrated positions.

DISADVANTAGES As with all complex planning vehicles and governance structures, there are disadvantages particularly in the areas of increased administration, regulatory oversight, reporting, and costs. For PTCs these include:

- PTCs are relatively untested entities, although a growing number of states are adopting statutes to promote their use and there is an increasing body of knowledge and experience among tax and legal advisers regarding their use and requirements.
- When family members are involved in a PTC, there is the potential for family conflict if the trustee is not truly independent of family control.
- In addition to having high initial capitalization and start-up costs, a PTC has continuing administration costs.
- In cases of mismanagement, breach of trustees, or poor investment performance, family members may have little practical recourse against the fiduciary, as compared to recourse afforded by a corporate trustee (such as a bank or trust company).
- There are potential adverse estate, gift, generation-skipping transfer (GST), and income tax consequences if certain family members retain too much influence over specific PTC activities, such as distribution decisions.
- There are numerous regulatory, oversight, and financial reporting requirements.

PTC FORMATION Wealthy families typically choose family members, advisers, and/or commercial trustees with whom they have had personal, professional, or business relationships over the years to be their trustees. PTCs allow these individuals to continue to participate in the family operations and also provide them with additional governance, structure, and support, all while dramatically reducing their personal liability and providing many other key advantages.

A PTC is generally a limited liability company (LLC) or corporate entity that is typically 100 percent owned by the family and qualified to do business in the PTC jurisdiction, usually after acceptance by the jurisdiction's Division of Banking (DOB). The PTC then typically works with the family office, often located in the family's resident jurisdiction, via a service agreement to provide related services, such as investment advisory and management and asset allocation, as well as illiquid asset, real estate, and private equity management.

PTCs may be either regulated or unregulated. The regulated PTC generally receives a charter, and the unregulated PTC usually receives a license. The question of whether to establish a regulated or an unregulated PTC is important (as discussed next). The formalities associated with the regulated PTC, such as a charter, capital requirements, state audits, policy and procedures manuals, and compliance all help to ensure that the PTC is a properly functioning entity and trustee. Some unregulated PTCs also follow many of the formalities of the regulated PTCs to strengthen their position as viable trustee alternatives and hopefully prevent the ability to pierce the corporate veil. Other unregulated PTCs simply have the corporate agent keep their license in a drawer without many (if any) formalities, which could prove to be problematic.

SELECTING A JURISDICTION Typically, the PTC is located in a jurisdiction with favorable PTC laws, as well as favorable trust, asset protection, and tax laws. Some of the more popular PTC jurisdictions are Nevada, New Hampshire, South Dakota, Texas, and Wyoming, and some of the newer jurisdictions enacting PTC legislation include Florida, Ohio, and Tennessee. Family offices should consult with their attorneys to obtain an updated list of states that have enacted PTC statutes. When selecting a PTC jurisdiction, many families typically consider the following aspects:

- The jurisdiction's PTC laws
- Support of the PTC from the state legislature and governor
- Whether the jurisdiction has an accredited DOB with experience in and support for handling PTCs
- A corporate agent in the jurisdiction with experience in assisting with the PTC's formation, ongoing operation, compliance, and formalities
- A trustee agent in that jurisdiction with experience in providing trust administration
- Trust, asset protection, and tax laws of that jurisdiction
- Dynasty trust/rule against perpetuity statutes
- The economic conditions of the PTC jurisdiction

OWNERSHIP STRUCTURE The PTC ownership structure varies with each family. The most popular organizational entity for the PTC is generally an LLC, which is usually one or more of the following: (1) owned outright by the senior family member; (2) a purpose trust with dynasty provisions and no beneficiaries, whose sole purpose is to care for and perpetuate the PTC; (3) a nonpurpose dynasty trust with family member beneficiaries; and (4) a family trust.

The internal governance of the PTC (figure 11.2) is generally structured similar to a corporation, with a board of managers or directors that specifically appoints and works with separate committees, each comprised of family members and their trusted advisers. Typically, these committees are responsible for trust distributions and trust investments. Sometimes the investment and distributions committees are combined as one, or even made part of the board of managers. The requisite number of board members varies among the PTC jurisdictions, generally ranging from three to twelve. Further, while a few of the PTC jurisdictions may not require it, most families prefer to have at least one resident board member provide a closer nexus to the PTC, which can prove to be very beneficial.

SITUS REQUIREMENTS The PTC formation jurisdiction will often require the regulated PTC to have an office located there. Families will typically hire the services of a corporate agent in the PTC situs jurisdiction to fulfill this requirement. Consequently, the corporate agent provides a local nexus and gives a family the minimum statutory contacts necessary for the jurisdiction's PTC application process, as well as for the ongoing operation of the PTC. For example, a corporate agent in a regulated PTC jurisdiction might maintain three contracts with a family office in that jurisdiction: (1) a lease for the office and vault space; (2) a service agreement to answer the telephone, receive faxes, forward mail, and provide service of process; and (3) an arrangement for the corporate agent to serve as the local PTC director. These services generally provide the requisite contacts with the PTC jurisdiction without burdening the family with seeking out, hiring, and monitoring a staff in the jurisdiction, although many families elect to hire staff in the jurisdiction.

Moreover, while a corporate agent will generally satisfy the statutory situs requirements of a PTC, it may not be sufficient for maintaining a trust situs in the PTC jurisdiction. If this added benefit is desired,

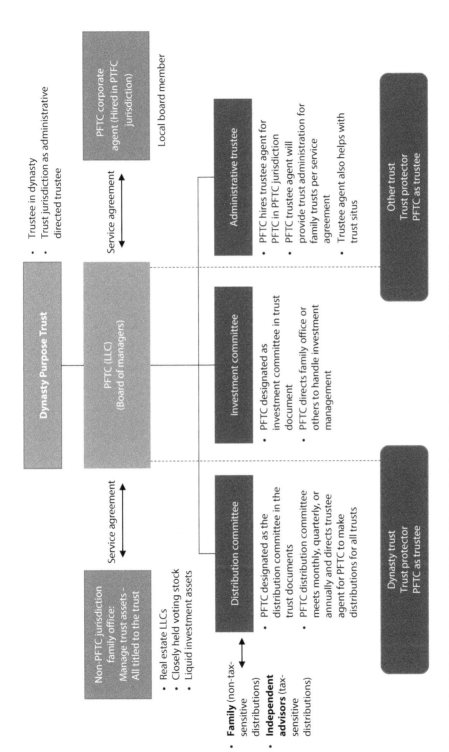

Figure 11.2 PTC chart *Source:* Al W. King III, South Dakota Trust Company, LLC (SDTC), 2016.

some corporate agents can also act as trustee agents to accomplish this goal, or, alternatively, the PTC can hire separate trustee agents that are independent of the corporate agent. A trustee agent hired by the trustee PTC can provide the necessary trust administration services in the PTC jurisdiction to validate trust situs in the jurisdiction, allowing the family to benefit from the favorable trust, asset protection, and tax laws of the jurisdiction, if the PTC is properly structured. Alternatively, most regulated PTC jurisdictions have reciprocity with other jurisdictions, thus possibly allowing the trust administration by the PTC to be done in the family's resident jurisdiction. This reciprocity usually applies only if the PTC is regulated. However, taking advantage of such reciprocity will generally preclude the PTC from taking advantage of the favorable trust, asset protection, and tax laws of the PTC jurisdiction because the trust needs to be administered properly in the PTC jurisdiction to accomplish this goal.

FORMALITIES It is extremely important to exercise the proper formalities with a regulated PTC regarding the PTC's ongoing operation. Generally, the key formalities include (1) shareholder, board, and committee meetings and minutes; (2) creation of and compliance with a policy and procedures manual; (3) annual trust account reviews; (4) trust investment policy statement reviews; (5) proper decision-making and documentation regarding trust distributions and investments; and (6) the PTC jurisdiction's DOB audits.

As a result of the PTC being owned by the family and named as a trustee for the family trusts, the family must be careful with the operation to avoid estate tax problems. While the Internal Revenue Service (IRS) no longer issues private letter rulings (PLRs) regarding the estate tax consequences of a family-owned PTC, it has offered some guidance by issuing IRS Revenue Notice 2008–63 and has determined that if structured and operated properly, a PTC will not result in any negative estate tax consequences. Although not binding, prior PLRs provide some additional guidance.

DECISIONS TO MAKE Once a family office chooses to establish a PTC, it must make several decisions. For example, in which jurisdiction should the PTC be established? Should it be regulated or unregulated? How will the PTC be organized? What kind of entity will it become (e.g., a corporation or LLC)? What about its ownership and governance structure? How will the PTC be compensated for services?

The first step is to determine the jurisdiction in which the PTC should be formed and, depending on that jurisdiction, whether the trust will be regulated or unregulated. A regulated PTC is chartered to offer trust services and is regulated under state or federal law. An unregulated PTC is incorporated in a state that allows a "limited purpose corporation," thus recognizing the unregulated PTC as providing fiduciary services to a single family.

Most states require that a PTC be fully regulated and have formal capital and policy requirements, as well as regulatory oversight and reporting requirements. A regulated PTC isn't required to register with the SEC as an RIA, and the state regulatory process makes independent review possible. This is because a trust company, which is supervised by state or federal authorities, satisfies the definition of a bank and isn't considered an investment adviser under the IAA (Investment Advisers Act of 1940).

By contrast, an unregulated PTC isn't chartered as a state trust company and generally is not subject to supervision, though it may perform limited fiduciary services. This kind of trust company may not create a common trust fund, although it offers families more privacy and is less expensive than a regulated PTC to form and operate. Consequently, such unregulated PTCs may have to satisfy the SEC's family office exemption rule to avoid its registration requirement.

Once a family office decides whether to formulate a PTC, its decision about whether to be regulated or unregulated will affect the choice of jurisdiction available to it. Family offices should check with their legal advisers to understand which states permit PTCs, and to receive guidance regarding the best jurisdiction in light of these and other family-specific needs and concerns. These concerns include the following:

- Costs of forming a PTC in addition to capital requirements
- The state's income taxes and their impacts on PTCs, trusts, grantors, and beneficiaries
- The state's applicable fiduciary laws and investment standards affecting the trustees and the trust

As a practical matter, the PTC's geographic location may also be a factor. Bear in mind that legal matters involving a trust must be handled in the trust's jurisdiction. For some families, having a PTC in a distant state may pose too many logistical difficulties because of the time and travel involved.

GOVERNANCE There are many issues to address when structuring a PTC, such as determining its purpose, as well as the roles and responsibilities of its shareholders, directors, and investment and distributions committees.

PTCs often take over the functions and formalize the structure of an existing family office and help preserve family privacy. In addition, the PTC creates a separate identity for dealing with the business world; centralizes administrative functions for the family, such as tax preparation and investment management; and segregates the family and investment functions from other family entities, such as a closely held family business.

There are two basic levels of governance and their composition:

- **Shareholders:** These people are responsible for electing the board of directors, approving amendments to bylaws and articles of incorporation, and approving extraordinary corporate actions, such as a merger and a recapitalization.
- **Directors:** These people are elected by the voting shareholders and are responsible for the daily business of the PTC, including hiring and compensation, operational matters, and appointing committees to assume specific functions. One to three directors are a practical size for this group, and they should include at least one person who's independent, with no beneficial interest in any trust for which the PTC acts as trustee, and should not be related or subordinate to a grantor or beneficiary of the trust. One independent director must serve at all times.

Potential adverse estate, gift, GST, or income tax consequences may arise if certain family members retain too much influence over specific PTC activities. Examples include when a grantor retains too much power over trust property and when a grantor may alter, amend, revoke, or terminate enjoyment of that property and cause unintended grantor status for tax purposes.

In selecting directors, shareholders need to bear in mind that the PTC's bylaws must prohibit any director or member of the trust's distributions committee from acting on or approving any discretionary distribution from a trust that such person or their spouse created or has a beneficial interest in. A "discretionary distribution" is defined as a distribution for any purpose in excess of health, education, maintenance, and support (known as an "ascertainable standard"). Such a limitation, therefore, heightens the importance of selecting independent directors for the trust.

Other Considerations

One of the benefits of establishing a PTC is that it allows the fiduciaries and employees to get to know the beneficiaries better than is typically possible with a corporate fiduciary. This provides both groups with greater insight into the needs and desires of the beneficiaries. This helps promote cohesion among the family and the trust company employees. It also facilitates governing the trusts in a manner that addresses the idiosyncratic needs of trust beneficiaries.[4]

ASSESSMENT AND ISSUES SURFACED

What Did We Learn?

John is enjoying having all his family with him during the holiday season and reflecting on his life and accomplishments. The children have also started to form adult identities, with jobs, interests, and families of their own. John is starting to think about governance mechanisms for both overseeing the family office and giving ongoing guidance to his children. This is a particularly important issue now, as John cannot, necessarily, plan for when there might be a need for a transition in the family office. These transitions require time to develop and integrate into how the family office operates and makes decisions. There is also an open question about the desired level of involvement by John's children and when and how they might be involved.

Case Questions

- What role can the family office play in helping John address and manage these concerns?

- Where might the family office look for guidance about appropriate governance structures and best practices?
- What are some key considerations for implementing governance structures and procedures for within the family office?
- Which governance processes and structures would make the most sense for the family at this point?
- Which governance processes and structures might make the most sense for the family in ten or twenty years?

RECOMMENDED SOLUTIONS

Responses to Case Questions

What role can the family office play in helping John address and manage these concerns?

In many ways, family offices should take the lead in introducing discussions about broader governance and related leadership succession issues. Principals of family offices often do not want to address this issue or postpone doing so because it entails both dealing with one's mortality and potentially giving up control. In this case, while John is the one introducing the topics, the family office should take the lead in developing and suggesting structures to John. Michael, in light of his experience and connections, is in a great position to gather information about how other family offices that are similar to John's in terms of size and family makeup govern themselves and provide mechanisms for succession.

Where might the family office look for guidance about appropriate governance structures and best practices?

Due to the ubiquity of governance issues for closely held family businesses, there is a great deal of academic study on the subject and numerous consulting resources available to these families. Family office professionals can look to this academic research and engage with consultants to learn about common approaches to succession and governance that can be tailored to the unique needs and attributes of their particular family office.

What are some key considerations for implementing governance structures and procedures for within the family office?

Governance structures should be developed around the unique needs, stakeholder makeup, and interpersonal dynamics within each family office. As a result, they vary even for very similar-looking families. This is also the reason why involving consultants can be very helpful in working with the family and family office to design governance policies and structures.

In the case of the Thorne family's evolution, formal governance procedures and structures are just starting to be implemented. This is because the family office is still largely controlled by John, and the children are still quite uninvolved. As a result, the family has no familiarity with or perceived immediate need for more formal governance, save for the intellectual arguments why some are needed and would be beneficial. In these cases, the family office can introduce more formal governance processes and structures in a measured way as they conduct their daily business and engage with family members.

Which governance processes and structures would make the most sense for the family at this point?

Regardless of any initial governance efforts, the family office should suggest and help the family host family meetings. These will be the first formal efforts to bring the family members together around common interests and needs, help promote communication, and provide an efficient recurring forum for education.

The family office could form an investment committee and start including the children in overseeing their investment portfolio. While the children may not be expected to actively engage initially, given their backgrounds and historic lack of involvement, involving them will start to acclimate them to a way of making decisions that has broader applications across other areas of governance need. In essence, the children will learn by watching how to behave, make decisions, and raise and resolve disputes.

Finally, the family office could suggest to John and Sofia that they consider developing a family constitution or important subelements of such a governing document, like a mission or vision statement. If they decide to do so, the family should engage with outside consultants to help them develop the statement, engage the children, draw out commonalities and differences, and mediate discussions.

Which governance processes and structures might make the most sense for the family in ten or twenty years?

In ten to twenty years, the family's makeup and needs will be quite different than they are today. As a result, the governance structures and mechanisms will also be different. Key changes will include a much larger and more diverse group of family members and a management structure that by necessity includes select family members, outsiders, or both. At this point in the future, it would not be unlikely to have a number of governance structures, including a family assembly that represents all the family members, a family council that includes selected family members who represent various constituent groups, and perhaps an advisory board for the family office leadership and professionals themselves. The family might also consider creating a PTC to formalize many of these governance needs and efforts via a more institutionalized process by outside professionals, but where they can retain a level of control.

CHAPTER TWELVE

Succession and Leadership Insights

CASE STUDY

Summary

- Ten years after the creation of the Left Seat Management family office
- Michael is retiring, and John is hiring a new chief executive officer (CEO) to replace him
- Insights into what Michael has learned

Key Words/Concepts

- Succession within a family office
- Leadership insights

Challenge

For the last few years, Michael had been preparing John and Sofia for the fact that he intended to retire in the next few years. During his years running the family office, he had become very close to both of them and knew the significance of this change. The family office was not just a resource to John and Sofia; their professionals were an extension of their family, much as the senior management team had been at Rybat Manufacturing. However, in this case, the importance of maintaining this unique and important relationship could not be overstated due to how deeply the family office touched and affected the lives of everyone, particularly the children.

Michael understood and appreciated these facts and took his responsibilities for this transition very seriously. Three years earlier, he began planning his retirement. This included communicating his intentions to John, Sofia, and the senior professionals at Left Seat Management; instituting a number of important governance structures; and developing important wealth education programs for the children.

He also engaged a recruiter to help the family find a suitable replacement for him. The recruiter worked with John, Sofia, and Michael to identify candidates with both the professional and personal qualifications that would be needed to oversee such an important job. This was a lengthy process and had taken the better part of a year. They had found a great CEO successor, someone uniquely suited to help the family office manage not only its current challenges, but those that lay ahead of them due to the changing needs and roles of the various stakeholders.

The new CEO, Tracey (age fifty), had been a partner at a well-respected venture capital firm based in Minneapolis. In this role, she invested in both companies and people and as a result had great insights into managerial and governance best practices. This would be important as the family office transitioned over the next several years from mainly serving the needs of only John and Sofia to those of a wider and more complex infrastructure of family members, structures, and activities. Tracey also had significant private investing experience, which was important given the large and growing commitment that the family office was making to direct investing. Finally, she worked extremely well with the Thorne children and was closely connected to them, by virtue of both age and areas of investment interest, particularly impact investing.

Tracey, however, did not have private client experience, certainly as it related to managing a large family office. It was in this area that Michael felt that he could be a great immediate resource for her. He scheduled a meeting with her to discuss many of the unique managerial and service dynamics that come with working for a wealthy family and within a family office.

BACKGROUND INFORMATION

Succession

Transitions in senior personnel at a family office can be very challenging and tremendously disruptive to both the principals and the family office staff. This is not unique to family offices, but most family offices are quite small, with select individuals that have an outsized influence over the organization, and very few have an experienced second-in-command who can take over.

Further complicating transitions is the fact that great senior leaders at a family office are deeply connected with family members on a personal level, and the family has placed their confidence and trust in them over many years. This relationship can be hard to replace, and it is very difficult to assess these qualities in candidates for the top job. While a great deal of work can and should be put into assessing fit at this level, there is always an amount of unpredictability.

Finally, relatively newer family offices, as well as those created by the primary generation after a liquidity event, are likely still undergoing a series of changes and adjustments as responsibilities increase, principals become more experienced, and the family grows in age, service needs, and expectations. Transitions in leadership create both an opportunity and a challenge in this respect. For some families, hiring a new leader who will continue to manage the family office and guide the family in a manner similar to the way their predecessor did can be a positive or a negative enterprise. As families evolve and mature, so do their needs, and occasionally the nature of leadership needed by the family office as well. Examples include families transitioning from one generation to the next; those that have strategically or behaviorally decided to focus more on one particular area (such as direct or impact investing); and ones where oversight and management need to be conducted through formal governance vehicles, structures, and committees, as opposed to by individuals, whether it be a family member or family office CEO. In these cases, it is possible that the family office not only needs new leadership, but also different skills and experiences in that leader.

Determining the Path Forward

For many of the reasons stated previously, a transition in leadership provides a wealthy family with the opportunity to assess what they have relative to what they need. They should consider their priorities, preferences, and requirements, both now and in the immediate future. For some families, this will be the first time that they do this sort of strategic planning. Further, families should reflect on what they like and do not like about the family office and services that they have provided.

Perhaps there were some needs not being met in an adequate or timely way, which would warrant hiring someone who can better focus on delivering these. They might consider whether certain functions should be outsourced, thereby allowing them to allocate time, personnel, and resources to other more important needs. Finally, the family and family office professionals could consider inviting other families to use the services of the office, thereby creating a multifamily office (MFO), particularly if the family office is overseeing the needs of a diverse group of next-generation, adult family members or branches. For obvious reasons, engaging in these types of discussions informs the decision about whom they need to hire because they help clarify what the family office should do going forward.

Process

When hiring for senior leadership positions within a family office, principals should follow the prescribed process outlined in Section One, including giving serious consideration to the use of a recruiting firm. The family office industry is still quite small relative to both the number of family offices (as compared to other industries) and the prevalence of senior professionals who have both the relevant skills and the necessary personality and demeanor. For these reasons, relying on experts who are both connected to qualified candidates and experienced at assessing fit has paramount importance.

This process should include having candidates spend time with not only the principals and senior family office staff, but also any adult children and important outside advisors. These are all important stakeholders who will be interacting with and relying upon the new leader. While it is possible that a great candidate will present themself early, it is also often the case that a search can take many months, if not years. Families should not be put off by this because making the wrong hire is often difficult to unwind, and not only that, it may cause more damage than waiting for the right hire.

Leadership Insights

Family offices have many basic characteristics in common with commercial businesses, particularly professional and financial services firms. This is because they provide services and advice to wealthy, complex "clients" and because the organizational structures and staffing are, by necessity, similar. Indeed, a number of family offices evolve into providing services to numerous families, both related and unrelated, and in so doing compete against traditional professional and financial services firms (so-called MFOs).

Yet, as it pertains to leadership (and in other areas), they differ in a number of material respects due to (1) the unique nature of family offices (e.g., initially controlled by involved principals), (2) the captive nature of the environment for both the family and the family office personnel (e.g., exclusive versus multiple service providers for the family, and single versus multiple clients for the employees), and (3) the intimate nature of the services they provide (e.g., bill paying, lifestyle, and concierge). Moreover, family offices are idiosyncratic and unlike each other in myriad ways, which is typically the result of the personalities of the principals and what was referred to in chapter 1.

The following are a number of unique leadership insights gleaned from those who have worked for and with family offices.[1]

Understanding Motivations

Family offices are not in the business of making a profit, at least by the standards applied to businesses. This can make it hard for a family office to orient their activities and resources toward quantifiable goals such as shareholder value, revenue growth, and net income. Yes, family offices invest money and often have return or risk targets and ranges. They also have budgets and financial forecasts that indeed are measurable and quantifiable.

However, these are seldom the most important motives for principals and/or their family members. It is, therefore, important for family office executives to understand what drives family members so they can properly orient the family office and its activities toward helping them achieve their goals. Examples of these categories are lifestyle, philanthropy, direct investing, hobbies, and family harmony, the measurement of which can be quite subjective depending on family members' interests. Despite the challenges of measuring outcomes in these areas, family office executives should endeavor to identify them and do their best to manage their time, the office, and the staff to ensure that the principals and/or their family members have the greatest chance of success at achieving them.

Leadership through Teaching

There is a well-known saying among equestrians: "You can't force a horse to do something, only suggest it." The same goes for family office principals. Family offices are, at the end of the day, simply management organizations established to oversee the wealth and personal affairs of the principals. It is their money, after all, and senior executives at family offices are wise to remember this fact.

Leadership within a family office is often best conducted through education and behavioral examples, as opposed to by executive fiat. While the term "servant leadership" typically describes a leadership style that emphasizes the education and growth of employees, it can be modified in the context of family offices to include educating principals through leadership actions. As has been discussed many times throughout this book, the issues that come with substantial wealth are not necessarily those with which a principal is familiar, whether it is managing complex assets, overseeing a large liquid and nonliquid investment portfolio, or pursuing philanthropic ambitions. Senior leadership within a family should anticipate this point and recognize that solutions to many of these challenges must be introduced, explained, and addressed in a manner that educates and acclimates very successful and confident principals.

Aligning Focus and Resources

It is often said that there are three "who's": who we think we are; who others see us as; and who we really are. In the context of family offices, there are three "what's": what the family office spends its time on; what they should be spending their time on; and what the principals would like them to spend their time on (in either stated or unstated goals).

Probably the best example of this is in the area of accounting and finance. Chief financial officers (CFOs) of family offices will almost universally say that they spend more time and resources on this than what they think they should. And, for most principals, this is not an area of great interest to them, other than making sure that the bills get paid, there is proper reporting, and that both are done in a timely and accurate fashion.

In resource-constrained family offices—usually newer ones that have not yet invested in the resources and personnel to manage this imbalance—this often means that the time invested by leadership and staff in this area does not align with either what senior leadership believes should be required or the key areas of interest of the principals. Senior executives need to be mindful of this and make sure that they request and receive (if possible) the resources they need so they can devote an appropriate amount of their time, and the staff's time, on matters and opportunities of greater interest to the principals and their families. This might include, for example, sports teams, philanthropy, and direct investments.

Service Expectations

Not unsurprisingly, principals and their family members have high expectations for service, responsiveness, execution, and insights. This can create a challenge for family office employees, inasmuch as it sets a high-water mark in terms of service and its delivery, whether by the family office or outside advisors. For understandable reasons, the family office will not be able to ensure excellence in execution across all the various service and advisory needs of wealthy families. For example, there are only so many times that the office can secure backstage passes to the Rolling Stones, obtain timely backup pilots, or ensure that the hotel in Italy properly accommodates and treats the family. However, they must be prepared for, and be able to handle gracefully, both reasonable and (occasionally) unreasonable demands and criticisms.

Differing Perspectives

Family office executives often make the mistake of consciously or unconsciously applying their own standards and beliefs to decision-making for allocations of capital, resources, or time by, or on behalf of, the principals. This is understandable inasmuch as family office professionals, particularly less senior staff, have neither the means of nor close personal experience with individuals of significant wealth. In so doing, they run the risk of failing to understand, anticipate, and suggest opportunities and solutions that make sense for the principals applicable to their perspective. This might include things like seemingly extravagant expenditures, excessive liquidity, or vanity investments that are sure to lose money. It is important for executives and staff to be mindful of this, and to balance providing thoughtful advice about cost/benefits with an appreciation for the relative impact of choices that the principals make from their financial perspective.

ASSESSMENT AND ISSUES SURFACED

What Did We Learn?

Having gone through a very thoughtful and extended process to find his successor, Michael is now focused on helping set Tracey up for success by making sure that she understands many of the unique dynamics that come with working for wealthy families. These are often things that executives don't realize and learn until they have been on the inside of the workings of a family office.

Case Questions

- What are a number of challenges that family offices face when trying to find and hire new employees, and in particular senior leadership?
- What did Michael do well to help manage these challenges?

- What examples might Michael share with Tracey of unique managerial issues with respect to each of the key leadership areas, whether at Left Seat Management or in a hypothetical scenario?

RECOMMENDED SOLUTIONS

Responses to Case Questions

What are a number of challenges that family offices face when trying to find and hire new employees, and in particular senior leadership?

While the family office industry is indeed maturing and professionalizing, it is still early in its evolution relative to other industries. As a result, established hiring practices, resources, and industry-knowledgeable applicants are in short supply. In addition, principals at family offices are often loath to use recruiters and instead prioritize hiring individuals with whom they are familiar because the CEO of the family office is such an important and personal role. Furthermore, even if they are open to using a recruiter, principals rarely know where to go for help or how to assess candidates properly.

What did Michael do well to help manage these challenges?

As a former wealth management industry professional who worked with wealthy families and family offices before, Michael was well aware of these issues and instituted a professional process for finding his replacement. This process included a number of important steps, including the following:

- Communicating early his intention to retire in order to socialize it with the family and allow them time to process, prepare, and plan
- Using the services of a recruiter to not only help them source candidates, but also to evaluate the candidates in light of the family's unique needs and members' personality types
- Sitting down with Tracey to provide her with some unique insights that pertain to family offices generally, as well as the Thorne family specifically

What examples might Michael share with Tracey
of unique managerial issues with respect to each of the
key leadership areas, whether at Left Seat Management
or in a hypothetical scenario?

UNDERSTANDING MOTIVATIONS John has a number of great interests, including private aviation and direct investing. Likewise, Sofia is increasingly active and interested in a number of specific areas of philanthropy. The family office dedicated resources to each, including developing a flight department and initiating strategic discussions with philanthropic consultants. However, it is clear through the investments that Michael made in these areas, such as hiring a CIO and an analyst and creating a flight department, that he recognized the importance of each of these areas to John and Sofia.

LEADERSHIP THROUGH TEACHING While John was certainly an accomplished businessman, he did not have a great deal of experience investing across multiple asset classes, and certainly not at his newfound level of wealth. Michael, on the other hand, had spent his career in financial services and understood both the space and its players quite well. However, John was used to managing his own affairs, including indulging his penchant for private investing. As a result, he initially relied on his legacy advisers to bring him ideas from which he would choose investments.

To be successful, Michael would likely have taken his time executing a new investment strategy by "bringing John along" through a combination of specific recommendations and education, as opposed to by executive fiat (to the extent that such a power exists within a family office). The migration to a more institutional portfolio management approach, away from John's long-standing financial advisers, would be one example.

ALIGNING FOCUS AND RESOURCES It is difficult to say, based on the limited case study information provided, whether Michael and the family office aligned their resources properly relative to John's and Sofia's stated (and unstated) needs and desires. The success that Michael had by staying in his position for ten years and the respect and affection he developed with both of the principals suggests that he did a good job. Where understanding the importance of aligning focus and resources might be better illustrated is in the area of consolidated reporting. As was made clear in the case study, the demands of keeping track of all the investments and related activities had outstripped the personnel resources and technologies of the family office at one point. As a result, the office made changes that allowed them to address the need for timely and accurate reporting in a manner that did not divert resources from other areas of greater importance to John and Sofia.

While this may seem like an obvious and inevitable area where family offices recognize the need for change in order to align focus and resources properly, that is not always the case. It is quite common for family offices to retain outdated and time-consuming technologies in spite of the impact on time and resources needed elsewhere. This lack of proper attention to the needed realignment of focus and resources can manifest itself in constant delays or mistakes in reporting that will be noticed by the principals, and for which senior executives at the family office will be held accountable.

SERVICE EXPECTATIONS There are a number of areas where service expectations by wealthy families set a high bar for family office staff. While there are not many examples where the professionals at Left Seat Management failed to meet or even exceed the expectations of John and Sofia, it is not hard to imagine the areas where this could happen. Examples include problems with making the plane available due to pilot staffing, broken lights at the Cabo San Lucas house because staff failed to check which ones needed to be replaced, and an embarrassing spelling mistake made on the invitations that Sofia sent out for a charity fundraising gala. While it is impossible to avoid mistakes or to be able to anticipate service errors or disruptions by third-party vendors, family office professionals must pay strict attention to each and every detail in all areas of service to family members. Further, they must be able to handle the problems or issues that inevitably come up right away, and in a professional manner.

DIFFERING PERSPECTIVES One of the most obvious examples where wealthy families can (and do) spend a great deal more than they otherwise need to is in the area of private aviation. While there are numerous legitimate reasons to fly privately—from time efficiency to scheduling flexibility to personal security—it is for many

principals an indispensable luxury and one for which the brutal economics of owning a private plane are not considered. While it was
mentioned, but not discussed in detail, John's choice for a jet, the
Challenger 350, was more than he needed to ferry his family to and
from Cabo San Lucas. There are many less expensive planes that
could make that trip without stopping, and given his relatively infre-
quent use, there also are more cost-effective options, such as charter
or fractional planes.

Industry Data and Resources

ONE OF the reasons behind publishing this book is that data on family offices, while increasingly available, is dispersed across multiple providers through episodic surveys, reports, and white papers. (The same can be said of technical reference materials across the multitude of service and advisory areas.) There is no single repository for this data when it comes out from the various wealth management and professional services firms, consultants and advisers, service providers, trade organizations, academic institutions, and networks and clubs.

The authors have endeavored to collect much of this information and make it available in one location with the express permission of the parties involved. This information can be found at www.thefamilyofficebook.com, which catalogs select surveys, reports, and white papers of relevance to academics, students, principals, practitioners, advisers, and vendors interested in learning more about family offices, their practices, and their behaviors across multiple areas, as well as the industry overall.

This section provides data collected about family offices through a number of surveys, reports, and white papers in the following areas:

- Demographics
- Investment allocations
- Costs
- Compensation
- Risk and threat management

CHAPTER THIRTEEN

The Numbers

DEMOGRAPHICS

How many family offices are in operation today? No one really knows. Their penchant for privacy and avoiding the limelight helps most of them to remain largely anonymous. Many are embedded within private companies, further shielding them from public awareness. If and when those companies are sold, the founding families may set up formally dedicated entities to handle their affairs and manage the wealth derived from their business sales. Sometimes family office functions are supported on an informal basis by family members or operating company employees, with no separate legal entity established for that purpose. In other cases, families may pool their resources to jointly hire professionals to serve them and thus benefit from economies of scale. Whatever their approach, these families have several characteristics in common: They face the challenges of managing substantial wealth. They need ongoing services from dedicated professionals. Also, they often want to delegate significant leeway and authority to those professionals in handling their day-to-day wealth management needs.

One way to gauge the number of family offices is by identifying the number of families that have a sufficient net worth so that the issues and challenges of substantial wealth typically exist, and the requirement to rely upon others for assistance can be reasonably assumed.

Globally, there are approximately 18,000 ultra-high-net-worth (UHNW) families worth $250 million or more.[1] While it is unknown whether these families all have family offices, or leverage a family office solution through one of the various forms discussed in Section One, what is known is that the issues that warrant a family office easily present themselves at this level of wealth. It can be reasonably assumed, therefore, that most will be employing multiple professionals to help them manage their affairs. Contrariwise, many families with less than $250 million also find reason to establish a family office and so the actual number of family offices will differ but could easily be higher based on the methodology we are employing. Figure 13.1 provides an approximate distribution of family offices around the world for those UHNW families worth $250 million or more.

These families control an extraordinary and disproportionate amount of wealth. Of the approximately $32 trillion in global wealth, UHNW families worth $250 million or more control approximately $16 trillion.[2] This represents half of all the wealth controlled by UHNW families globally.[3]

An increasing number of surveys are being done on family offices, although their use is somewhat limited to providing a snapshot in time over the respondents' *average* and *range* of investing behavior, compensation practices, operating costs, and trends and concerns. As a result, they are helpful inasmuch as they provide a look at the practices

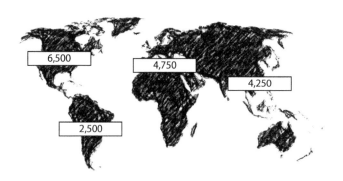

Figure 13.1 World map of family offices

of other family offices across a number of attributes. However, they are not necessarily definitive about how a particular family office should (or does) invest their assets, structure their organizations, compensate their employees, or prioritize concerns.

Included next are select survey results regarding family office asset allocations, operating and investment management fees and other costs, senior executive compensation, and risk and threat management concerns and practices.

INVESTMENT ALLOCATIONS

A 2019 survey of 360 families broadly dispersed globally (figure 13.2), and with approximately 80 percent of the respondents representing single-family offices (SFOs), as opposed to multiple-family offices (MFOs) (figure 13.3), found the following:[4]

- Global equities and private equity continue to constitute the top asset classes that family offices invest in, with portfolio shares of 32 percent and 19 percent, respectively (figure 13.4).
- Going forward, family offices aim to further diversify their portfolios, with significant numbers reporting that they plan to make larger allocations to developing market equities, private equity, and real estate.

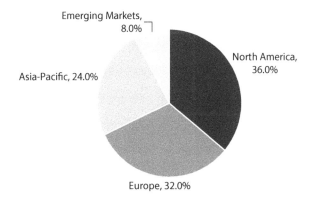

Geographic Location

Emerging Markets, 8.0%

Asia-Pacific, 24.0%

North America, 36.0%

Europe, 32.0%

Figure 13.2 World geography of family offices *Source*: Campden Wealth and UBS, "Global Family Office Report 2019," Campden Wealth and UBS, 2019.

Family Office Type

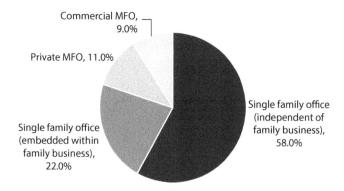

Figure 13.3 Types of family offices *Source*: Campden Wealth and UBS, "Global Family Office Report 2019," Campden Wealth and UBS, 2019.

Asset Allocation

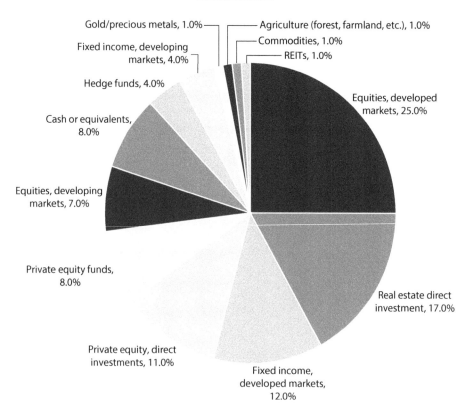

Figure 13.4 Asset allocation *Source*: Campden Wealth and UBS, "Global Family Office Report 2019," Campden Wealth and UBS, 2019.

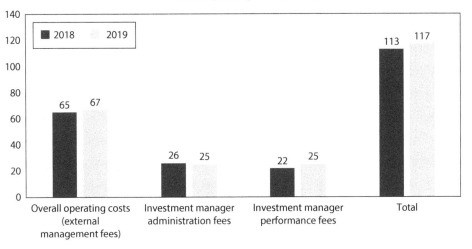

Figure 13.5 Operating costs *Source*: Campden Wealth and UBS, "Global Family Office Report 2019," Campden Wealth and UBS, 2019.

COSTS

The costs to run a family office vary greatly based on the number of employees; the office's location, responsibilities, and portfolio allocation; and the experience and backgrounds of both the principals and senior executives. Figure 13.5 shows the average expenses as a percentage of assets under management (AUM) according to the respondents to the 2019 global survey previously mentioned. It is important to note that the average wealth and AUM for the SFO respondents were $1.3 billion and $802 million, respectively. For family offices with fewer AUMs, the average costs will undoubtedly be higher as a percentage of assets managed. The findings included the following:

- In 2019, the total average spending of family offices on services stood at $11.8 million, including $6.8 million in operational costs and $5.1 million in external investment management administration and performance fees.
- Family offices spent an average of $1.5 million (14 basis points) on general advisory services, $2.5 million (25 basis points) on

TABLE 13.1
SFO and MFO costs of individual services from main service categories

	TOTAL SFO + MFO			SFO			MFO		
	Proportion of operating costs (%)	Operating cost of each service (BP)	Operating cost for the average FO (USD)*	Proportion of operating costs (%)	Operating cost of each service (BP)	Operating cost for the average FO (USD)*	Proportion of operating costs (%)	Operating cost of each service (BP)	Operating cost for the average FO (USD)
General advisory services	**22**	**14**	**1,515,000**	**21**	**14**	**1,196,000**	**25**	**16**	**2,474,000**
Financial planning		4.3	469,000		3.7	313,000		6.1	936,000
Tax planning		3.2	332,000		3.2	273,000		3.3	506,000
Estate planning		1.8	202,000		1.5	130,000		2.7	416,000
Legal services		2.4	237,000		2.6	220,000		1.9	285,000
Insurance planning		0.7	75,000		0.8	65,000		0.7	104,000
Trust management		2.1	202,000		2.3	194,000		1.5	227,000
Investment-related activities	**38**	**25**	**2,543,000**	**38**	**25**	**2,155,000**	**38**	**24**	**3,707,000**
Asset allocation		4.7	512,000		4.1	353,000		6.4	990,000
Risk management		2.0	219,000		1.9	160,000		2.6	396,000
Manager selection/oversight		2.9	316,000		2.7	230,000		3.7	574,000
Private banking		1.1	107,000		1.2	100,000		0.8	127,000
Traditional investments		1.8	182,000		1.8	158,000		1.7	256,000
Alternative investments		2.4	235,000		2.5	218,000		1.9	285,000
Real estate		2.8	269,000		3.2	276,000		1.6	245,000
Investment banking functions		1.4	144,000		1.4	121,000		1.4	214,000
Financial accounting/reporting		3.4	331,000		3.8	326,000		2.2	345,000

	$	BP	%	$	BP	%	$	BP	%
Global custody and integrated investment reporting	119,000	0.8		91,000	1.1		98,000	1.0	
Foreign exchange management	47,000	0.3		24,000	0.3		29,000	0.3	
Philanthropy	110,000	0.7		98,000	1.1		101,000	1.0	
Family professional services	**1,650,000**	**11**	17	**838,000**	**10**	15	**1,041,000**	**10**	15
Concierge services and security	123,000	0.8		151,000	1.8		144,000	1.5	
Family counselling/relationship management	260,000	1.7		92,000	1.1		134,000	1.2	
Family governance and succession planning	566,000	3.7		197,000	2.3		290,000	2.6	
Management of high-value physical assets (e.g., property, art, yachts)	312,000	2.0		175,000	2.0		209,000	2.0	
Support for new family business and other projects	388,000	2.5		222,000	2.6		264,000	2.6	
Administrative activities	**2,015,000**	**13**	20	**1,534,000**	**18**	27	**1,654,000**	**17**	25
IT costs	275,000	1.8		207,000	2.4		224,000	2.3	
Office overhead	882,000	5.7		555,000	6.5		637,000	6.3	
Accounting	603,000	3.9		495,000	5.8		522,000	5.3	
Other office services	255,000	1.7		277,000	3.2		271,000	2.8	
TOTAL:	**9,846,000**	**64**		**5,722,000**	**67**		**6,753,000**	**66**	
Administration/management	**3,854,000**	**25**		**2,061,000**	**23**		**2,510,000**	**24**	
Performance	**3,231,000**	**21**		**2,322,000**	**26**		**2,549,000**	**25**	

Source: Campden Wealth and UBS, "Global Family Office Report 2019", Campden Wealth and UBS, 2019.
* Figures may not sum to 100% due to rounding. Total costs (bps) do not match those in Figure s4.5 because the numbers in Figure 13.5 are based on participants who provided more data.
Note: BP = basis points; FO = family office

investment-related activities, $1 million (10 basis points) on family professional services, and $1.7 million (17 basis points) on administration activities.

- Family offices are, on average, spending less in 2019 compared to 2018 on internal investment-related services ($2.5 million), and more on family professional services ($1 million) and general advisory services ($1.5 million).

Costs (by Service Area)

Table 13.1 shows the costs for individual services according to the same survey respondents.

COMPENSATION

The following is a summary of findings from a family office compensation consulting firm that the authors believe most accurately represent the level of compensation paid to family office senior executives as of mid-2020 (notwithstanding caveats regarding the application and accuracy of the data due to things such as the geographic location of the office, backgrounds of the principals, experience and backgrounds of the candidates, etc.).[5]

The positions shown in tables 13.2 through 13.5 include chief executive officer (CEO), chief investment officer (CIO), chief financial officer (CFO), and chief operating officer (COO), respectively. Compensation data for the following additional positions can be found at www.thefamilyofficebook.com:

- General counsel
- Comptroller
- Portfolio manager
- Tax manager
- Investment analyst
- Accountant
- Executive assistant
- Bookkeeper
- Property manager

TABLE 13.2
CEO compensation

More than $2 billion	10th percentile	25th percentile	Median	75th percentile	90th percentile
Base salary	$449,300	$524,900	$682,300	$830,400	$1,288,800
Total cash comp	$639,500	$734,800	$946,200	$2,173,000	$3,096,800
Total direct comp	$639,500	$734,800	$946,200	$2,204,500	$3,186,800
$1-$1.9 billion	**10th percentile**	**25th percentile**	**Median**	**75th percentile**	**90th percentile**
Base salary	$342,200	$452,800	$572,100	$734,800	$1,028,200
Total cash comp	$451,600	$579,300	$903,300	$1,369,500	$1,736,500
Total direct comp	$476,000	$579,300	$935,800	$1,491,300	$2,118,700
$500–$999 million	**10th percentile**	**25th percentile**	**Median**	**75th percentile**	**90th percentile**
Base salary	$296,500	$346,400	$394,700	$524,900	$606,800
Total cash comp	$418,300	$497,900	$665,100	$861,900	$1,396,200
Total direct comp	$418,300	$503,700	$682,200	$972,900	$1,396,200
$300–$499 million	**10th percentile**	**25th percentile**	**Median**	**75th percentile**	**90th percentile**
Base salary	$220,700	$283,600	$380,300	$465,200	$551,100
Total cash comp	$232,000	$365,100	$433,600	$549,900	$739,000
Total direct comp	$232,000	$365,100	$433,600	$561,600	$783,100
$100–$299 million	**10th percentile**	**25th percentile**	**Median**	**75th percentile**	**90th percentile**
Base salary	$199,800	$249,300	$314,900	$406,800	$550,100
Total cash comp	$237,200	$291,000	$393,700	$556,400	$651,000
Total direct comp	$237,200	$295,300	$410,500	$572,100	$787,300

Source: Trish Botoff, Botoff Consulting, 2019.

TABLE 13.3
CIO compensation

	10th %tile	25th %tile	Median	75th %tile	90th %tile
More than $2 billion					
Base Salary	$357,400	$368,600	$478,700	$873,600	$1,271,300
Total Cash Comp	$498,600	$608,700	$805,400	$1,096,100	$2,800,100
TDC	$530,200	$675,000	$881,000	$1,249,500	$2,800,100
$1–$1.9 Billion	**10th %tile**	**25th %tile**	**Median**	**75th %tile**	**90th %tile**
Base Salary	$332,000	$367,400	$446,200	$500,600	$601,100
Total Cash Comp	$372,500	$454,400	$761,100	$1,037,700	$1,745,900
TDC	$435,500	$486,500	$761,100	$1,198,900	$1,774,300
$500–$999 Million	**10th %tile**	**25th %tile**	**Median**	**75th %tile**	**90th %tile**
Base Salary	$230,800	$271,700	$419,900	$485,500	$552,800
Total Cash Comp	$373,800	$471,000	$543,300	$657,800	$860,800
TDC	$373,800	$471,000	$567,200	$743,900	$900,000
$300–$499 million	**10th %tile**	**25th %tile**	**Median**	**75th %tile**	**90th %tile**
Base Salary	$196,100	$219,200	$277,000	$362,500	$391,000
Total Cash Comp	$265,100	$300,200	$373,300	$416,800	$522,300
TDC	$265,100	$300,200	$396,300	$518,400	$725,100
$100–$299 million	**10th %tile**	**25th %tile**	**Median**	**75th %tile**	**90th %tile**
Base Salary	$201,600	$241,000	$271,700	$337,400	$456,600
Total Cash Comp	$237,800	$294,800	$367,400	$484,800	$693,400
TDC	$237,800	$294,800	$367,400	$563,100	$748,000

Source: Trish Botoff, Botoff Consulting, 2019.

TABLE 13.4
CFO compensation

More than $2 billion	10th percentile	25th percentile	Median	75th percentile	90th percentile
Base salary	$265,900	$316,300	$393,700	$469,100	$495,000
Total cash comp	$332,400	$388,400	$472,400	$672,500	$811,600
Total direct comp	$332,400	$412,000	$506,800	$672,500	$893,400
$1-$1.9 billion	**10th percentile**	**25th percentile**	**Median**	**75th percentile**	**90th percentile**
Base salary	$225,700	$262,400	$314,900	$362,200	$614,100
Total cash comp	$264,300	$367,400	$446,200	$566,900	$723,100
Total direct comp	$289,500	$367,400	$446,200	$618,400	$723,100
$500-$999 million	**10th percentile**	**25th percentile**	**Median**	**75th percentile**	**90th percentile**
Base salary	$194,600	$212,600	$283,400	$333,800	$438,300
Total cash comp	$278,200	$314,900	$419,800	$549,900	$631,500
Total direct comp	$278,200	$314,900	$423,000	$549,900	$631,500
$300-$499 million	**10th percentile**	**25th percentile**	**Median**	**75th percentile**	**90th percentile**
Base salary	$195,300	$233,600	$254,000	$276,100	$333,300
Total cash comp	$244,600	$269,200	$274,500	$308,400	$439,300
Total direct comp	$244,600	$269,200	$274,500	$308,400	$439,300
$100-$299 million	**10th percentile**	**25th percentile**	**Median**	**75th percentile**	**90th percentile**
Base salary	$148,000	$189,000	$227,800	$262,400	$307,600
Total cash comp	$168,000	$205,800	$262,400	$320,200	$392,000
Total direct comp	$168,000	$205,800	$265,400	$320,200	$436,100

Source: Trish Botoff, Botoff Consulting, 2019.

TABLE 13.5
COO compensation

More than $2 billion	10th percentile	25th percentile	Median	75th percentile	90th percentile
Base salary	$269,000	$360,700	$575,400	$944,500	$1,800,500
Total cash comp	$365,200	$417,100	$663,900	$1,559,100	$1,937,500
Total direct comp	$365,200	$442,200	$663,900	$1,574,900	$1,937,500
$1-$1.9 billion	**10th percentile**	**25th percentile**	**Median**	**75th percentile**	**90th percentile**
Base salary	$290,100	$312,900	$376,000	$418,600	$529,800
Total cash comp	$357,400	$417,200	$500,500	$632,600	$1,036,500
Total direct comp	$378,300	$431,100	$500,500	$632,600	$1,036,500
$500–$999 million	**10th percentile**	**25th percentile**	**Median**	**75th percentile**	**90th percentile**
Base salary	$223,100	$262,400	$288,700	$373,900	$550,100
Total cash comp	$317,600	$334,700	$418,300	$577,400	$619,400
Total direct comp	$317,600	$334,700	$418,300	$629,900	$708,300
$300–$499 million	**10th percentile**	**25th percentile**	**Median**	**75th percentile**	**90th percentile**
Base salary	$200,600	$226,200	$258,300	$316,700	$372,000
Total cash comp	$233,500	$282,400	$376,300	$384,200	$399,500
Total direct comp	$233,500	$282,400	$376,300	$397,500	$461,600
$100–$299 million	**10th percentile**	**25th percentile**	**Median**	**75th percentile**	**90th percentile**
Base salary	$157,500	$174,100	$207,300	$245,400	$323,400
Total cash comp	$175,100	$196,900	$232,000	$278,800	$529,800
Total direct comp	$175,100	$199,100	$232,000	$278,800	$558,400

Source: Trish Botoff, Botoff Consulting, 2019.

RISK AND THREAT MANAGEMENT

The following data provides additional information on risk and threat management concerns and practices for family offices.[6] These findings come from a 2020 survey conducted of more than 200 family offices regarding their perceptions of various risks and threats and what they are doing to mitigate them. The survey uncovered a number of insights about the risk and threat management state of the industry. The following are a number of interesting findings from that survey.

Over 25 percent of family offices have been hacked.

These figures, which are in line with other surveys in the family office space, demonstrate the grave threat that families face from a cybersecurity perspective despite their concentrated efforts to lower their public profile and the risk mitigation mechanisms already in place (figure 13.6).

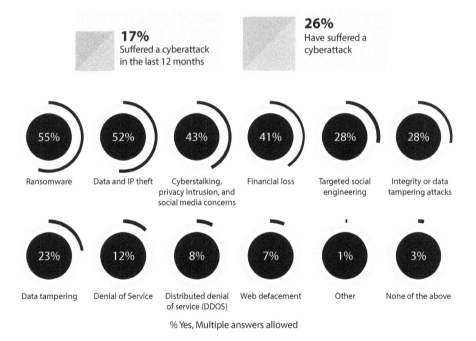

Figure 13.6 Hacking of family offices *Source*: Boston Private, Dentons, McNally Capital, The Chertoff Group, and Data Tribe, "Family Office Risk and Threat Management," 2020.

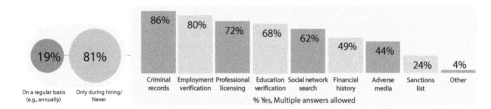

Figure 13.7 Background checks at family offices *Source*: Boston Private, Dentons, McNally Capital, The Chertoff Group, and Data Tribe, "Family Office Risk and Threat Management," 2020.

Only 19 percent of family offices conduct background checks of staff on a regular basis.

The data on background checks on family office employees highlights a large problem, but it also presents a great opportunity that family offices across the board can focus on (figure 13.7). By failing to create a systematic and regular review of employees, families open up the risk of insider threats—whether intentional or accidental. Partnering with risk management professionals to create a review system will improve the risk and threat posture for these families.

Mitigating tail risk is a primary focus when considering investment risk.

Figure 13.8 provides some insight into the mindset of families during the 2020 COVID-19 pandemic and economic fallout around the topic of investments. It clearly shows a focus on mitigating tail risk in portfolios. Further study over a longer period of time would be valuable to determine if these concerns change over time and under different market conditions.

Family offices only sporadically evaluate threats and risks using third-party vendors.

Family offices tend to ignore the threats that result from third-party vendors for a variety of reasons, including awareness of risks, costs of evaluating, and lack of ability to properly contrast and compare various suppliers. Figure 13.9 shows responses to the survey question "When

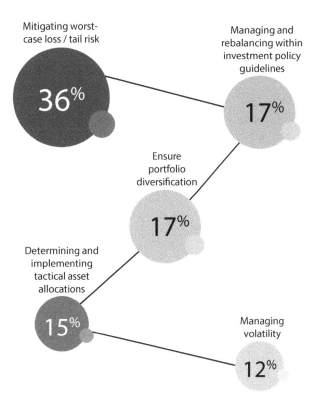

Figure 13.8 Investment risk concerns *Source*: Boston Private, Dentons, McNally Capital, The Chertoff Group, and Data Tribe, "Family Office Risk and Threat Management," 2020.

was the last time your team conducted a review of the risks and threats to family members or family office clients using third-party vendors? How can a family office know which risk vendor is best for them and their situation? To lower their supply-chain risk, family offices would benefit from working with risk management professionals to establish protocols to select and monitor vendors and advisers.

A total of 59 percent of family offices say there should be more conferences where they can network and learn more about emerging threats and best practices in risk management.

Many family office conferences and associations are available, in all parts of the globe. Family offices are private in nature but tend to

| 20% | 18% | 20% | 4% | 10% | 28% |

| In the last 6 months | 6 months to 1 year | 1 to 3 years | More than 3 years ago | We haven't yet but we are planning to | Never |

Figure 13.9 Third-party vendors *Source*: Boston Private, Dentons, McNally Capital, The Chertoff Group, and Data Tribe, "Family Office Risk and Threat Management," 2020.

appreciate opportunities to collaborate with peers. The results shown in figure 13.10 indicate a demand for more connectivity around risk and threats. Advisers to family offices should consider developing additional risk and threat management content for existing programming.

There should be more conferences where family offices can network and learn about emerging threats and best risk management practices

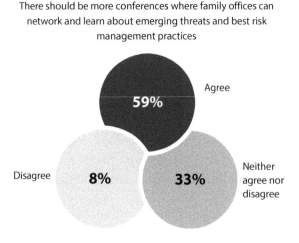

Agree
59%

Disagree
8%

Neither agree nor disagree
33%

Figure 13.10 Demand for network conferences *Source*: Boston Private, Dentons, McNally Capital, The Chertoff Group, and Data Tribe, "Family Office Risk and Threat Management," 2020.

The top two obstacles to implementing risk management measures in a family office are underestimating threat levels and complacency.

As discussed previously in chapter 7, the nature of how principals and family office executives view risk management presents potential pitfalls. These problems often show up as underestimation and overlooking of threats, frustration concerning effective protective measures, and a reactionary mindset in the family office. The survey results provide additional evidence and insights into this issue (figure 13.11). Knowing that these issues exist, families can work with risk professionals to build better protection systems and general threat awareness in the family office.

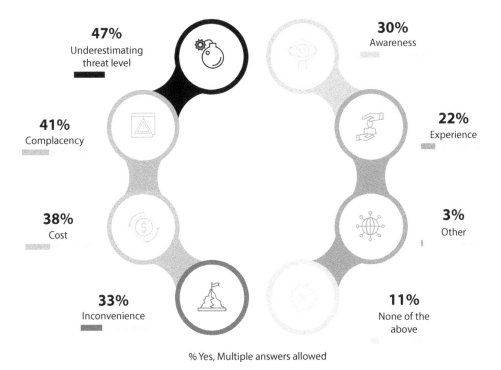

47%
Underestimating threat level

30%
Awareness

41%
Complacency

22%
Experience

38%
Cost

3%
Other

33%
Inconvenience

11%
None of the above

% Yes, Multiple answers allowed

Figure 13.11 Obstacles to risk management *Source:* Boston Private, Dentons, McNally Capital, The Chertoff Group, and Data Tribe, "Family Office Risk and Threat Management," 2020.

INDUSTRY RESOURCES

For Students and Academics

The study of family offices and instruction regarding their various classifications, organizational and behavioral types, services provided, and unique dynamics are just now becoming a common part of graduate business school curricula, whether as part of a master of business administration (MBA), master's of professional studies in wealth management (MPS), executive education, or professional studies program. This book was written in large part using problem-based learning pedagogy to assist educators in presenting information on these topics.

In further support of these programs, the authors have developed a number of additional educational resources for academics to use in discussing and presenting family offices to their students. Access to this information can be found at www.thefamilyofficebook.com.

For Principals, Practitioners, Service Providers, and Vendors

As discussed throughout this book, there are an increasing number of family office networks, clubs, conferences, and academic programs that can be invaluable resources to principals, practitioners, service providers and vendors.

Given the ever-changing nature of this information, it is not possible to list it all here. Instead, the authors have developed a list of certain networks and programs that can be accessed at www.thefamilyofficebook.com.

Conclusion

IN THE beginning of *Anna Karenina*, Tolstoy famously writes, "Happy families are all alike; every unhappy family is unhappy in its own way." Family offices are no different. To be sure, family offices differ because they reflect each principal's distinctive personality and preferences. However, this does not necessarily mean that the solutions to common challenges that they face are so different. It's the application of those solutions that tends to distinguish family offices from one another.

We wrote this book to share those solutions that we believe explain why successful family offices are far more alike than they are different. We did so by providing detailed insights into the challenges that wealthy families face, the solutions they adopt, and how they manage them, all from the perspective of a particular family as they addressed these issues and implemented solutions.

It is our sincere hope that this book serves its purpose of being a broad resource for those interested in learning about family offices, whether students and academics, principals and practitioners, or service providers and vendors.

Appendix

Book Website

For up-to-date information on this work and the family office industry, please visit the dedicated book website: www.thefamilyofficebook.com. Here, you will find numerous resources, including questions to ask when starting a family office; teaching materials and templates; and access to events, podcasts, interviews, and much more.

Appreciations

It would be impossible to name all of the individuals who contributed to this book, either directly through their advice and/or contributions as we wrote it, or indirectly, through the guidance they provided us throughout our careers. However, we endeavor to do so with the following list (presented in alphabetical order). We apologize in advance for any omissions or oversights.

Lon Augustenborg, President, Novus Intelligence
Jennifer Bailey, Vice President, Internet Services, Apple Pay at Apple
Milton Bearden, retired Central Intelligence Agency executive
Daniel Berick, Esq., Partner and Global Head of Family Office, Squire Patton Boggs (US) LLP
Trish Botoff, Managing Principal, Botoff Consulting
David Braham, Braham Consulting Limited
Stewart Brenner, retired financial services executive

Tom Broderick, retired managing director at WTAS

Jason Brown, Strategic Advisor, SEI Family Office Services, and Chairman, Proteus Capital.

Wesley Bull, Chief Executive Officer, Sentinel Resource Group LLC

Paul Carbone, President and Managing Partner, Pritzker Private Capital, LLC

Robert Casey, former editor of Bloomberg Wealth Management

Frank Dazzo, PhD, Professor, Michigan State University

Beth DeBeer, Chief Executive Officer, iImpact Consulting Network

Anthony DeChellis, Chief Executive Officer, Boston Private Bank & Trust Company

Brad Deflin, Founder and President, Total Digital Security

Anthony DeToto, Senior Vice President, Bank of America Private Bank

Allan Dunlavy, Esq., Partner, Shillings

John Dvor, Helge Capital

William F. Farren, President, My Accountant, Inc.

Rick Flynn, Managing Partner, Flynn Family Office

Randy Gantenbein, Founder and Chief Executive Officer, Vestis Collection, Inc.

Michael Gray, Esq., Partner, Neal, Gerber & Eisenberg, LLP

Suzanne Hammer, President, Hammer & Associates

Thomas Handler, Esq., Partner, Handler Thayer, LLP

Dennis T. Jaffe, PhD

Al King III, Co-founder and Co-Chief Executive Officer, South Dakota Trust Company LLC

Jeremy King, President, Benchmark Executive Search

Jay Frederick Krehbiel, Managing Director, KF Partners, LLC

David Friedman, Co-Founder, WealthQuotient, Co-Founder, Wealth-X

Neil Kreuzberger, Founder, Kreuzberger Associates, LLC

David Lansky, PhD, Principal Consultant, the Family Business Consulting Group

David Linnemeier, Founder, Linnemeier Aviation Advisors

Kevin Lorenz, Chief Investment Officer, Katz Group

Will Lymer, investor and cybersecurity expert

Anne Lyons, Founder and Chief Executive Officer, Tapestry Associates, LLC

Linda Mack, Founder and President, Mack International

Michael McAndrews, Principal, Abbot, Stringham & Lynch

Jamie McLaughlin, Founder, J. H. McLaughlin & Co.

Ward McNally, Founder and Managing Partner, McNally Capital

Mike McNamara, Chief Executive Officer, Dentons US

Brian Mefford, Chief Executive Officer, Wooden Horse Strategies

Michael Montgomery, Chief Executive Officer, Brush Street Investments

Charles Moorcroft, Owner, Charles Moorcroft, Inc.

Darren Moore, Esq., Bourland, Wall & Wenzel

Steven Oyer, Chief Executive Officer, i(x) investments

Joel Palathinkal, PhD, Chief Executive Officer and General Partner, Sutton Capital

George Pavlov, Chief Executive Officer, Bayshore Global Management

Jon Preizler, RH Capital

Stephen Prostano, Head of Family Advisory Services, PKF O'Connor Davies

John Prufeta, Chairman, Medical Excellence International

Waldek Raczkowski, Kedlaw Capital

Kathy Reilly, Chief Executive Officer, Lifestyle Advisory

Angelo Robles, Founder and Chief Executive Officer, Family Office Association

John Rompon, Marjo Investments, LLC

Rick Ross, Partner and Global Chair, Hotels and Leisure and Global Co-Chair, Family Office and High Net Worth Dentons

James Ruddy, President and Chief Executive Officer, Dillon Trust Company

Eric Schreiner, Chief Financial Officer, Pritzker Group

H. E. "Bud" Scruggs, Managing Director, the Cynosure Group

Ladislav Sekerka, Partner, Consillium Family Office

Chris Sidford, MD, Founder and Medical Director, Black Bag

Molly Simmons, Partner, McFarland Partners

Brian Smith, Assistant Editor, Columbia University Press

Parks Strobridge, Managing Director, UBS

Chad Sweet, Co-Founder and Chief Executive Officer, The Chertoff Group

Keith Swirsky, Esq., President, GKG Law, P.C.

Mike Szalkowski, Adjunct Professor, UNC Kenan-Flagler Business School

Geoff Teall, Owner, Montoga, Inc.

Steve Thayer, Esq., Partner, Handler Thayer, LLP

John Thiel, former Head of Merrill Lynch Wealth Management

Myles Thompson, Publisher, Columbia University Press

Mark Vorsatz, Global Chairman and Chief Executive Officer at Andersen

Ingo Walter, PhD, Professor, New York University—Leonard N. Stern School of Business

Tracey Brophy Warson, former Head, Citi Private Bank, North America

Glossary

Advisers Act: The Investment Advisers Act of 1940.

Advisory board: Independent advisors to the principal and senior executives of the family business or family office who typically do not hold voting rights.

Aircraft management company: A business that helps owners oversee some of or all the management of their private aircraft.

Business e-mail compromise (BEC): A cyber scam where e-mails appear to come from legitimate sources; used to induce behaviors that often end in fraudulent transfers of money.

Cessna 172: A four-seat, single-engine, fixed-wing aircraft popular with private aviation enthusiasts.

Concours d'Elegance: A well-known car show typically held in Pebble Beach, California, each year.

Consolidated reporting: Comprehensive reporting of all investable assets held by a wealthy family across multiple managers and custodians, including nonmarketable assets such as private equity, hedge funds, and real estate.

Custodian: A financial institution that holds customer securities (either physically or electronically) for safekeeping to minimize the risk of their theft or loss.

Dodd-Frank Act: The Dodd-Frank Wall Street Reform and Consumer Protection Act enacted on July 21, 2010. Passed after the Great Recession during and following 2008 and 2009, it overhauled federal financial regulatory agencies and much of the financial services industry.

Estate management: The oversight and periodic care and maintenance of personal residences, vacation homes, ranches, and other real estate holdings.

Executive: Refers to a senior professional who works for a family office. Also referred to as a "practitioner."

Executive recruiter: See *Search consultant.*

Family assembly: The universe of family members, often delineated by major family groups.

Family constitution: A statement of the principles that outline the family commitment to the core values, vision, and mission of the business, or as the case may be, the family office.

Family council: A working governing body that is elected by the family assembly among its members to deliberate on family business or family office issues.

Family Office Rule: A provision of the Dodd-Frank Wall Street Reform and Consumer Protection Act (Dodd-Frank Act) that provides guidelines by which family offices could be excluded from the definition of an "investment adviser" under the Investment Advisers Act of 1940 (Advisers Act).

FBO: Fixed Base Operator.

Federal Aviation Administration (FAA): An agency of the United States with powers to regulate all aspects of civil aviation within its borders, as well as its surrounding international waters.

Financial sponsor: A private equity firm, particularly one that invests in leveraged buy-outs.

Fixed base operator (FBO): A business located at most airports to assist private aircraft owners with fueling, hangaring, maintenance, and similar services.

Flight department: An entity created by a wealthy family to allow them to formally employ pilots and support staff.

General ledger: The accounting system used to record all transactions relating to a company's revenues, expenses, assets, and liabilities.

Governance: The manner and systems by which organizations are overseen and controlled at the highest levels.

Hedge fund: A private investment partnership or fund following proprietary strategies to invest or trade in various securities and assets in order to generate returns at reduced risk.

Impact investing: Investments intended to have both financial returns and positive societal or environmental effects.

Investment committee: The governing board that oversees investment management for a wealthy family, including development of an investment policy statement (IPS), selection of strategies and third-party managers, rebalancing of the portfolio to IPS guidelines, and the involvement and education of family members.

Investment policy statement (IPS): The governing document that provides strategic guidance for the planning and implementation of an investmnt management program related to governance, asset allocation, implementation, monitoring, and reporting.

Lifestyle management and concierge: General description of meeting the personal service needs of wealthy families, including finding and hiring assistants and household staff, making travel arrangements and reservations, and planning special events.

Lift: A term used to denote the various ways in which wealthy families fly privately.

Major domus: During the Roman Empire, a term for the manager of a household and/or numerous estates.

Managed service provider: An information technology (IT) company that provides users with outsourced access to the servers, networks, and specialized applications to help them run their organizations.

National Business Aviation Association (NBAA): An organization designed for companies that rely on general aviation aircraft to help make their businesses more efficient, productive, and successful.

Part 135: Federal aviation regulations that govern commercial aircraft and their operators. Generally, these rules set more stringent standards within private aviation for commuter and on-demand charter operations.

Partnership accounting: Complex financial and tax reporting for asset ownership vehicles used by wealthy families, usually partnerships or limited liability companies (LLCs), particularly when family members and entities used for their benefit have different profits or capital ownership interests.

Principal: The individual for whom the family office is established. Also referred to as the "patriarch" or "matriarch." A family office can have more than one principal.

Private trust company (PTC): A legal entity established by a wealthy family to provide a form of governance, via a privately owned, professionally run trust company, over which the family has some level of control.

Ransomware: A cyberattack where files or systems are locked until a victim pays a ransom (usually in the form of cryptocurrency).

Renaissance: Transitional period in Europe during the fifteenth and sixteenth centuries that marked the transition from the Middle Ages to modern times.

Search consultant: Firm that specializes in finding and assessing executives and staff within a particular industry or industries.

Securities and Exchange Commission (SEC): A government agency created to monitor and regulate investments and the national banking system for the protection of investors.

STEM: An acronym for educational programs that focus on science, technology, engineering, and math.

Ultra-high net worth (UHNW): A term typically used to refer to families with a net worth of $30 million or more.

Wealth education: A term referring to a broad range of integrated activities that provide next-generation family members with the education, resources, and tools needed to become successful stewards of the wealth of themselves and/or the family in general.

Notes

INTRODUCTION

1. When used throughout this book, the term "wealthy families" means families with $100 million or more of net worth.

BACKGROUND INFORMATION FOR CASE STUDIES 1 THROUGH 3

1. The ages listed in this summary are those of each person at the time of the sale of Rybat Manufacturing.

3. LEADERSHIP AND STAFFING

1. Linda Mack, "Recruiting and Retaining Top Leadership Talent," Family Office Association, 2017, http://www.mackinternational.com/documents/Family-Office-Association-Recruiting-and-Retaining-Top-Leadership-Talent.pdf.

2. Trish Botoff, "Compensation Trends, Best Practices, and Market Data," (unpublished report, August 25, 2020), typescript.

BACKGROUND INFORMATION FOR CASE STUDIES 4 THROUGH 9

1. Left Seat Management, LLC, is the corporate name of the family office management company for the Thorne family.

4. FINANCE

1. The authors would like to thank William Farren of My Accountant for his contributions to this chapter. William F. Farren, "Bill Paying Services," (unpublished manuscript, July 24, 2020), typescript.

2. Jason Brown, "Innovations in Private Wealth Technology and Reporting," SEI Archway, 2018, https://resources.archwaytechnology.net /innovations-in-private-wealth-technology.

3. The authors would like to thank Stephen Prostano, Gemma Leddy, Thomas Riggs, and Marc Rinaldi of PKF O'Connor Davies' Family Office Group for their contributions to this chapter. Stephen Prostano et al., "Tax Reporting," (unpublished manuscript, August 19, 2020), typescript.

4. Brad Deflin, "Family Office Cybersecurity IT and Trends," Total Digital Security, March 8, 2018, https://www.totaldigitalsecurity.com/blog /it-and-cybersecurity-for-the-family-office.

5. LIFESTYLE

1. The authors would like to thank Kathy Reilly of Lifestyle Advisory for her contributions to this chapter. Kathy Reilly, "Lifestyle Management and Concierge," (unpublished manuscript, July 24, 2020), typescript.

2. The authors would like to thank Anne Lyons and Judy Boerner-Rule of Tapestry Associates for their contributions to this chapter. Anne Lyons and Judy Boerner-Rule, "Estate Management," (unpublished manuscript, July 24, 2020), typescript.

3. The authors would like to thank Keith Swirsky of GKG Law for his contributions to this chapter. Keith G. Swirsky, "Private Aviation" (August 19, 2019), typescript.

4. This section benefited greatly from many conversations with David Linnemeier, Founder, Linnemeier Aviation Advisors.

6. INVESTMENTS

1. Daniel G. Berick, Karina Abolina, and Amy E. Gilbert, "The Family Office Rule under the Investment Advisers Act," Squire Patton Boggs, Family Office Insights, 2017, https://www.squirepattonboggs.com/-/media/files /insights/publications/2017/06/family-office-insights-the-family-office -rule-under-the-investment-advisers-act/26895-2017_june_family-office -insight_-family-office-exemption.pdf.

2. World Economic Forum, "Direct Investing by Institutional Investors: Implications for Investors and Policy-Makers," November 2014, http://www3.weforum .org/docs/WEFUSA_DirectInvestingInstitutionalInvestors.pdf.

3. This section benefited greatly from many conversations with Ward McNally, Managing Partner, McNally Capital.

4. This section benefited greatly from many conversations with H. E. "Bud" Scruggs, Managing Director, the Cynosure Group.

5. This section benefited greatly from many conversations with Paul Carbone, President and Managing Director, Pritzker Private Capital.

6. Steve Thayer, "Risks and Opportunities for Family Offices in the Direct and Co-Investment World," Handler Thayer, LLP, July 23, 2020, https://stevenjthayer.com/2020/07/23/risks-and-opportunities-for-family-offices-in-the-direct-co-investment-world/.

7. The authors would like to thank Joel Palathinkal of Sutton Capital for his contributions to this chapter. Joel Palathinkal, PhD, "Investing in Venture Capital," (unpublished manuscript, August 16, 2020), typescript.

8. Beth deBeer, "Impact Investing and Family Offices," Impact Consulting Network, 2020.

9. Mary Elizabeth Klein, "The Democratization of Art and Its Impact on Family Offices," Family Office Association and Angelo Robles, 2018, http://familyofficeassociation.com/wp-content/uploads/2020/04/klein_family_office_art-1.pdf.

7. RISK MANAGEMENT

1. Boston Private, "Demystifying Risk Management for Family Offices," 2020, https://files.bostonprivate.com/file/Demystifying-Risk-Management-for-Family-Offices.pdf.

2. The authors would like to thank Chad Sweet of the Chertoff Group for his contributions to this chapter. Chad Sweet, "Family Office Risk Management Practices," (unpublished manuscript, October 1, 2020), typescript.

3. The authors would like to thank John Prufeta of Medical Excellence International for his contributions to this chapter. John Prufeta, "Healthcare Advisory and Advocacy," (unpublished manuscript, August 15, 2020), typescript.

4. The authors would like to thank Chris Sidford of Black Bag for his contributions to this chapter. Chris Sidford, MD, "International Travel Medical Needs," (unpublished manuscript, September 1, 2020), typescript.

5. The authors would like to thank Michael Gray of Neal, Gerber & Eisenberg, LLP, for his contributions to this chapter. Michael B. Gray, "Legal Services," (unpublished manuscript, January 30, 2021), typescript.

6. This section benefited greatly from numerous conversations with Daniel G. Berick, Americas Chair of Global Corporate Practice, Squire Patton Boggs (US) LLP.

8. PHILANTHROPY

1. The authors would like to thank Suzanne Hammer of Hammer & Associates and Vahe Vartanian of Global Family Office Community for their contributions to this chapter. Suzanne Hammer and Vahe Vartanian, "Family Philanthropy," (unpublished manuscript, July 30, 2020), typescript.

2. Michelle Coleman-Johnson, Bourland, Wall & Wenzel, P.C., "Creating a Family Foundation," *GPSolo*, Law Trends & News, Estate Planning, Volume 2, Number 2, February 2006.

3. The authors would like to thank Darren B. Moore of Bourland, Wall & Wenzel for reviewing and updating the information contained in this section.

9. NEXT GENERATION

1. The authors would like to thank Dennis Jaffe for his review of this chapter.

2. Dennis T. Jaffe and James A. Grubman, "Acquirers' and Inheritors' Dilemma: Discovering Life Purpose and Building Personal Identity in the Presence of Wealth," 2007, https://dennisjaffe.com/download/acquirers-and-inheritors-dilemma-discovering-life-purpose-in-the-presence-of-wealth/.

3. Dennis T. Jaffe, "The Five Challenges for Wealth Inheritors to Develop a Positive Wealth Identity," 2018, https://dennisjaffe.com/download/the-five-challenges-for-wealth-inheritors-to-develop-a-positive-wealth-identity/.

10. COMMUNICATIONS AND PLANNING

1. This section benefited greatly from many conversations with Michael Montgomery, Chief Executive Officer, Brush Street Investments, LLC.

11. STRUCTURES

1. International Finance Corporation, World Bank Group, *IFC Family Business Governance Handbook*, International Finance Corporation, 2008, https://www.ifc.org/wps/wcm/connect/topics_ext_content/ifc_external_corporate_site/ifc+cg/resources/guidelines_reviews+and+case+studies/ifc+family+business+governance+handbook.

2. David Lansky and Jennifer Pendergast, "Is Good Governance Different in the Family Office Setting?" Family Business Magazine, 2010, https://www.familybusinessmagazine.com/good-governance-different-family-office-setting-0#:~:text=Taken%20together%2C%20these%20observations%20suggest,environment%2C%20if%20not%20more%20important.

3. Al W. King III, "Tips from the Pros: The Private Family Trust Company and Powerful Alternatives," WealthManagement.com, January 28, 2016, https://www.wealthmanagement.com/estate-planning/tips-pros-private-family-trust-company-and-powerful-alternatives; Matt Tobin and Tom Cota, "Nine Reasons to Start a Private Family Trust Company," Family Office Exchange, January 9, 2018, https://www.familyoffice.com/insights/nine-reasons-start-private-family-trust-company.

4. This section benefited greatly from many conversations with James Ruddy, President and Chief Executive Officer, Dillon Trust Company.

12. SUCCESSION AND LEADERSHIP INSIGHTS

1. This section benefited greatly from many conversations with George Pavlov, Chief Executive Officer, Bayshore Global Management.

13. THE NUMBERS

1. Wealth-X, "Ultra Wealthy Population Analysis: The World Ultra Wealth Report 2019," September 25, 2019, https://www.wealthx.com/report/world-ultra-wealth-report-2019/.

2. Wealth-X, one of the leading wealth intelligence companies, defines UHNW as meaning families with $30 million or more in net worth.

3. Wealth-X, "Ultra Wealthy Population Analysis: The World Ultra Wealth Report 2019," September 25, 2019, https://www.wealthx.com/report/world-ultra-wealth-report-2019/.

4. Campden Wealth Limited and UBS, "Global Family Office Report 2019," 2019, http://www.campdenwealth.com/article/global-family-office-report-2019.

5. The authors would like to thank Trish Botoff of Botoff Consulting for her contributions to this chapter. Trish Botoff, "Compensation Data Tables," (unpublished spreadsheet, August 25, 2020), spreadsheet file.

6. Boston Private, Dentons, McNally Capital, The Chertoff Group, and Data Tribe, "Family Office Risk and Threat Management Survey," 2020, https://www.bostonprivate.com/our-thinking/vault/articles/surveying-the-risk-and-threat-landscape-to-family-offices-2571.

Index

Page numbers in *italics* indicate figures or tables.